THE ESSENTIAL GUIDE TO BEING POLISH

Anna Spysz & Marta Turek

Anna Spysz, Editor

THE ESSENTIAL GUIDE TO BEING POLISH

Anna Spysz & Marta Turek

FOREWORD BY Lech Wałęsa

WITH A CONTRIBUTION BY
Tomasz Zubilewicz

Anna Spysz, EDITOR

New Europe Books

Published by New Europe Books, 2013
Williamstown, Massachusetts
www.NewEuropeBooks.com

ISBN: 978-0-9850623-0-9

Cataloging-in-Publication Data is available from the Library of Congress.

Printed in the United States of America on acid-free paper.

10 9 8 7 6 5 4 3 2

TABLE OF CONTENTS[1*]

page

Foreword ix
Preface xi
Timeline xiii
Maps xiv
Pronunciation Guide xix

PART I: POLAND IN CONTEXT
  1 Poland! My Homeland!—featuring "On Polish Weather"
     by TV weatherman Tomasz Zubilewicz 3
  2 Matka Nature 11
  3 Legendary Tales 16
  4 Polish History in a Nutshell 23
  5 Kings & Queens 28
  6 Capital(s) 35
  7 Neighborly Relations 41
  8 Jews in Poland 48
  9 Poles at War 55
10 The People's Republic 64
11 Postcommunism: Now What? 72
12 Poland Gets Down to Business 78
13 Language: Logic Has Nothing to Do With It 84
14 (The Politics of) Religion 98
15 All Saints' Year 104
16 The Ol' White and Red 111

---

1 * Chapters 4, 7–12, 20, 21, 34, 35, and 37–50 written by Anna Spysz.
   Chapters 1–3, 5, 6, 13–19, 22–33, and 36 written by Marta Turek.
   All translations by the respective authors unless otherwise noted.

PART II: POLES IN POLAND

17 The Polish Mentality 118
18 Superstitions: Hold Your Thumbs! 123
19 Names: From Ania to Zenon 129
20 Polish Women: Mothers of the Nation 133
21 Polish Men: Stereotypes and Reality 139
22 How to Survive a Polish Wedding 144
23 *F* for Family 148
24 Going Shopping 151
25 Home Sweet Polish Home 155
26 Polish Food: From *Bigos* to *Żurek* 160
27 (Famous) Polish Hospitality 171
28 Drinking in Poland: *Na Zdrowie!* 175
29 Back to School 180
30 Here Come the Holidays 187
31 Folk Traditions 192
32 The Highlander Life 197
33 Poles on Vacation 202

PART III: POLES IN THE LIMELIGHT

34 Writers & Poets: Beyond Miłosz & Mickiewicz 210
35 Theater (& Cabaret) of the Absurd 218
36 Capturing Reality on Film 222
37 Polish Artists: Framed by History 227
38 Composers & Music: More than Chopin 232
39 Scientists: Polonium & More 238
40 Sports & Athletes: *"Polska Goooooooool!"* 244
41 Protestors, Rebels, and Rabble-Rousers 249

PART IV: POLES AROUND THE WORLD

42 Nationhood (& Lack Thereof) 256
43 Exile & Emigration 261
44 Polonia—the Polish Diaspora 266
45 New Neighbours: Poles in the UK 271
46 Taking Over the Continent: Poles in Europe 276
47 *Jackowo!* Poles in the Americas 280
48 Non-Native Realms: The Arts in Emigration 286
49 Bring on the Funding: Poland in the EU 292

PART V: POLES IN A NUTSHELL

50 The Essence of Polishness 298

Index 303
About the Authors 316

Foreword

Poles have the Freedom Gene

When I think about what common denominator could be used to describe Poland, the Polish people, and the Polish soul, I come to the conclusion that, regardless of the time period or historical and political circumstances, what connects and defines us Poles is . . . the freedom gene.

The Polish freedom gene is encoded somewhere deep within us and passed on from generation to generation. In the days of occupation it ordered us to take up independence missions, sometimes even hopeless ones, and in times of democracy it teaches us how to deal with the freedom we have won. And if we look at our homeland after more than twenty years of political transformations, we can see that we are doing quite well, that we are building a modern country that is open and prosperous, even if it is not free of problems.

It was the Polish freedom gene that in 1980 brought about the birth of the Solidarity movement among many millions of people, which not only allowed us to introduce systemic changes in Poland, but—following the voice of our great compatriot, the blessed John Paul II—also helped us "renew the face of the land" in Europe and even in the world. It was in turn this Solidarity message that, carried to the world, came upon fertile ground—as it entered the hearts of many people and nations for whom the freedom gene has for generations been a constant point of reference.

I believe that today the same freedom gene will lead us in building a free world that is based on moral values, human solidarity, and peace. And it will not allow us to fully experience inner peace for as long as the desire for freedom has not been fully satisfied in any corner of the world.

I invite you on this journey into the depths of the Polish soul as described on the pages of this book. And I invite you to Poland—a land of freedom and solidarity.

—Lech Wałęsa, cofounder of the Solidarity movement, Nobel Peace Prize laureate, former president of Poland (1990–1995)

PREFACE

"We're talking about Poland. Nothing is usual there."
–Andrzej Sapkowski, Polish fantasy writer

The Essential Guide to Being Polish is just that: a guidebook for the lapsed Pole, non-Pole living in Poland, or anyone remotely interested in Polish culture, history, and the essence of Polishness. Within its pages is a cursory introduction to the long and often turbulent history of Poland, and how it has affected everything from the arts to where Polish populations reside to modern economics in the country. It is an attempt to answer an impossible question: What is the essence of being Polish?

This book is not intended to be read cover to cover, but rather each chapter is a self-contained piece of the Polish puzzle. This is why certain themes are sometimes repeated, and other chapters are frequently referenced as background material. No extensive knowledge of Polish or European history is required, though those with little exposure to Poland should start with the first four chapters. *The Essential Guide to Being Polish* is not an instruction book that will teach readers how to be Polish, though it might give aspiring citizens a head start. It is aimed not at scholars, but rather anyone with an interest in discovering what makes Poland and its people, well, *Polish*.

This book is also not an academic work, though care has been taken to ensure that the most up to date figures and accurate historical accounts have been presented. In writing this book, the authors relied on their own knowledge, expert opinions, anecdotes, and their personal experiences of being Polish and living in Poland as well as being a part of Polish communities abroad. Each chapter contains a "further reading" section, provided for those who would like to dive deeper into a particular topic. Though many of those books have been used as reference materials, the lists are not bibliographies, just suggestions. The authors hope that their introduction to these essential aspects of Polishness will whet the appetites of readers and encourage them to read more about Poland, and if possible, travel through Poland to experience this enigmatic land for themselves.

ACKNOWLEDGMENTS

Anna Spysz would like to thank Nick Hodge and Piotr Krasnowolski for their incredibly helpful feedback on initial drafts, Dara Bramson, Marek Kamiński, Phil Manchester, and Duncan Rhodes for help with individual chapters, as well as all of her male Polish friends who offered much-needed assistance in writing Chapter 21. Above all, she would like to thank her parents, who kept the language and spirit of Poland alive far away from Polish lands, her friends and family in Poland and elsewhere for their steady encouragement, and Kevin Hudson for his unending support.

Marta Turek would like to thank Kazimierz Turek for providing extensive comments on Polish history, Anna Mojska for her insightful remarks on Poland in general, and friends and family far and wide for their unlimited support and inspiration.

Both writers would first and foremost like to thank Paul Olchváry for giving us this chance to tell the story of the Polish people, as well as Tomasz Jankowski and Professor Emeritus Thaddeus V. Gromada for taking the time to read earlier versions of the manuscript and offering their scholarly advice.

We especially wish to express our deepest gratitude to the former president of Poland, Lech Wałęsa, for promulgating the Polish spirit of freedom and solidarity and for his utmost support in our endeavor.

— *Anna Spysz, Krakow, February 2013*
— *Marta Turek, Rokietnica, February 2013*

A Brief Timeline of Polish History

- 966—Christianity introduced to Poland by Mieszko I
- 1025—Bolesław the Brave is crowned the first Polish king
- 1333–1370—Casimir the Great unites Poland, with Krakow as the capital
- 1364—Jagiellonian University founded
- 1410—Battle of Grunwald fought between Polish and Lithuanian forces and Teutonic Knights
- 1543—Nicolaus Copernicus publishes *On the Revolutions of the Celestial Spheres*
- 1569—Union of Lublin signed, creating the Polish–Lithuanian Commonwealth
- 1596–1609—Poland's capital moved from Krakow to Warsaw
- 1655-60—Swedish Deluge destroys Warsaw and much of Poland
- 1772—First Partition of Poland
- 1791—Adoption of the Constitution of the Third of May
- 1793—Second Partition of Poland
- 1795—Third Partition of Poland
- 1830—November Uprising against Russian rule
- 1863—January Uprising against Russian rule
- 1914—World War I begins
- 1918—Poland regains independence at the end of WWI
- 1920–1921—Polish-Russian war, followed by adoption of Polish constitution and establishment of borders
- 1939–1945—World War II
- 1945-1947—Establishment of People's Republic of Poland, new borders, and adoption of constitution
- 1980–1981—Formation of Solidarity trade union, declaration of martial law
- 1989—Round Table Agreement signed, first partially free elections
- 1990—Lech Wałęsa elected president
- 1999—Poland joins NATO
- 2004—Poland joins European Union
- 2010—Smolensk plane crash kills President Lech Kaczyński
- 2011—Poland holds rotating EU presidency

Polish-Lithuanian Commonwealth from the Union of Lublin, 1569 to 1667

(Courtesy of *Poland: A Country Study,* Library of Congress, 1992)

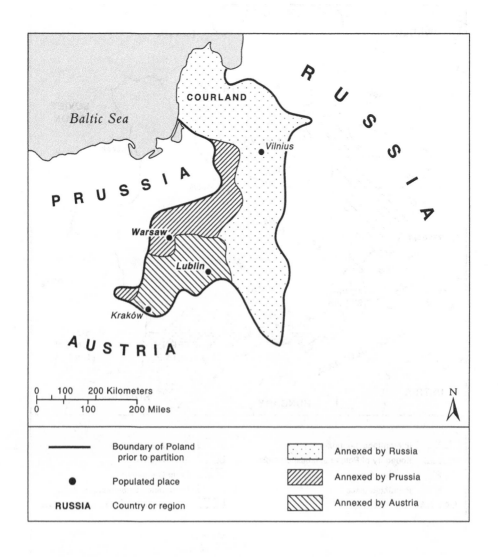

The 1795 dismemberment of Poland by the Third Partiton. Solid line: Poland's borders prior to the Partition. (Courtesy of *Poland: A Country Study*, Library of Congress, 1992)

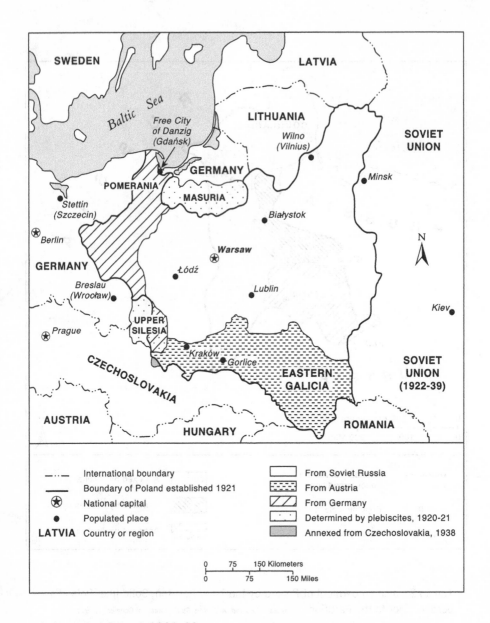

Independent Poland, 1920–39 (Courtesy of *Poland: A Country Study,* Library of Congress, 1992)

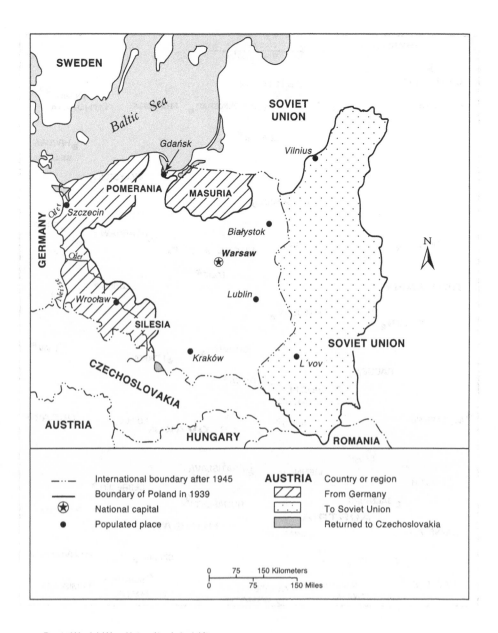

Post–World War II territorial shifts (Courtesy of *Poland: A Country Study*, Library of Congress, 1992)

Poland in postcommunist Europe (Shutterstock.com)

A Brief Guide to Polish Pronunciation

At first glance, Polish is a difficult language, particularly for the English ears (and eyes—where are the vowels?). While it takes years of study and the patience of a *święty* to master Polish, luckily its spelling is completely phonetic and its pronunciation is actually fairly simple once you become familiar with a few basic rules, listed below.

Vowels and vowel combinations

a	ah	u	oo
ą	awn or on, nasalized, e.g. wesołych swiąt = veh-soh-wikh shvyont	y	ih, like the y in "rhythm"
e	eh	aj	iy, as in the word "eye"
ę	en, e.g. Lech Wałęsa = leh vah-wen-sah	ej	ay
i	ee	oj	oy
o	oh	ia	yah
ó	oo	ie	yeh

Consonants

c [+anything but i]	ts, e.g. Górecki = goo-rets-kee, Katowice = kah-toh-vee-tseh	r	r, rolled as in Italian or Spanish
ć, cz*	ch, as in "church"	rz	zh, like the s in "measure," e.g. Krzysztof Penderecki = kzhihsht-off pen-deh-rets-kee
ci	chee, e.g. Oświęcim = ohsh-vyehn-cheem	ś, sz*	sh
ci [+vowel]	ch, e.g. ojciec = oy-chets	ść, szcz	sh-ch, an odd sound found also in Russian: say the words "fresh cheese," then remove the "fre" and the "eese"
ch	kh, lightly gutteral, as in German "Bach"	si	shee, e.g. Zanussi = zah-noo-shee
dź, dż, dzi	j, e.g. Włodzimierz = vwoh-jee-myehsh	si [+vowel]	sh, e.g. Harnasie = har-nah-sheh
g	g, always hard, as in "get"	w	v, or also f at the end of a syllable, e.g. Lutosławski = loo-to-swahf-skee
j	y, as in German "Johann"	ź, ż*	zh, like the s in "measure"
ł	w, e.g. Wrocław = vrohts-wahf	zi	zhee, e.g. Kazimierz = kah-zhee-myehsh
ń	ny, a palatalized n, like French/Italian gn	zi [+vowel]	zh, e.g. ziemia = zhehm-yah

*Technically ć and cz are not the same sound, nor are ś and sz or ź and ż, but we defy anyone who wasn't born in Poland to tell the difference.

Pronunciation guide used with permission of Chris Wendl, pronunciationguide.info

PART I

POLAND IN CONTEXT

CHAPTER 1

POLAND! MY HOMELAND!

Lithuania! My homeland! Thou art like fine health.
How much thou should be appreciated, will only know
One who has lost thee. Thy beauty today, in all its splendor
I behold and portray, for I long after thee.
–Adam Mickiewicz, Pan Tadeusz

Poland is a beautiful country. And if you've ever taken a train through the Polish countryside, it probably reminded you of a ruffled patch-work quilt sewn from rich shades of color and a variety of textures—from the lightest, yellowish brown to the darkest, velvety green. After all, the name itself holds the essence of what much of the country's terrain is—*pola*, which literally means "fields." Golden patches of wheat fields are spotted with crimson poppy flowers and purplish-blue cornflowers. Tall, wild grasses rustling in the wind or short, lush, bottle green grass, reminiscent of a smooth carpet, draw you in. The train will take you through dark, quiet forests where you may even spot a startled roe-deer or a shy red fox, and then will pass through, or even stop at, lazy-looking towns with their century-old train stations, places where the concept of time seems to abide by its own rules.

Poland extends 649 km[2*] from its northwestern border (the Baltic Sea) to its southern border (the Sudeten and Carpathian Mountains). If we were to take a virtual train along Poland's seacoast we would have to travel 524 km. From the western border to the eastern border the country spans 689 km. If we wanted to take our train along the border of every country neighboring Poland we would have to travel about 210 km along the border with the Russian Federation, 103 km along the border with Lithuania, 416 km with Belarus, 529 km with Ukraine, 539 km with Slovakia, 790 km with the Czech Republic and 467 km with Germany. In all, Poland covers a surface area of 312,685 km2—placing it tenth on the list of European countries. Population-wise, it ranks eight, with about thirty-eight million citizens.

There are specific regions in Poland known for their historic and ethnographic significance, such as the Podlasie or Masuria regions, and the country is divided into sixteen administrative units, or provinces, which are called voivodeships (*województwa*). This funny-looking word originates from the twelfth century, when a *wojewoda* was a military leader, roughly speaking, if you can count a group of twenty or so knights a military.

The northern part of the country, with the Pomerania (Pomorze), Kashubia (Kaszuby), Warmia, and Masuria (Mazury) regions, is a varied landscape consisting of gently rolling hills, many forests and lakes, which Poland has plenty of, with several thousand postglacial lakes, known as the Great Masurian Lakes, located in the Masuria region. This area is extremely popular with Polish vacationers, and campsites and rows of recreational boats line the shores of most lakes.

The Pomerania region lies along the Baltic Coast, which is dotted with popular seaside resorts, such as Kołobrzeg or Międzyzdroje, with its major cities of Szczecin to the west and Gdańsk to the east. Southwest of Gdańsk is the Kashubia region, an ethnographically distinct

---

2 * That's about 406 miles. In the interest of presenting Poland as its residents measure it, this book is all metric. Since one mile = 1.6 kilometers (km), one easy way to convert is to divide the km figure by half, and add 25% of the result (e.g., half of 649 is around 325, and 25% of that is 81; 325 + 81 = 406). Even easier, if less exact: the mile figure is somewhere between half and the full km amount. As for meters (m), one of them is a bit more than a yard; and centigrade, well, 40 is pretty hot, 0 is freezing, and -40 is about as cold as it's ever been in Poland. As for kilograms (kg), double the figure and add a tiny bit, and that's how many pounds you're talking about (put more exactly: 1 kg = 2.2 pounds).

Old engraved illustration of Gdansk. Trousset Encyclopedia, 1890s.
(Shutterstock.com)

part of Poland. The entire picturesque landscape boasts well-preserved forests and hundreds of postglacial lakes. Along the Vistula (Wisła) River lies Mikołaj Kopernik's Toruń, the finest example of a bustling medieval Gothic town.

The Warmia and Masuria regions are also known for their castles, many of which were built by the German Teutonic Knights starting from the thirteenth century. Here we can stop by the picturesque town of Malbork, where the Gothic castle of the Teutonic Order overlooks the Nogat River. This is the largest brick building in Europe and the largest castle in the world in surface area. The Warmia-Masuria voivodeship also boasts the Elbląg Canal, an 80.5 km-long complex system of inclined planes to raise boats between the different water levels connecting Lake Drużno and Lake Jeziorak—with differences in water levels sometimes reaching 100 m. In a 2007 poll conducted by one of Poland's national papers, *Rzeczpospolita*, both Malbork Castle and the Elbląg Canal were chosen by readers as two of the Seven Wonders of Poland (although with typical Polish indecisiveness, readers voted for a total of eighty-seven places). Poland's average elevation is 173 meters above sea level, and the lowest point is near the mouth of the Vistula River in this region's Żuławy delta area—at 1.8 m below sea level. Located in a small village called Raczki Elbląskie, a tall, red pole has been placed in this very spot with blue wavy lines drawn on it. The wavy lines show the sea level, so if you stand next to the pole you can see whether your head would be above or below the Baltic Sea's waves. This is tourist fun at its best.

Poland is mostly covered by lowlands along its central belt, and this is where some of its historically significant regions lie: Greater Poland (Wielkopolska), called the cradle of Poland because the first foundations of the Polish state were formed there, Kujawy, Lower Silesia (Dolny Śląsk), Mazovia (Mazowsze) and Podlasie. This middle stretch of Poland is mostly agricultural and is known as the country's breadbasket.

The Greater Poland region houses many historically significant places, such as Biskupin, the oldest surviving fortified settlement in Poland, Gniezno, Poland's first capital from the tenth century, and Poznań, the main seat of Poland's first rulers. The Warta River runs through this historic area, which is also home to the Piast Route (Szlak

ON POLISH WEATHER

by Tomasz Zubilewicz

There is no such thing as bad weather—you can only go wrong in your choice of apparel! I often repeat this maxim in my weather forecasts.

We Poles, just like the British, can talk about the weather for hours, anytime and anywhere. We have reasons to do so, for the weather in our country is unique, as rarely in the world can one find a relatively small country with such a diverse climate.

Let's look at a map of Europe. All of the different air masses collide exactly above where Poland lies; the moist air from the Atlantic and "Brother Ivan's" dry air from Siberia meet the cold arctic air from Scandinavia and the hot African air from the south. Sometimes the rain that falls over Poland has a red or orange hue, and this is due to the strong wind that blows in sand all the way from the Sahara!

That is why you can have two different seasons of the year at the same time. I am not kidding. When tractors are already working the fields and larks are singing in the March sun of the Silesian Lowland, at that same time the lakes of the Suwałki region near the border with Lithuania are still covered in ice! Another example? In eastern Poland there may be a cover of snow for over three months, whereas at the Baltic Sea it is just twenty days. Here the winter is the shortest and the warmest.

If you want to experience Poland's climatic epicenter, head toward the city of Suwałki, and then to the tiny village of Wiżajny. This is our Polish North Pole. It is a spot that regularly witnesses the country's coldest temperatures, from twenty to even thirty degrees below zero. Sometimes there is so much snow that the only means of transport is by sleigh. Stories have been told of people taking a horse-drawn sleigh to go shopping, only to come out of the store and find that their horses were nowhere to be seen. It was so cold at times that the animals simply decided to return to the farm by themselves, without waiting for their owners.

Another weather record point is the Valley of Five Lakes in the Tatra Mountains. A ridge that runs along part of the Polish-Slovak border receives the most rainfall in Poland, with a yearly average of up to 1.8 meters, almost three times more than that of Warsaw.

And to sum up, here are some of Poland's weather records of the twentieth century: maximum temperature: 40.2 degrees Celsius in Prószków near Opole on July 29, 1929; minimum temperature: −41.0 degrees Celsius on January 11, 1940 in Siedlce.

Now, you can feel free to talk about the weather with Poles anywhere and at any time. And remember: there is no such thing as bad weather.

Photo provided by Tomasz Zubilewicz

*Meteorologist **Tomasz Zubilewicz**, Poland's most popular TV weather forecaster, is head of the weather team at the internationally broadcast television network TVN.*

Piastowski) that can be taken through the towns and places where the Polish state was formed. Centrally located between Greater Poland and Mazovia is the ethnographically distinct region of Kujawy. The region of Lower Silesia stretches along the Odra River, home to Wrocław, Poland's fourth largest city and its main tourist attraction, with its mixture of Polish, German, and Czech architectural styles.

The Mazovia region is mostly a flat plain with infertile soil and freely growing groups of willows, a tree that has served as a source of inspiration for poets, painters and writers. The region's historic and cultural center is the capital city of Warsaw (Warszawa in Polish), which lies on Poland's longest, 1,047-km long river, the Vistula. The city is said to be protected by the river's most famous inhabitant, the Warsaw Mermaid, whose sister can be found on the distant shores of Copenhagen in Denmark.

If we travel west of the capital we can visit Żelazowa Wola, the manor house (*dworek*) where Poland's most famous composer, Fryderyk Chopin, was born (see Chapter 38). Nearby is Kampinos National Park (Puszcza Kampinoska), one of Poland's largest protected parks. Płock, the capital of Mazovia long before Warsaw, has one of Poland's oldest cathedrals situated on a beautiful clifflike hill overlooking the Vistula River. The medieval town of Pułtusk, also internationally known for its Dom Polonii, a place where Poles from all over the world come to meet, is one of the Mazovia region's most picturesque towns.

The Podlasie region, which runs along the Polish-Belarusian border, is an ethnically distinct area of Poland mostly covered by forests, marshes and rivers. It is also a natural sanctuary and home to four national parks: Białowieski, Biebrzański, Narwiański, and Wigierski, protecting some of Poland's most endangered wild animals, such as the *żubr* (European bison), of Żubrówka fame (see Chapter 28). Close to the border is Janów Podlaski, with its world-renowned stud farm specializing in breeding some of the finest Arabian horses.

Further south the terrain rises, and here lie the uplands of Upper Silesia (Górny Śląsk) and Lesser Poland (Małopolska). The region of Górny Śląsk has always been Poland's main source of coal deposits and the steel industry, mostly centered in medium- and large-sized cities around Katowice. This industrial area, with its coal mines, heavy

Dunajec river in the Pieniny Mountains (Poland). From Meyers Konversations-Lexikon, 1897.

(Hein Nouwens / Shutterstock.com)

industry but also high-tech factories is the most densely populated, and unfortunately most environmentally polluted, part of Poland.

The Lesser Poland region of green valleys and gently undulating hills dotted with villages and towns is located in Poland's central, southeastern part, called by some "the most Polish" of regions. It boasts three of the Seven Wonders of Poland, all of which are also UNESCO (the United Nations Educational, Scientific and Cultural Organization) World Heritage Sites. Most notable is Krakow, with its two main historic centers, the Old Town and the Wawel Castle. Speaking of the number seven, the Wawel is said to be home to one of only seven Chakra stones in the world, believed by some to have been thrown by the Lord Shiva himself and to possess mystical energies. These days, though, it attracts more New Agers than gurus.

Another wonder is the Wieliczka Salt Mine, an absolutely breathtaking underground museum and cathedral carved, by miners, entirely out of rock salt. The third is Zamość, a town perfectly planned, designed, and built in the best Renaissance tradition. The region also comprises the central Lesser Poland Upland, with its oldest mountain range, the Holy Cross Mountains (Góry Świętokrzyskie), the Krakow-Częstochowa Upland to the west, and the Lublin Upland to the east.

The Krakow-Częstochowa Upland has interesting smooth rock formations and dozens of castle ruins, which can be visited en route the Eagle's Nest Trail (Szlak Orlich Gniazd). The only things missing would be medieval clothing and a horse-drawn carriage to complement the atmosphere. This region is also home to the monastery of Jasna Góra in Częstochowa, the destination of millions of pilgrims who come to pray in front of the miraculous painting of the Black Madonna. The hundreds of canes, prosthetics, golden necklaces, and other personal mementoes left hanging on the walls inside the shrine can attest to the painting's effectiveness.

If we travel yet further south we will come upon the Sudeten and Carpathian mountain ranges. The Sudeten Mountains are famous for the Góry Stołowe, literally called the Table Mountains, because their peaks are as flat as tabletops. The Karkonosze in the Sudeten Mountains are home to the third highest mountain, Mt. Śnieżka (1,602 meters a.s.l.). The Tatras are the highest mountain range in the Carpathian Mountains and boast the highest peak in Poland, Mt. Rysy (2,499 m), a magnificent observation point itself, from which nearly a hundred other Tatra peaks can be seen on a clear day. At the foot of the Tatras lies the Podhale region with bustling Zakopane, Poland's favorite winter holiday destination as well as the "in" place to be all-year-round, especially for those Polish fashionistas who can occasionally be spotted on hiking trails in, yes, high heels. In the vicinity is the Valley of Five Lakes (Dolina Pięciu Stawów), a picturesque area with emerald-green lakes, the most notable of which is Lake Morskie Oko—literally, the "Eye of the Sea." There's also a postglacial lake that lies so high in the mountains that it remains frozen for nearly ten months out of the year.

We have taken this virtual train through the regions of Poland, which literally lies in the heart of Europe, where we passed by historic towns, bustling cities and quaint villages, through stretches of grassland full of magical lakes, winding rivers, and forests marking some of those regions' natural boundaries

So, why do the first lines of Poland's most famous epic poem refer to Lithuania? The answer is simple—Mickiewicz, considered to be one of Poland's greatest bards, described the natural beauty of his homeland when Poland and Lithuania were joined as the Polish-Lithuanian Commonwealth. Taught early in Polish schools, almost every adult knows the beginning of the invocation by heart.

M.T.

CHAPTER 2

Matka Nature

Rano kawka, wieczorem żubr.
A jackdaw bird (coffee) in the morning, a żubr (beer) in the evening.

Żubr stawia się czasem.
Sometimes a żubr will not heed (a Żubr beer on the house).

Dobrze posiedzieć przy żubrze.
It's good to sit next to a żubr (beer).
(Wordplay slogans from famous TV commercials for Żubr beer)

When it comes to natural riches, Poland has its bases thoroughly covered. The country has twenty-three national parks that are visited by nearly eleven million guests on a yearly basis. The parks cover, in total, 3,167 km² and about 1% of the country's entire surface area. Nearly all types of natural ecosystems are protected by these parks, including mountain ranges (nine parks), the highlands (two parks), the lowlands, wetlands, forests, lakes and rivers kept in their original, natural form (ten parks), and lake area ecosystems along the Baltic coast (two parks). Eight parks are listed as UNESCO Biosphere Reserves.

The Białowieża National Park (Białowieski Park Narodowy) is the oldest national park in Poland and one of the oldest in Europe. Originally established in 1923, and in its current form since 1947, it is the only park in Poland to be listed as a UNESCO World Natural

Heritage site, which places it among such sites as the Serengeti in Tanzania or the Grand Canyon in Arizona.

The park is situated in the Podlasie region, close to the north-eastern border with Belarus, and constitutes a small part (about one-tenth) of the vast and wild Białowieża Primeval Forest (Puszcza Białowieska), which is the last, and largest, remaining primeval—never deforested—stand of evergreen and mixed forest of the European lowlands. This immense forest range dates back to 8000 BC and is the only remaining example of the original forests that once covered much of Europe. Thus, almost 90% of the park is covered with European primeval lowland mixed forest and protects many indigenous species of trees, such as pine, beech, oak (some over 500 years old), alder, and spruce as well as unique plants and shrubs. The park's total area is 105 km2, and nearly half is under strict environmental protection. It is home to the elk, wild boar, lynx, wolf, badger, otter, beaver, ermine—a weird little weasel-like creature made famous by a certain lady in a certain da Vinci painting—and bats. Its bird species include the white-tailed eagle, white stork, peregrine falcon, and eagle owl.

In medieval times, the Białowieża Forest was the property of Polish monarchs and was the setting of their private hunting excursions. After Poland's partitions in the nineteenth century (see Chapter 42), it became the property of the Russian tsars. During World War I the forest was extensively exploited by the Germans, who cut millions of cubic meters of timber, thus destroying large parts of the forest's fragile ecosystems. Luckily, much of the forest survived in almost unaltered form.

The Białowieża National Park is inhabited by the *żubr*—the European bison—the largest land mammal in all of Europe. Called the uncontested king of the forest, the *żubr* was an almost extinct species that was reintroduced into the park in 1929.

The story of the European bison goes back to sixteenth-century Bavaria, when parks were established to protect these wild animals, but by 1800 they had become nearly extinct in Europe. After 1755 they were only present in Poland, where they unfortunately continued to be hunted as wild game. After the Partitions, Russian tsar Alexander I ordered that the vast forest and its wild animals be protected, which meant the local people living there, along with any potential poachers, were removed by force. This did not stop the bison from dying out further, as entire herds were often decimated by a natural culprit—disease. In 1919 the last *żubr* living in the wild was, sadly enough, killed by a poacher. Thus, after World War I no European bison were to be found roaming free, and only forty living individuals remained in various zoos scattered all over Europe. The Society for the Protection of European Bison was formed, with Poland, Germany, the UK, and Sweden as members, and twelve bison living in captivity in Polish zoos were bred and reintroduced into the wild. Today, bison live in the wild in the forests and parks of many regions of Poland and other countries of Europe, but all are descendants of those twelve individuals.

An adult male *żubr* weighs almost one ton. Females are smaller and bear one young, weighing a mere 30 kg, every two years, which in part explains their population problems. Although large and heavy, these bison are also fast and agile, but they avoid contact with humans, as they are known to be extremely shy—though this doesn't mean curious tourists should approach them, despite any television commercials that suggest otherwise. European bison live in herds, graze in the meadows and glades and love to roll around in the dirt and sand. They are still considered to be a critically endangered species. The *żubr* is the Białowieża National Park's symbol and great source of pride, and currently about 950 individuals live in the wild all over Poland.

The Białowieża Primeval Forest is also a reserve for the returning species of *tarpan*, a descendent of a small, wild forest horse that unfortunately followed in the footsteps of the dodo bird. In medieval times there were great numbers of these horses all over Europe, until they were intensely hunted and killed. Around the year 1786 the remaining few wild *tarpans* were collected from the forest and placed in a private wildlife reserve, but when that had to be closed down in 1808 due to a lack of funds, they were given away to local farmers, who crossbred them with their own domestic horses. The last known true *tarpan* died at the end of the nineteenth century. In the early 1920s the Polish professor Tadeusz Vetulani started studying these crossbreeds and introduced the term *konik polski* (Polish pony) to denote this new breed of the extinct species. Before World

The mighty *Żubr* (AlexanderZam / Shutterstock.com)

War II he had begun intensive scientific research on restoring the lost species of *tarpan* via breeding the Polish pony, but during the war the project was destroyed by the Germans, and thirty such ponies were deported to Germany. After the war Vetulani tried to recover these lost ponies to continue his work in restoring the extinct species, but to no avail.

The Biebrza National Park (Biebrzański Park Narodowy) is the largest park in Poland. Established in 1993, it lies in the Podlasie region, mainly in the basin of the Biebrza River, and covers an area of 592 km². It is also the longest park and covers some of the wildest and most remote terrain in Poland. The park is Central Europe's largest natural bog area (Bagna Biebrzańskie) and protects some of the largest marshes and beat bogs in this part of the continent. With damp forests and vast river sprawls, it contains unique flora as well as rich and diverse fauna, with large numbers of species of birds, such as storks, cranes, and owls—the sandpiper is the park's symbol. It is home to the wolf, wild boar, fox, roe deer, otter, and beaver. It is also a natural sanctuary for the elk (moose), which was on the verge of extinction, but is now common in Poland and considered the king of this park.

Poland currently has one of the best and most elaborate environmental protection systems in the world. Besides its natural parks it has a plethora of nature reserves, landscape parks, natural monuments, protected landscape areas and botanical gardens. Even Polish kings in the early Middle Ages knew that nature had to be protected, thus they introduced edicts forbidding the hunting of certain animals or on certain grounds by establishing royal game reserves. But royal edicts could not stop heinous poaching, an example of which is the fate of the *tur*, an ancestor of today's domestic cattle, which was, as a species, able to survive the longest in Poland—the last living *tur* was killed by a poacher in 1627 in the Mazovia region. Only later did people start to understand that the wild and vast ecosystems in which these animals lived also had to be protected.

In 1529, a Lithuanian statute ordered that beavers and their lodges be protected by landowners. But by 1945 only two populations of beavers remained in all of Poland, and since 1974 they have been specially bred and reintroduced into the wild. Currently there are 14,000 beavers in the country. Another interesting story is that of the marmot (*świstak*), similar to a groundhog, whose fat was believed to have certain healing properties. Thus it was heavily poached, especially during the winter hibernation period, when entire colonies were dug up by poachers. In the nineteenth century the marmot was an endangered species in the Tatras, and in 1868 a Groundhog Protection Act, the first of its kind in the world, was introduced. But most interesting of all is that in 1875 two local notorious poachers in the Tatra region were hired as the first forest rangers to protect the very animals they had been hunting illegally. They became the marmot's most faithful and conscientious guardians, and there was a visible increase in the number of groundhogs in this mountainous region.

M.T.

CHAPTER 3

LEGENDARY TALES

"What cannot survive in nature can only survive in legends. Only
legend and myth do not know the limits of possibility."
–Andrzej Sapkowski, Polish writer, *Granica Możliwości*

Poland's rich collection of legends will take you back in time to ethe-
real people, events, and places constituting the core of Polish identity.
Although they differ by region, all carry a message that is universal
in character, yet one that constitutes the core of Polish identity. Some
of Poland's most well-known legends can roughly be divided into
four themes—those about the provenance of the Polish state, stories
about ominous creatures and, more tangibly, about menacing kings
and valiant heroes.

LECH, CZECH, AND RUS
O Lechu, Czechu i Rusie tells the story of three brothers who set out
to find better lands for their peoples. The Slavic tribes led by Lech,
Czech and Rus all lived peacefully side by side in a vast and sunny
valley where there was want for nothing. As the years passed, the
tribes expanded and their people grew in number. The land was over-
crowded, there was less game in the forests, and the fish in the rivers
did not suffice. The brothers knew that hunger would soon befall their
people, and discontent might lead to war between their tribes. Thus,
they decided that after harvest time they would set out together with
their people in search of new lands to settle, and all prepared for the
long journey well by packing food and whatever belongings they had.

The people of the three tribes traveled for weeks on end, until one day they came upon a majestic view, as monumental mountains with snow-capped peaks grew before their eyes. Czech galloped forward on his horse and, standing on a mountain ridge, saw fertile valleys with crystal-clear rivers running through thick forests. His heart sang with joy. "Here my people and I shall stay," Czech stated, and added, "Let us promise that no brother shall ever stand against brother." The brothers agreed and embraced one another warmly. Then the two remaining brothers, Lech and Rus, set out together with their people again to look for new lands.

The leaves started turning golden brown and the nights became cooler as they approached a vast plain. Grasses covered the plain like an endless ocean and the water spilling out of the rivers glistened in the sun. Overjoyed, Rus could not take his eyes away from the view. "My heart belongs here, this is the land my people and I have always dreamed of," he said solemnly. Thus, the two brothers departed, Rus to the east and Lech to the north.

The morning frost had already begun to cover the grass as Lech and his people headed forward, with some already becoming disheartened that they were passing over good lands, but Lech would not stay, and he was not wary—"This is not the place yet," he firmly stated. One day, as the sun was beginning to set, Lech and his people stopped to rest in the middle of a forest clearing. Surrounded by large, old trees, they noticed a nest (*gniazdo*) in the tallest tree of the forest, and in it a beautiful white eagle. The eagle majestically spread its wings, as if to pompously welcome the newcomers. Lech's heart was filled with joy. "This is the sign I have been looking for," he said. "Here we shall build our settlement and—" he pointed at the white eagle standing against the red background of a setting sun "—that shall be our coat of arms."

The place Lech chose came to be called Gniezdo, now known as Gniezno, and the settlement was to become the first capital of Poland.

KING POPIEL

O Popielu is the story of a king who made one too many sinister choices. In a fortified castle in Kruszwica near Lake Gopło there lived a king by the name of Popiel, who had been humble, righteous and wise before being chosen king. Afterward, Popiel took a liking for precious fabrics, silverware, and costly furs. He also chose a wife for himself, and not one from among his own people, but a foreigner, Hildegard, who turned out to be just as evil and cunning as he was to become. Together the king and queen delighted in worldly excesses as their people fell into deeper poverty and misery.

One day King Popiel's serfs came to pay him a visit, hoping that he would listen to what his people had to say and change his evil ways. Popiel wanted to hear none of it and shouted, "I will sooner be eaten by mice than allow you to tell me how to rule!" Thus the serfs left and Popiel lost a loyal serf army that would no longer come to his every call. "We will hire a foreign army," said Hildegard, "no need for you to worry."

The years passed by and the king and queen wallowed in luxuries, hosting expensive tournaments and pompous feasts, while the common people had nothing to eat. On a cold, rainy day an old woman knocked on the castle's great gate doors. "Take me to the king," she begged, shivering from the cold in her old rags. The guards told her the king would oust any beggar. "But I am his mother!" the old woman said. She was led before King Popiel and begged him to have mercy on his people, but Popiel only shouted, "Let me be eaten by mice if you are my mother!" and he ordered the guards to throw the old woman out into the dark, rainy night.

King Popiel was warned soon after that the people were ready to choose a new king from among his uncles. "Invite your uncles," said Queen Hildegard, "and leave the rest to me." The uncles were greeted accordingly, with a great feast and many a toast, entirely unaware that Hildegard had poisoned the wine they were drinking. This was to be the last feast of their lives. "Let me be eaten by mice if someone dares to threaten my rule now!" sneered King Popiel as he had the last of his uncles' bodies thrown into the waters of Lake Gopło.

As Popiel said these words the sky turned a dark hue and an ominous wind began to blow, and mice began creeping out of the dark lake's waters, quietly heading toward Popiel's fortified castle in rows of thousands. They started coming out of every corner, nook and cranny, ferociously biting and blocking any way of escape. Popiel tried to chase the mice away, but they were everywhere. "Let us flee to the island in the middle of the lake, to the high tower," he shouted to Hildegard, believing the mice would not be able to follow them there. How wrong he was, for even in the tower the mice surrounded him, crawling up his shoes, pockets, and into his sleeves. The mice ate Popiel alive, and the tower, called Mysia Wieża (Mouse Tower), stands in the town of Kruszwica as a living reminder still today.

THE WAWEL DRAGON

O smoku wawelskim takes us to times so distant that dragons still walked the earth and wreaked havoc in the lives of the common people. Dragons were a menacing breed that cared for no one, much less for the people that sometimes stood in their path. They spewed fire and devoured innocent victims, be it animal or human. This is the story of the Wawel dragon and the brave shoemaker who knew how to deceive the baleful creature.

In times long past there lived a king whose name was Krak. He was much loved and admired by his people for he was a just king, but he could not reign in peace, as the town was threatened by a bloodthirsty dragon that lived in a cave on the Wawel hillside. The dragon ate any animal that came its way, and the more it ate, the hungrier it became. It was a huge dragon, tall as a house, with thick, scaly skin, a long tail and huge wings. Fire came out of its huge mouth and puffs of smoke burst out of its large nostrils. Its feet had claws as long as a grown man's arm. The king had called together his advisors many times, but no spells or poisons could make the treacherous beast go away.

As its appetite grew, the dragon began roaming nearer the town and terrorizing its inhabitants. "Enough!" said King Krak, "there must be some other way to stop this unsightly beast! Go and tell all the people that whoever has enough courage and strength is to come forth before the king, for we are in great danger! Whoever defeats this murderous monster will receive a sack of gold, and will be the king's guest of honor!"

Surely enough, several undaunted men came forth—some for the gold, others for glory, and still others due to their patriotic love for their hometown. But no honestly brave heart, no wit and strength, no luck or courage, or even providence itself, could save them from the dragon's flames of fire. They all perished, turning into a heap of ashes before the dragon's dreadful cave.

A humble shoemaker by the name of Skuba, saddened by the evil dragon's treacherous ways and the brave men's defeats, sat down and thought intensely about how to help his townspeople. Finally, he came up with an ingenious plan and went forth to stand before the king. "You are but a shoemaker," said the worried king, "How do you plan to overcome this loathsome beast?" The shoemaker stood on sure feet, "It is not by strength that I will defeat the dragon, but by deceit." "Do as you feel is right," said the king, "for we all shall sooner perish." Skuba the shoemaker bought a ram, returned home and commenced work on the idea that had developed in his mind. He had to kill the poor animal, took out its bowels and filled its insides with sulfur. The next day, before sunrise, he placed the stuffed ram in front of the dragon's cave.

The dragon came out in the morning as usual, roaring, spitting fire and looking for a generous meal. Tempted by the ram's smell of flesh from afar, it quickly pounced upon the stuffed animal and swallowed it in one fiery gulp. Suddenly, the burning started inside its great stomach, moving upwards along its throat and tongue. The dragon ran for the Vistula River and drank and drank its water to lessen the burning pain, it drank so much that its stomach became bloated like a balloon and burst into a thousand pieces. The treacherous sound awakened the king and the townspeople.

The smell of sulfur and burnt dragon skin filled their nostrils as the people came out of their homes, but their hearts quickly filled with joy, for they understood that the dragon had been defeated and their lives were no longer in danger. They cheered loudly and proudly carried the humble shoemaker to the king's castle, where he was treated as a hero and guest of honor. Everyone could live in peace once more, and the town of Krakow was never to see so hard-fought a beast again.

THE SLEEPING KNIGHTS

O śpiących rycerzach takes place near Zakopane, in the heart of the mysterious Tatra Mountains. They say an army of valiant knights lies there in repose, patiently awaiting the day they will be awakened once more. They say this fearless cavalry arrived with King Bolesław the Brave, fought bravely and shed blood for their beloved homeland, but the people for whom they fought became unworthy of seeing them in all their majesty, thus they lay to sleep in the deep, secret, mountainous caves and will awaken when the time comes, when people will be able to tell good from evil...

It all started a very, very, long time ago when a little shepherd boy was tending to his flock of sheep high up in the mountains. He had wandered so far from the green pasture on which his sheep were grazing only to find himself in a place he had never been before. Surrounded by large, granite rocks and tall, thick evergreen trees, it seemed dark and foreboding. The shepherd boy did not know from which way he had come and which way to go to return to his grazing sheep, thus he called out bravely to hear his own echo. The echo came back, and along with it a musical sound so loud it sounded as if a thousand church organs were playing in unison. The shepherd boy was frightened, but even more so when he looked in awe as two large boulders on the side of the mountain suddenly parted in two, and a great knight in full regalia, with sword in hand, stood in the sun's glory.

"Who calls us forth?" he shouted loudly, looking around, "Who dares to awaken us from our slumber? Has the time come already?" The shepherd boy could not utter but a word, and then the knight saw him and said calmly: "Do not be afraid, for I am a warrior who has fought for our country. If your voice has awakened us from our slumber then you must be a good and just child. Come with me, for you will then tell the others what you have seen!" They entered the crevice that had formed from the two parting rocks, and the boy found himself in a cave greater than the interiors of any church he could have ever imagined. They passed by underground sky-blue lakes, chapels and waterfalls, all as if frozen by the eternity of time. They then entered a great hall that was as wide and as long as the eye could see. And there, standing before the little shepherd boy, were hundreds of rows of fully armored knights on splendidly decorated horses, shields and swords in hand, with great wings mounted on their backs. They were waiting anxiously, ready to fight.

"These are hussar knights, young lad," the knight continued, "they have shed much blood for our country and have been waiting. The time shall come when people will gain the wisdom necessary to differentiate right from wrong, when they will throw away the shackles binding them and, with great faith, will send a messenger, just like you. He will be the chosen one, from among millions, one with integrity so great that we will hear his call and awaken once more. There will be thunder and lightning, the waters will stir uneasily and spill out from the lakes and streams, and rains will cover the earth. Great rocks will fall from the mountains, the sun will hide and a great fog will allow no light. There will be great fear, weeping, and lamentation. And then silence shall befall the earth. But the sun will rise again and there will be light and rejoicing."

The shepherd boy was very moved and promised, "I will tell everyone what I have seen and heard. I want to teach people great wisdom and faith, so that perhaps one day what you have told me will come true!" The knights stirred uneasily on their horses, and so the messenger knight shouted, "The time has not yet come!" With these words the entire army of hussar knights and their horses suddenly froze still and returned to their slumber. The knight led the shepherd boy back to the entrance of the cave and said, "Go, and tell the others! For it will not be you who will return here again," and with these words the large boulders closed shut and he disappeared in the depths of the mountain to rest once more.

The boy ran home as quickly as his small legs could carry him. He told his father the great wonders he had seen and heard. "Son, you have been chosen to go forth and spread word of these wondrous things!" Thus his father sent his shepherd son to school to educate and prepare the boy for his life-long mission. The boy then went among the people, traveling near and far, and spreading, with great faith and truth, word of what had happened on the mountainside. The people who listened to him have been repeating those words of wisdom, faith, and love until today. But the time shall come that everyone will understand their important message. Then the just, chosen one will come to the same place in the Tatra Mountains to awaken the sleeping knights, and he will call out to them, "The time has come!"

M.T.

FURTHER READING

The Dragon of Krakow and Other Polish Stories by Richard Monte. Frances Lincoln Children's Books, 2008.

Old Polish Legends by F. C. Anstruther. Hippocrene Books, 1997.

CHAPTER 4

POLISH HISTORY IN A NUTSHELL

"Poland has been a source of trouble for over five hundred years."
–Franklin D. Roosevelt

There's no easy way to say this: Polish history is a long and complicated beast. Nonetheless, while it's a complex and often tragic tale, it is a fascinating one as well, and anyone interested in Poland and its people would be amiss to not have at least a cursory understanding of it. While you hardly need to be a historical scholar to live in Poland (and just like anywhere in the world, many Poles are ignorant of the lesser details of their own history), if you truly want to understand the Polish psyche, start with history.

First, one has to comprehend that Poland's history is above all shaped by two things: its neighbors (see Chapter 7) and war (Chapter 9). Most of the events that determined its fate are a result of those two factors (with a bit of rotten luck thrown in). During the many times in its history when it was occupied, whether under imperial or communist powers, the Polish nation held together through shared nationalism and religion. Though it's seen as a very Catholic nation today, both its Catholicism and its status as a nation only began in the tenth century.

In 966, Mieszko I brought Christianity to the heathens and the Kingdom of Poland was established in 1025. Not content with rule over a significant portion of the European continent, King Sigismund II Augustus, the last monarch of the Jagiełło clan, joined Poland with its northern neighbor Lithuania, forming the Polish-Lithuanian

Commonwealth. The fate of the two peoples was sealed in the mid-sixteenth century with the Union of Lublin, and though the two states were equal on paper, in reality, Poland dominated the partnership, and the Commonwealth's capital was Krakow at first, then Warsaw. So while the rest of Europe was mucking around exploring the New World, the Polish-Lithuanian Commonwealth grew to become one of the largest and most populous kingdoms during the sixteenth and seventeenth centuries, stretching from the Baltic to the Black Sea. It was also one of the first attempts at a quasi-democratic system, with an elective monarchy that was held accountable by a parliament comprised of the nobility—not to say that it was a democracy, as the nobility comprised at best 10% of the population and the peasantry did not fare particularly better than in other medieval kingdoms. Nonetheless, Polish monarchs were limited in their powers, and Poland was also uniquely religiously tolerant for the times.

Of course, all good things must come to an end, and for Poland that happened thrice over. Over the course of the eighteenth century, the Commonwealth was cut into pieces until there was nothing left (see Chapter 42). One by one, the Cossacks, the Swedes, the Russians, the Prussians, and the Hapsburg Austrians invaded, snatching up land as they came through. The constant invasions and warfare took their toll in the form of population loss and economic decline. However, the crisis also gave rise to a period of intellectual and artistic enlightenment, and the May 3 Constitution (now known mostly for creating four-day weekends together with the May 1 Labor Day holiday), passed in 1791, became the first modern constitution in Europe, as understood in the contemporary, largely American definition. Unfortunately, it didn't do much good for the declining state and only lasted as long as it took Russian troops to march into Warsaw. With the third and final partition of Poland in 1795, the Polish-Lithuanian Commonwealth ceased to exist, and Poles found themselves now citizens of Russia, Prussia, or Austria.

Though Poland disappeared from European maps for 123 years, Poles fought hard to keep their culture intact and even thriving, and widespread rebellions like the 1830 November Uprising kept morale (as well as body counts) high. During this period, the great Polish tradition of emigration (Chapter 43) began, a practice quite popular

January Uprising (against the Russian Empire), which started in January 1863 and was crushed the following year." Delete this part of the 2nd sentence: "Created by Worms after Boni, published on *L'Illustration, Journal Universel*, Paris, 1863. (Antonio Abrignani / Shutterstock.com)

to this day, with figures like Adam Mickiewicz, Cyprian Norwid, and Fryderyk Chopin all packing their bags to make their names outside Poland. Eastward, various Polish puppet states came and went, but for the most part the Polish nation remained under the rule of the three afore-mentioned powers.

World War I brought conflict across Europe, but its end brought Poland's return to the globe, as the 1919 Treaty of Versailles officially recognized it as a country once again. During the Polish-Soviet War of 1919-1921, the Polish army took advantage of Russia's preoccupation with its own civil war to invade and annex old Commonwealth lands in Lithuania, Belarus, and Ukraine. This didn't last long, as Stalin got those lands back and then some thanks to the Molotov–Ribbentrop Pact and invasion by both Nazi Germany and Soviet Russia in September 1939 (Chapter 9).

The devastation of Poland and near-elimination of what had previously been a thriving Jewish community followed during World War II. For Poles, this is the volume of history that lives on to this day, in part because there are those around who still remember it, and in part because its impact can still be felt and seen. The end of the war left Poland missing one third of its population—roughly six million people, half of them Jews, lost their lives, while many more were displaced. It also lost one third of its land area, as the borders shifted westwards, with Poland losing its eastern territories to the Soviet Union and gaining former German lands—without their native German populations—which were often forcibly removed by Polish communists (with Soviet backing and large popular support) under the guise of the Potsdam Agreement.

The next forty-five years were a different type of occupation: officially, Poland was an independent "People's Republic." In reality, its fate was controlled by Moscow, and if it showed signs of rebellion, it was swiftly and brutally punished. The worst came between the years 1948 and 1956, which included a systematic elimination of Poland's middle and upper classes and intelligentsia, consisting of academics, scientists, artists, poets and the like. Though overall everyday life went on under the communist system, two very important events would lead to the end of Soviet rule, first in Poland and then the rest of the Soviet Bloc.

The first was the appointment of a (relatively) young Polish cardinal named Karol Wojtyła as Pope John Paul II. While the Pope did not bring down communism single-handedly, he as well as the Catholic Church in Poland created a mental and spiritual space that was separate from the communist sphere dominating all other aspects of daily life. With his visit to Poland in 1979, Pope John Paul II drew millions to an event not sponsored by the state—this was utterly unheard of during the previous forty years. The Church would also provide the physical spaces for underground meetings, theater productions, and art shows that were deemed "antisocialist" by the authorities. Meanwhile, that spark of hope created by the Pope's visit, together with an ever-worsening economic situation and general unrest, led to the largest series of organized strikes in the nation and the formation of the first independent trade union in the Soviet Bloc: Solidarity. Though it would take another nine years for Poland to hold its first semi-free elections, and then another year for it to truly become independent as the Soviet system collapsed, the seeds of revolution had been sown in 1980.

The 1990s were a hard decade for Poles (see Chapter 11). Yes, the Third Polish Republic was established in 1990, with Solidarity hero Lech Wałęsa elected president that December. However, the communist system had left Poland with crippling debt and failing infrastructure. What followed was a period called "shock therapy," which saw factories closed, industries privatized, people losing their once always-secure jobs, funding for the arts dropping, and prices rising dramatically as the country opened its markets to the world for the first time in fifty years. Poland emerged from its growing pains stronger than ever, however, joining NATO in 1999, the European Union in 2004, and drawing in foreign investment by the busload (Chapter 12).

Today, Poland still struggles with the legacy of its past while trying to preserve its memory. Young Poles have more in common with their counterparts across Europe than their grandparents, though that doesn't stop them from listening to stories of the "good and bad old days." So if you meet an elder Pole today lamenting about how much better things were under the "old system" or recalling their forefathers' tales of war, just smile and give an understanding nod.

A.S.

FURTHER READING

God's Playground (Volumes I & II) by Norman Davies. Columbia University Press, 2005.

Heart of Europe: The Past in Poland's Present by Norman Davies. Oxford University Press, 2001.

The Polish Way: A Thousand-Year History of the Poles and Their Culture by Adam Zamoyski. Hippocrene Books, 1993.

CHAPTER 5

KINGS & QUEENS

"He came to a Poland built of wood and left it built of brick."
(A Polish saying about Casimir III the Great, king of Poland)

The most famous collection of portraits of Poland's entourage of kings and queens was painted by Jan Matejko, one of Poland's, and Europe's, most prominent representatives of historical paintings (see Chapter 37). Matejko not only paid particular artistic attention to historical detail in the costumes, weapons, and interiors he depicted, but also tried to genuinely breathe some life into his portraits of Polish rulers by ensuring that their facial expressions and postures reflected the kinds of people they might have been, why they had made certain decisions and undertaken the actions that historians without fail so scrupulously analyzed and described in voluminous history books—all of which sometimes seems so distant to modern-day Poles. What kind of people were some of these kings and queens of Poland's rich historical past? What could they have been like in everyday life? This we will try to discover by looking into some of their lives in more detail...

POLAND'S FIRST RULERS—THE PIAST DYNASTY

Mieszko I (reigned ca. 963–992), the first official ruler of the country of Poland, known as *Polonia* in Latin, reigned over peoples that were entirely pagan. With the neighboring Holy Roman Empire eager to take political control over these Slavic pagans by converting them, Mieszko

Mieszko I of Poland and Bolesław the Brave. Old illustration of bronze group statue in Posen cathedral. Created by Stal, published on Magasin Pittoresque, Paris, 1845. (Antonio Abrignani / Shutterstock.com)

I quickly realized that accepting Christianity would be the only politically and culturally rational choice in keeping the uninvited evangelizing (read: colonizing) guests out of his territories. He turned instead to the Czechs, who had already sought and accepted Christianity for their court, and asked to marry their Bohemian princess Dobrava (Dąbrówka in Polish), a devout Christian. They married in the year 965, but upon arriving the princess stated firmly that she would have none of his preposterous, barbaric ways, and that he would have to throw off the hurdles of paganism and accept the Christian way of life before they consummated their marriage as husband and wife (probably not the first or last example of such demands in history). On Mieszko's behalf, this meant parting with the seven pagan wives that shared his bed. It is said that both Jordan, the first known missionary cleric in the Polish court, and the newly wed princess Dąbrówka "worked very hard" to change the ways of Mieszko I and his courtiers. In 966 Mieszko I and his court were considered ready to accept the sacrament of baptism, and after this christening ceremony Poland formally became a part of European Christendom. Accepting Christianity meant direct association with, as well as future papal protection from, Rome. It also meant avoiding an imminent war with the German Roman Emperor. Above all, Poland's official baptism meant it had joined the cultural and political Western world of Christianity. This one religion was to introduce organizational order through the learned Christian clerics, who began helping run the state and treasury and introduced literacy in state institutions through Latin—the official language of the Church and Western diplomacy. Wanting to emphasize this independence of the Polish lands he had fought so hard to unite, Mieszko I took one more political step in officially laying down the boundaries of his realm by placing them under the protection of the Pope in a document he drew up shortly before his death, called the *Dagome Iudex*.

Bolesław the Brave (Bolesław I Chrobry) (reigned ca. 992–1025) was the firstborn son of Mieszko I and Dobrava. Sent as a child to the imperial court of the Holy Roman Empire as a guarantee of political peace between the two nations, he later had to fight, upon his return, to regain power from his three half-brothers and their widowed German mother, Oda, who had come to be Mieszko I's second wife. Bolesław wanted to continue the unifying policy his father had started, thus he banished his stepbrothers, along with their mother, and began reigning in 992—the year of his father's death. He made sure that relations with the Holy Roman Empire were favorable and wanted to use the Christian faith, just as his father had before him, to strengthen Poland's internal policy. Such an opportunity appeared in 996, when a missionary monk, Wojciech (Vojtěch in Czech), was sent by Pope Sylvester I to Bolesław's court. This new missionary, the Bishop of Prague, had come with the mission of evangelizing the non-Slavic Prussians, a pagan people inhabiting lands northeast of the Vistula River. Hostile and unwilling to accept these new Christian beliefs he was trying to introduce, a small group of Prussians attacked and murdered Wojciech as he was celebrating Holy Mass. Wojciech's untimely death could not have come at a more convenient time for Bolesław, who quickly reacted and bought what was left of the Bishop's tortured remains for their weight in gold, which he then laid to rest in the Cathedral of Gniezno. Wojciech was canonized by the Pope in 999, and Bolesław was fortunate enough to have the saint's relics in the capital of his country. This, in turn, led to a pilgrimage visit by the new Emperor Otto III, who had been a good friend of the late martyr saint (see Chapter 15). Otto III was greeted with grandeur and reverence as stories of miracles attracted large numbers of faithful pilgrims to the saint's tomb. This new martyr cult raised the status of the Polish Church. Bolesław the Brave further expanded Polish territories and cemented Poland's position and borders—he was crowned the first king of Poland with the official permission of Pope John XIX in Gniezno in 1025. This royal power came directly from God, as Bolesław was officially named "pomazaniec Boży"—"divinely anointed"—and was to be treated on equal terms with the other European kings.

Bolesław III Wrymouth (Bolesław III Krzywousty) (reigned 1102–1138) was called such either because he had a deformed face or due to his cunning and sardonic personality. The mistake his ruling father, Władysław Herman, had made upon his deathbed took a full turn when Bolesław himself was to draw up a testament. But let us start from the beginning…

Bolesław's father had been forced to divide Poland between Bolesław and his older brother, Zbigniew. Bolesław, however, decided to rule single-handedly and drove his brother out of the kingdom in 1107. Zbigniew turned to the Emperor Henry V for help and together they invaded Poland in 1109. Bolesław defeated the Emperor's army near Wrocław as well as regaining control of Pomerania, where a gradual German invasion had weakened Poland's position. Three years later he agreed to peacefully accept his brother Zbigniew back, only to have him captured and cruelly blinded by gouging out his eyes. Zbigniew died shortly after this brutal attack, and Władysław, to show signs of repentance, mortified his flesh and took part in various pilgrimages. He also made the rulers of West Pomerania accept Christianity and sent evangelizing missions there. Despite being able to successfully establish a strong state in this region and to uphold Poland's place as a sovereign country in Central Europe, he was never crowned king and ruled as a duke until his death. So, what very unfortunate mistake did he make? In order to avoid any fratricidal rivalry among his own progeny, he too decided to divide Poland into five duchies, each of which was to be ruled by one of his five sons. The eldest son was given reign in his own duchy of Krakow, power to exert suzerainty over his four other brothers and to oversee the entire country's foreign affairs. This son however, Władysław the Exile (Władysław Wygnaniec), was, as his name suggests, soon driven from the country's territories by his brothers, each of whom wanted to reign on his own. This fateful division of Polish lands was to have many negative repercussions in Poland's international and internal policy, and was to last almost two hundred years.

Casimir III the Great (Kazimierz III Wielki) (reigned 1333–1370) became king of Poland at the age of twenty-three. He was tall, handsome, loved the company of women, good food, and wine—thus there were no promising signs that his reign would be successful, much less exceptional. He turned out to be a man of great wisdom, understanding, and foresight. The famous saying refers to his having introduced a building program where brick and stone, instead of wood, were to be used—sixty-five new fortified towns, fifty-three new castles as well as great fortified walls for twenty-seven existing towns were built. This doubled the number of existing towns and building structures before his reign. He had the stone cathedrals of Gniezno and Krakow erected along with many more churches—the Collegiate Church of Sandomierz in particular. He introduced a codified legal system, one for Greater Poland and the other for the Lesser Poland region, and entirely reformed the fiscal system. He also established a state monarchy where the king, gentry, clergy, bourgeoisie, and peasantry had their own specific rights and duties. He granted Jewish and other minority groups their own rights and laws. The Great Plague of 1348 had decimated all of Europe, but most Polish territory remained unaffected due to its sparsely populated areas, which lacked dense concentrations of people. After the plague came a widespread famine, and Poland's population grew as survivors roamed all over Europe in search of a refuge—this was especially true for the Jews, who had become a sort of scapegoat in some of the greatest anti-Jewish atrocities that befell them in medieval Europe. They fled east, mainly to Poland, where they were welcomed and given religious freedom. This allowed for a growth of industry, with an influx of skilled artisans and merchants, manufactured goods, banking, and other facilities. Casimir changed existing salt deposits into profitable salt mines, bringing huge revenues to the state budget, and had a canal constructed linking the salt mines of Wieliczka with the capital of Krakow. Finally, he founded a university, the first in Poland and only second in all of Central Europe—the Krakow Academy—in 1364, later to be known as the world-renowned Jagiellonian University. Called "the Great" during his lifetime, he was married four times but left no legitimate heir of his own, thus becoming the last representative of the great Piast dynasty that had ruled Polish lands for nearly 400 years. His successor was the king of Hungary, Louis of Anjou (Ludwik Andegaweński).

THE JAGIELLON DYNASTY

Sigismund II Augustus (Zygmunt II August) (reigned 1548–1572) was the son of Sigismund I the Old (Zygmunt I Stary) and Queen Bona Sforza. He was crowned king of Poland upon his mother's insistence at the tender age of ten. His first wife, Elizabeth Habsburg, died two years after their marriage. He then fell in love with the beautiful Lithuanian Barbara Radziwiłł (Radziwiłłówna). Supposedly egotistic and capricious in character, she was accepted neither by the gentry, the subjects, nor other members of the royal family, with the king's mother, Queen Bona Sforza, leading the pack. He loved Barbara dearly nevertheless, and showered her with opulent luxuries and precious jewels. They were secretly married in 1547, and the king had her crowned at Wawel three years later—with Queen Bona unwillingly accepting her as a new daughter-in-law. But the newly found happiness was not to last long. Barbara grew gravely ill in the following months and, much to the king's utter despair, the royal physicians could do nothing to save her. His beloved wife died five months after her coronation. Sigismund dressed entirely in black as a sign of mourning until the end of his days and kept her belongings as if they were

John III Sobieski. Engraved by J. Thomson and published in *The Gallery Of Portraits With Memoirs*, United Kingdom, 1833.
(Georgios Kollidas / Shutterstock.com)

relics. He also reluctantly married for a third time—this time it was his first deceased wife's sister, Katherine of Habsburg. The marriage ended in failure as he was physically repelled by his new wife, which even became a concern of the state and Church. With no heirs he became the last king of the great Jagiellonian dynasty, whose founder had been **Ladislaus II Jagiełło** (Władysław Jagiełło), the Grand Duke of Lithuania who accepted Christianity for himself and his people when crowned king of Poland. It had been Jagiełło under whose command, in the year 1410, allied Polish and Lithuanian forces defeated the Teutonic knights at the Battle of Grunwald—one of the greatest victories in Polish history.

ONE KING TO RULE THEM ALL

John III Sobieski (Jan III Sobieski) (reigned 1674–1696) lived during a time when there was a culmination of Polish-Turkish wars. He became king of Poland in 1674 after triumphantly having defeated the Ottoman Turks with his army at Chocim the year before. A brilliant military strategist and skillful soldier, he fought in numerous battles against the Muslim Tatars and Turks, who saw Europe as a territory to execute their *jihad* and whom he considered constant foes in a general crusade against the infidels. In a broader aspect this meant ongoing rivalry between a Christian Europe and a Muslim front from the southeast. A decade later, in 1683, the sultan proclaimed another *jihad* and a great Ottoman army rapidly advanced into Europe and laid siege to Vienna. The fifty-four-year-old Polish king, who marched his great army of 36,000 from Poland in a matter of fourteen days, stood in command of his own men and the allied troops of the Habsburg Empire—70,000 soldiers altogether who had formed a front over 11 km long—with the especially impressive *Husaria*, the unrivalled Polish heavy cavalry. Some of the Turkish military leaders who had fought his troops in other battles turned back in defeat on the Viennese battlefield, and as many as 10,000 to 15,000 Turks out of the 90,000 present on that day were killed. John III Sobieski victoriously defeated the Ottoman leader, Kara Mustafa, freed Vienna and, in a greater context, saved Christian Europe from the hands of the Muslims. That same day he is said to have sat down and written a letter to his beloved wife, whom he tenderly called Marysieńka, for Sobieski has also come down in history as a prolific letter-writer, producing nearly one letter a day for twenty years, all of which were faithfully addressed to her, the French Marie d'Arquien. Poland was at that time the largest state in Europe, and Sobieski's personal ambition was to establish a new Polish dynasty, which he believed would strengthen the country. Yet, in order for the monarch's rule to be effective, he needed the approval and support of the magnates, but enforcing reforms and the magnates' accepting his strong position as a monarch turned out to be futile, as they had never failed to forget that he had been one of their own. With these dynastically minded dreams in mind, Sobieski had a majestic, baroque palace built in Wilanów (near Warsaw).

These Polish rulers from Matejko's collection of royal portraits, men and women of flesh and bone, were just some of the many to reign over Polish lands.

M.T.

FURTHER READING

Kingdoms of Europe by Gene Gurney. Crown Publishers, Inc., 1982.

An Outline History of Poland by Jerzy Topolski. Interpress Publishers, 1986.

The Polish Way. A Thousand-Year History of the Poles and Their Culture by Adam Zamoyski. Butler & Tanner Ltd, 1987.

CHAPTER 6

CAPITAL(S)

CAŁY NARÓD BVDVJE SWOJĄ STOLICĘ
THE WHOLE NATION BUILDS ITS CAPITAL
(An inscription on the façade of a post–WWII building in Warsaw)

As Poland's borders have shifted over the years, so has the nation's capital, from Gniezno to Poznań, Krakow, and Warsaw—in that order. In the beginning, there was no official capital as we understand it today, because the "capital" was where the country's ruler, duke, or king resided with his trusted team of advisors, and they tended to move from one fortified settlement to another. It was Gniezno that, according to legend, was chosen as prime real estate for the Polish nation by the Slavic Lech and his people (see Chapter 3).

THE "NEST" OF THE EARLY KINGDOM
Probably established around the eighth century, **Gniezno** is considered the cradle of the first state, when in the tenth century the leaders of the *Polanie* tribe unified the other tribes throughout the region and made Gniezno their main stronghold. The year 966 marked Mieszko I's baptism there, which further strengthened Gniezno's position. It was mainly from the fortified castle in Gniezno that rulers of the Piast dynasty presided over the land.

Otto III's pompous visit in 1000 further strengthened Gniezno's position. This emperor of the Holy Roman Empire was at that time considered the greatest and most powerful ruler on the

European continent. Fervently devout, he dreamed of creating a universal Roman Empire that would embrace all Christianized lands beyond his own, which is why he fully accepted Mieszko I's eldest son, Bolesław the Brave (Chrobry), as a sovereign ruler of the Polish territories. Gniezno thus became an important religious center with its newly established archbishopric in 1000, and in 1025 Bolesław the Brave was crowned the first Polish king in the fortified settlement's cathedral.

But it was in **Poznań** that Mieszko I had obtained permission to establish the first missionary bishopric years before Gniezno's archbishopric was established. From a chronological perspective the first cathedral was also built in Poznań, and both Mieszko I's and Bolesław the Brave's remains were laid there—for Polish kings were buried in Poznań, not in Gniezno. In this sense, Poznań was more important politically than Gniezno at that time.

The term Greater Poland (Wielkopolska), the region where both Gniezno and Poznań are situated, comes from the Latin *Polonia Major*, whose meaning emphasized its historic importance in the founding of a sovereign, Polish state. But all of this changed when the Bohemians (the Czech variety, not the hippie kind), led by Duke Bretislaus I, raided and plundered the area of Poznań and Gniezno in the years 1038-1039, and the seat of power moved to Krakow in the Lesser Poland region, which was seen as a more peaceful and secure place from which to reign. Nevertheless, Polish kings continued to be crowned in Gniezno until the end of the thirteenth century, and it also retained its position as the ecclesiastical capital of the Polish Catholic Church.

ROYAL KRAKOW

The region of Lesser Poland, in turn, was called *Polonia Minor* in Latin to signify that it was the "younger Poland." A bishopric was established in **Krakow** in the year 1000, and around 1040 this fortified settlement was chosen as the royal capital of the Piast kingdom. The Wawel Castle and the several churches encircling it were built in the eleventh century, and Wawel became the residence of the Jagiellonian (Jagiełło) dynasty's rulers. Krakow was thus to become the place of coronations, burials, and the seat of Poland's

Wawel Castle, Krakow. Trousset encyclopedia (1886–1891). (Morphart Creation / Shutterstock.com)

rulers for over five hundred years—you can still visit the tombs of over a dozen Polish kings, saints, and bards at the Royal Cathedral at Wawel.

World War II left Krakow more or less intact, thus the city has a plethora of historic buildings in the architectural styles of different periods. Its historic center, medieval buildings, monuments, and priceless art collections were included in UNESCO's first World Cultural Heritage list of 1978. The city has its own magical atmosphere of historically based tradition mingling with innovative ideas in art, film, music, cabaret, and theater. Home to the second oldest university in Central Europe, the 600-year-old Jagiellonian University, it is where learning and science have always prospered, and it remains the cultural and artistic heart of Poland—something no proud Cracovian will fail to mention, particularly to a rival Varsovian.

THE MOVE TO WARSAW

Warsaw is today's capital of Poland, although historically it is its youngest. Several legends surround the city's origins and name, though most mention twins or a couple named Wars and Sawa and a tale of generous Polish hospitality during a royal visit. At the beginning of the fourteenth century Warsaw became the stronghold of the Mazovian dukes, and in 1413 it was chosen as their seat.

In 1526, when the last Mazovian duke died without an heir, the entire Mazovian region, including Warsaw, was reincorporated into the Polish kingdom and came under the direct rule of the Jagiellonian kings in Krakow. In 1569 the Sejm that had convened in Lublin to unify Poland and Lithuania as a single state voted that Warsaw, due to its centrally located position on the political map, would be the seat of the Sejm's debates. By 1573 Warsaw had also become the seat of royal elections, although Poland's kings would continue to reside in Krakow.

Finally, the main transfer of political and cultural life from Krakow came in the years 1596–1609, when King Sigismund III Vasa decided to move the capital to be geographically closer to the heart of the Polish-Lithuanian Commonwealth and, secretly, to Sweden, his homeland. Thus Warsaw has remained the capital of Poland since 1611—a year many Cracovians rue to this day.

The capital has suffered great damage and splendid growth throughout the torrents of the history that befell it; the Swedish invasion of 1655–1660 brought much damage (see Chapter 9), but the eighteenth century was to become Warsaw's period of great prosperity when many splendid churches and palaces were built. Its cultural and artistic life flourished under the reign of Poland's last king, Stanisław August Poniatowski, and 1791 marked the year of the signing of Europe's first modern constitution in Warsaw. The Third Partition of 1795 left the city under Prussian rule, and its status was degraded to that of a provincial town, but Napoleon reinstated it as a capital in 1807 with the creation of the Duchy of Warsaw.

After World War I, Warsaw was reinstated as the capital of an independent Poland, but not for long. On September 1, 1939 the first bombs fell on the city and it was taken over within one week by the Nazis. Despite its inhabitants' brave resistance, the city had to capitulate on September 28. Jews comprised a significant portion of the capital's population, and the five-year Nazi occupation period was marked by the creation of a Jewish ghetto, constant arrests, deportations, executions, and general terror.

The city was witness to two major uprisings during that time (see Chapters 8 and 9 for detailed descriptions). The Warsaw Ghetto Uprising in April 1943 was launched by the Jewish resistance as an effort to stop the final transport of the ghetto's population to Nazi extermination camps, with fighting lasting for almost a month. Despite additional help from Polish Resistance fighters, the Jewish quarter and its remaining population were annihilated completely, mainly through the burning blaze of Nazi flamethrowers and smoke bombs. The Warsaw Uprising, in turn, was orchestrated by the Polish Home Army (AK) to liberate the capital from Nazi German occupation before the Soviets could do the job, and raged on for sixty-three days beginning on August 1, 1944. The Nazis razed Warsaw to the ground, and the Red Army only moved in at the beginning of 1945 to help "liberate" what was basically a non-existent city.

Nearly 85% of Warsaw's buildings had been utterly destroyed, and over half a million of its inhabitants had died during the war—no other Polish city had suffered so much destruction and loss of human life—but a decision was made to rebuild the city, with its historic buildings, such as the Royal Castle, meticulously reconstructed in their entirety.

Warsaw had to raise itself from the ashes and ruins, and all of its surviving postwar inhabitants took part in this gigantic task of rebuilding the capital. Today skyscrapers designed by the world's most renowned architects stand next to monumental communist-era buildings. The most eye-catching and still controversial landmark is the Palace of Culture and Science, built in the years 1952–1955 as a "gift from the Soviet Union to the people of Poland"—or "Uncle Stalin's 'gift' to Warsaw" as many Varsovians say sarcastically. Whether one thinks of it as iconic or an eyesore, the Palace of Culture is an indispensable part of the modern Warsaw skyline.

Busy, cosmopolitan and progressive as well as the major center of Poland's dynamic political, economic, and cultural life, Warsaw is a frenzied mixture of small cafes, classy restaurants, funky art galleries, chic boutiques, state-of-the-art museums, as well as of the innovative architectural design of steel-and-glass constructions of the future.

M.T.

CHAPTER 7

NEIGHBORLY RELATIONS

"I judged the Poles by their enemies. And I found it was an almost unfailing truth that their enemies were the enemies of magnanimity and manhood. If a man loved slavery, if he loved usury, if he loved terrorism and all the trampled mire of materialistic politics, I have always found that he added to these affections the passion of a hatred of Poland. She could be judged in the light of that hatred; and the judgment has proved to be right."
– Gilbert Keith Chesterton

Life with neighbors can be hard. For Poland, sometimes it could be downright impossible. Historically, three of Poland's neighbors in particular have caused it periods of difficulty (to put it mildly) throughout the ages: Germany, Russia, and Austria. From a historical standpoint, the fact that Poland now finds itself in a stable partnership such as the European Union with two out of the three (and on good terms, relatively speaking, with the third) is nothing short of a miracle. That's not to say that Poland has always played the victim when it came to territorial disputes; in fact, those just beginning to learn about Poland's history will most likely be surprised at the number of times Poland has taken the role of aggressor (see Chapter 9). Nonetheless, more often than not, Poland's neighbors have shaped its fate.

GERMANY
The formation of both Germany and Poland as distinct cultural and national entities began at roughly the same time, in the tenth century.

It was also at that time that the Germans (then the Holy Roman Empire) and the Poles (then the Kingdom of Poland) clashed for the first time. The forces of Poland's Mieszko I met German Emperor Otto I the Great as the former was expanding his empire to the west and the latter to the east. Luckily, and not for the first or last time, major conflict was avoided through the clever use of marriage, and the two empires coexisted in an unsteady alliance for several centuries. It also helped that until the Reformation, the two peoples shared a common religion (Roman Catholicism), and were thus both under the dominion of the Pope.

From the thirteenth century, Poland began to receive settlers from German lands. In many ways, the two neighbors would continue to influence each other, with German immigrants populating western Polish towns and cities and helping to establish a merchant class. Meanwhile, up north the Germanic Teutonic Knights, first enlisted by Polish Duke Konrad Mazowiecki to help him attempt to conquer pagan Baltic lands and keep its people from fighting back, ended up conquering large swaths of Polish lands along the Baltic Sea, including the area of present-day Gdańsk. Fighting between the Teutonic Knights and the Poles continued well into the times of the Polish-Lithuanian Commonwealth, even when relations between Germany and Poland were relatively stable. The Battle of Grunwald (a big deal in Poland to this day) in the early fifteenth century ended with a victorious Poland-Lithuania defeating the Knights, who, while retaining most of their lands, never regained their former glory after the defeat.

As the Commonwealth began to decline and its central authority weakened in the seventeenth century, Poland's neighbors began to take advantage of its diminished state. On the German side, this meant that the newly dubbed Kingdom of Prussia took over Silesia from the Austrians (western Poland) in the mid-eighteenth century, then initiated the first Partition of Poland in 1772, taking over the areas of Pomerania (northwestern Poland) and Warmia (northeastern Poland) along the Baltic. Further Partitions in 1793 and 1795 gave the Prussians more lands to the south, including the city of Warsaw (though it would soon come under Russian rule).

The end of World War I resulted in the end of the Kingdom of Prussia and the start of the Second Republic of Poland. Poland regained its nationhood, and with it a part of Silesia. A small part of Pomerania became the Free City of Danzig (today's Gdańsk).

Sadly, peace was short-lived. On September 1, 1939, Hitler ordered his troops into Poland and the second German occupation of the country officially began (see Chapter 9 for a detailed account of World War II). Germany immediately annexed most of western Poland as far as Łódź, and under Hitler's orders, the Poles living in those lands were largely killed or "resettled" farther east. While the full wrath of Hitler was taken out on Poland's Jewish population (see Chapter 8), about 2.8 million non-Jewish Poles also died during the war, many in German labor and extermination camps—particularly members of the intelligentsia. Hitler's goal was nothing short of the elimination of the Polish race.

The Nazi war machine not only destroyed the lives and property of Polish citizens, but embittered Polish-German relations for the next half-century. In the aftermath, Warsaw stood almost completely leveled, Poland was once again under occupation (this time by the Soviets), and the future looked grim. As compensation, Poland received the former German lands of Silesia and Pomerania to the west and north, forming the present-day border along the Oder (Odra) and Neisse (Nysa Łużycka) rivers. Poland gained the cities of Gdańsk and Wrocław (while simultaneously losing Lviv and Vilnius in the east) as its borders were redrawn once again, which also lead to the mass expulsion of millions of ethnic Germans from those lands.

During the Cold War, the communist Polish government officially enjoyed good relations with East Germany; unofficially, many Poles were defecting to democratic nations in Europe, including West Germany. Relations finally began to normalize in the 70s and 80s, but it wasn't until the fall of the Iron Curtain that the two nations began to truly cooperate, starting with the newly-unified Germany's support of Poland's entry into NATO and later the EU.

Today, aside from the occasional xenophobic outburst from conservative politicians from both countries, Poland and Germany are partners within the EU. This has allowed for an active exchange of people between the two countries, whether between universities, for employment (generally Poles going to Germany) or for tourism. Former German cities are remembering and emphasizing their roots as they welcome German tourists. While tensions do crop up and plenty of cultural stereotypes remain (that of the Polish car thief stealing German cars is a mainstay of popular culture), these days, younger Germans and Poles share more similarities than differences.

RUSSIA

Considering the atrocities of the Nazis, present-day visitors to Poland might be surprised to learn that Russians, not Germans, are still viewed as "the enemy" by many Poles. Much of this has to do with recent history; after all, the Nazi occupation ended over sixty years ago, while it's been barely more than twenty years since Poland was freed from the Soviet yoke. And while the brutality of the Nazis lasted just six years, Poland was subjected to fifty years of hardship at the hands of the USSR—a fact not easily forgotten by the older generation in Poland today.

It wasn't until the sixteenth century that conflict between Poland (then the Polish-Lithuanian Commonwealth) and Russia (then Muscovy) truly began. While the western lands of Poland and Germany were defined by their Roman Catholicism from the tenth century on, the Russian states to the east were set apart by their loyalty to the Eastern Orthodox or Byzantine Church. This became a source of tension for several centuries, not least when Polish forces took Moscow in the early seventeenth century, taking advantage of strife within the Russian Tsardom to expand Polish territory.

When the Commonwealth began to decline, Russia (now the Russian Empire) was able to participate in the three Partitions of Poland, absorbing the country's eastern and northeastern territories, including the city of Vilnius. In the early nineteenth century the non-existent country of Poland received help from an unlikely source—Napoleon Bonaparte. As the French emperor and his forces marched eastwards, volunteer Polish troops almost 100,000 soldiers strong joined his army, not so much out of the goodness of their hearts, but in hopes of being rewarded with an independent Polish state. While that pipe dream failed to materialize, the short-lived Duchy of Warsaw, created by Napoleon from Prussian lands, gave Poles hope once again. That hope was dashed, of course, as the Russians chased Napoleon back west and occupied the new territory and partitioned it again, taking Warsaw for themselves this time. Thus a new "state" was created by the Congress of Vienna: the Kingdom of Poland.

The Kingdom of Poland (also known as Congress Poland) was created as an autonomous region within the Russian Empire from the lands that had constituted the Duchy. In reality, however, the Kingdom was a puppet state of the Empire. Never quite happy being occupied, the Poles would make trouble for the Russians for the next century or so, and the emperors would strike back with increasing restrictions on the Poles' freedoms. Thus life continued until the outbreak of World War I.

The war pitted Poland's three partitioners against each other, and ended with a free Polish state, though not without further Polish-Russian conflicts. The most significant of these was the Polish–Soviet War of 1919–21, in which a strong Polish offensive took on the newly-created Red Army and won… for the most part. The result was a return to similar borders as during the Commonwealth for the next twenty years.

In 1939, as Hitler's forces were marching across Poland from the west, Stalin's Red Army entered Poland, this time victoriously. The infamous Molotov-Ribbentrop Pact sealed Poland's fate as its neighbors carved it up once again, and when Hitler's forces grew overzealous and invaded the USSR, the Red Army marched on all the way to Germany.

While Nazi atrocities have been widely documented and publicized, many Soviet atrocities weren't acknowledged until the fall of the Iron Curtain. The worst among these is the 1940 Katyn Massacre, in which between 14,500 and 22,000 Polish officers and intellectuals were shot by the Soviet secret police and buried in several sites in the woods of western Russia (a very bitter topic to this day). All in all, hundreds of thousands of Poles were killed or sent to Siberia (generally a death sentence in itself) by the invading Soviet forces, including during the period of 1941–1945, when the two counties were "allies."

Another bitter topic for Poles is the Yalta Conference that followed the end of World War II. The words "betrayal" and "selling out" often follow a conversation on this topic, and not without reason. In a nutshell, the western Allies bowed to Stalin's demands and placed Poland within his control, thus creating the communist People's Republic of Poland, which would exist under the threat of Soviet tyranny until 1989 (see Chapter 10).

Though Poland regained its freedom once again in 1989, it wasn't until 1993 that the last Soviet troops left its soil and the country breathed a collective sigh of relief. Since then, relations between Poland and the Russian Federation have see-sawed over the years, with tensions reaching a high due to Poland's admission to NATO and the EU and thus its departure from the Russian sphere of influence. Poland's friendliness toward the U.S. has also been met with Russian resistance. More recently, however, relations improved when the Russian government and citizens gave an overwhelming show of sympathy following the 2010 Smolensk plane crash that killed the president and many high-ranking governmental and military officials (despite the prevalence of conspiracy theories that also arose on both sides). While many Poles remain suspicious of Russia today, politicians from both nations have strived to put on a friendly face and look toward the future.

AUSTRIA

As far as occupying forces go, most historians would agree that Habsburg Austria (later Austria-Hungary) was as good as it got. Though the country participated in the Partitions of Poland along with Prussia and Russia, the Polish territories that were lucky enough to fall within Austrian rule enjoyed the most freedom of the bunch.

Poland's southwestern neighbor famously benefited from Polish help during the Battle of Vienna in the late seventeenth century, during which, according to some, Polish King John III Sobieski single-handedly defeated the Ottomans and saved Vienna and thus Christendom from the Turks (in reality, the combined forces of the Holy Roman Empire and the Polish-Lithuanian Commonwealth won the battle that would be the turning point in the 300-year conflict between the Ottomans and the Habsburgs). Either way, the king's contribution was significant enough to warrant branding a vodka after him some centuries later.

Perhaps it was this remembered debt of gratitude that led the Habsburg monarchy to spare the Polish people in its territories many of the hardships their compatriots were being subjected to under Prussian and Russian rule. Though the Austrian-controlled territory was smaller than the other Partitions, it included the cities of Krakow and Lwów (now Ukrainian Lviv) and the surrounding territories known as Galicia.

While the Germans tried to assimilate the Poles and the Russians forbid the use of the Polish language and tried their best to suppress

Polish culture, from around the mid-nineteenth century Austria's Polish subjects were allowed the use of their language and even enjoyed some political autonomy with an elected parliamentary body. In addition, largely Catholic Austria allowed Poles a freedom of religion unknown in Protestant Prussia and Orthodox Russia. Thus, the Austrian-ruled Polish lands became a haven for Polish culture and the arts, and Krakow became the intellectual and artistic heart of the nation.

In 1918, the end of World War I brought an end to the Austro-Hungarian Empire, and Galicia once again returned to an independent Poland. The divisions following World War II resulted in Austria initially being divided between the Allied victors, while Hungary fell under the sway of the Soviet realm along with Poland.

POLAND'S NEIGHBORS TODAY

Modern-day Poland borders seven countries: Belarus, the Czech Republic, Germany, Lithuania, Russia (Kaliningrad), Slovakia, and Ukraine. Since it joined the European neighborhood with its entry into the EU in 2004, however, Poland's borders have opened as never before. Relations with fellow EU members are largely determined by Brussels, while recent conflicts have arisen between Poland and Belarus (over the Polish minority residing there) and Poland and Ukraine (over Poland's support of Ukrainian prodemocracy movements). There is still an undercurrent of animosity in Polish-Russian relations, though recent disputes have been over gas prices rather than borders. Luckily, these days clashes between Poland and its neighbors on the scale of the late eighteenth and mid-twentieth centuries seem to be a thing of the past.

A.S.

FURTHER READING

Bloodlands: Europe Between Hitler and Stalin by Timothy Snyder. Basic Books, 2010.

Central Europe: Enemies, Neighbors, Friends by Lonnie Johnson. Oxford University Press, 2010.

CHAPTER 8

JEWS IN POLAND

*"Despite the madness of war, we lived for a world that would be differ-
ent. For a better world to come when all this is over. And perhaps even our
being here is a step toward that world. Do you really think that, without
the hope that such a world is possible, that the rights of man will be restored
again, we could stand the concentration camp even for one day?"*
–Tadeusz Borowski, *This Way for the Gas, Ladies and Gentlemen*

When most people hear the words "Jews" and "Poland," their immediate first thought is the Holocaust. While that deeply tragic event
had the single most significant impact on Poland's Jewish population,
one might be surprised to know that Poland had a long and rich Jewish history before World War II, and even more surprised to hear that
the country's Jewish tale is still ongoing.

BEFORE 1939

Poland's Jewish history goes back a millennium. The first mentions
of Jews in Polish cities date back to the eleventh century, but historians believe they probably arrived even earlier, as Jewish communities
were establishing themselves in centers of trade throughout Europe
from the Middle Ages. Poland's first Jews spoke Slavonic and Hebrew,
and were most likely drawn to the region by trade opportunities as
well as the unique privileges Poland's early kings granted them. Over
several centuries, Jews in Polish territories formed a middle class of
merchants and tradesmen.

As a whole, medieval Poles were more tolerant toward other religions than Western Europeans—that is, until the Catholic Church had something to say about it. While the Church kept spreading intolerance toward Jews, Poland's Duke Bolesław the Pious issued a kind of bill of rights in the thirteenth century, which allowed Jews in Polish territories the rights to justice and freedom of worship, work, and movement. These were later extended by King Casimir (Kazimierz) the Great, who gets most of the credit today. That's not to say that there were no incidents of persecution or violence; but as a whole, if you were a Jew in medieval Europe, Poland was a pretty decent place to be. Which explains why at the end of the sixteenth century, Europe's largest Jewish population was to be found in Poland.

Under the Polish-Lithuanian Commonwealth, Jews and all religious minorities were granted unprecedented religious freedom, and Poland's Jewish community saw its golden age. Jewish schools, synagogues, and Hebrew printing houses were established. However, the unparalleled tolerance backfired in one regard: the freedom afforded to Jews led to the existence of Jewish communities completely isolated from the larger Catholic society, with Jews going to separate schools, speaking primarily Yiddish, worshipping separately, and even being tried under a separate legal system. This lack of integration led to feelings of "otherness" between Christians and Jews. Separation led to persecution, which led to further separation in a vicious cycle.

The decline of the Polish-Lithuanian Commonwealth led to a decline of tolerance toward minorities. As a result of invasions and new conflicts, Poland's Jewish population decreased, though it still remained the largest in Europe. After the Partitions, the bulk of the Jewish population found itself on Russian soil, and the Russian authorities encouraged Jews to assimilate; those who failed to were often subject to persecutions and pogroms (organized massacres of Jews).

During World War I, many Jews fought for Polish independence, while being simultaneously persecuted as Bolshevik supporters in Russia. Nonetheless, in the twenty years between the two World Wars, Poland's Jewish population flourished, and with it, Jewish theater, music, and cabarets. In 1939, Warsaw was the second largest Jewish city on earth, after New York.

Despite Jews largely being a part of Polish society, Poland was far from immune to the anti-Semitism spreading like wildfire throughout Europe. With three quarters of the Jewish population living in cities, Poland's vast countryside was largely intolerant and anti-Semitic. And the government at the time was not above blaming the country's many economic problems on the Jews, a trend that escalated after the death of Poland's interwar leader Marshal Piłsudski in 1935, who had been progressive in Jewish matters. Paradoxically, Polish society simultaneously became increasingly anti-Semitic and anti-Nazi in the years preceding Hitler's troops marching in.

The Holocaust

It might be enough to state that before the Holocaust, Jews numbered over three million and constituted Poland's largest minority; after the Holocaust, only about 300,000 remained. But sheer numbers fail to reflect the horrors, bravery, and resilience Polish Jews experienced between 1939 and 1945—and the bravery of the Poles who ensured that the final number was not zero.

When Hitler's forces marched into Polish territory, they brought with them his plans for the systematic elimination of the Jewish race. During the war, Jews not only died in concentration (and later death) camps, but were also starved or killed outright in ghettos or on the streets by the *Einsatzgruppen* (Nazi death squads). Some 100,000 Polish Jewish soldiers fighting with Polish forces were also killed or taken prisoner. In 1939, they made up over a tenth of the Polish army.

Under Nazi rule, all Jewish Poles were stripped of their rights, had to register, and were later made to wear a yellow Star of David. Most Jews in Polish cities were confined to ghettos, the most famous of which was the Warsaw Ghetto, with about 380,000 inhabitants. Jews caught trying to escape the ghetto or Poles caught smuggling in food were shot on site. In fact, Poles faced the harshest laws of all the Nazi-occupied lands. A Dutch or French citizen caught hiding or aiding Jews might be sent to prison; a Pole captured for the same crime was not only subject to the death penalty, but often that person's entire family was killed, together with the Jews they were hiding. Nonetheless, Israel recognizes more non-Jews who risked their lives saving Jews during the Holocaust from Poland than from any other nation.

One of the most famous of such citizens is Irena Sendler, a Catholic social worker and member of Żegota, the Polish Council to Aid Jews, an underground movement that hid and helped Jews—the only one of its kind in Nazi-occupied territories. Sendler rescued about 2,500 Jewish children, for which she was captured and tortured by the Nazis. Barely escaping death, she would go on to receive Poland's highest honor and be nominated for the Nobel Peace Prize.

However, no account of wartime Polish-Jewish relations could omit a mention of Jedwabne. The small northeastern Polish town was the site of the Jedwabne pogrom of 1941, during which at least 340 Polish Jews were killed. While historians are still debating what actually happened that day, most accounts state that a group of Polish men from the town gathered the local Jews in a barn that was then set on fire. Nazi forces stationed in the area shot those who tried to escape. Though the event was largely forgotten within the greater tragedy of the Holocaust, it resurfaced recently when a Polish-American historian published a controversial book on the subject.

While most of Poland's Jewish population fell under Nazi occupation, more than a third found themselves in what was now Soviet territory. Compared to the outright atrocities committed by the Nazis and the growing anti-Semitism of Poland's prewar government, it's no surprise that many Jews welcomed Soviet rule. Nonetheless, many were still persecuted by Stalin and sent to hard labor in Siberia—some of them would then return with Anders' forces and fight alongside Poles in Jewish units. Some 500–600 Jewish-Polish officers were killed at Katyn.

The apex of the Holocaust and Hitler's plans for the Jewish population was the Final Solution, which was best embodied in the Auschwitz II–Birkenau death camp. Located three kilometers from Auschwitz I, which was built by the Nazis in 1940 and mainly used as a labor camp for Polish prisoners of war, Birkenau's massive size alone illustrates the extent of Hitler's atrocities. The sole purpose of the camp was extermination, in the quickest and most effective way possible: gas chambers and crematoria—where the scent of death still lingers so many years later. Opened in 1942, Birkenau served as the final resting place of an estimated 146,000 Poles and 1.1–1.5 million Jews, many of whom arrived in overloaded train carts and were taken immediately for their "shower"—where instead of water, deadly Zyklon B gas rained down from the ceiling.

While the majority of Jews did die in concentration camps, there was still a strong resistance movement among those who managed to avoid deportation. The main one was the Jewish Combat Organization (ŻOB), whose largest act of defiance was the Warsaw Ghetto Uprising of 1943. The Ghetto's revolt was an effort to stop its inhabitants from being deported to the Treblinka extermination camp, and it was crushed mercilessly by the much larger and better armed Nazi forces. Many of the few survivors would go on to take part in the larger (and equally tragic) Warsaw Uprising the following year.

EMIGRATION AND COMMUNISM

Despite all the horrors both Jews and Poles lived through during WWII, despite the many instances of Jewish soldiers fighting for Poland and Polish civilians hiding Jews, tensions between the two groups were as high as ever as the war came to a close. How could this be? One explanation is that the roots of prejudice run deep, and even the horrors of war cannot always retract them. Another is that Poles saw Jews as communist sympathizers; anyone who colluded with or welcomed the Russians, who were forever The Enemy, was an enemy as well. From the point of view of Poland's Jewish community, the Soviets were a far lesser evil than the Nazis. In addition, the Soviet authorities, together with those of what would become the People's Republic of Poland (PRL), reached out to the Jewish community after the war, guaranteeing them rights under the new order, while the "true" Polish government, now in exile, remained largely anti-Semitic and had no such assurances in place. These tensions led to postwar pogroms, the most famous of which took place in Kielce in 1946.

In truth, it was a combination of these factors that led to the further expulsion and emigration of over 100,000 Jews from Poland in the years following the war. Of those who remained, some did indeed join the ranks of the Communist Party, with many taking prominent posts. This didn't prevent the communist authorities from turning on Polish Jews in 1967, after the newly formed Israel defeated the Soviet-backed Arab states. Faced with increasing restlessness from growing anticommunist youth movements, largely influenced by the Prague Spring rebellion next door, the PRL authorities decided to rile up Poland's anti-Semitic inclinations once again and led an anti-Zionist press campaign. Polish Jews, most of them completely assimilated, were removed from the Party and positions of power, and over 14,000 emigrated during the late 1960s. In 1989, only between 5,000 and 10,000 Jews remained in Poland. Full diplomatic relations between Poland and Israel would not be restored until communism fell.

RETURN

Perhaps one of the strangest phenomena to take place in recent Polish history is the reemergence of the nation's Jewish community, often from the most unexpected places. The most surprising Jews that "returned" to Poland were those who had never actually left; or, to be more accurate, their parents or grandparents had remained in Poland but had assumed Catholic names and traditions, and their children and grandchildren spent their lives completely unaware of their Jewish backgrounds—until suddenly it was safe to be Jewish again.

While not many Polish Jews returned when the Iron Curtain fell, these "new" Jews, estimated to number in the thousands, together with those who had remained, brought about a slow revival of Jewish life and culture in Poland's largest cities. But they're not the only ones: another recent phenomenon in Poland is the emergence of non-Jewish "pro-Semites" who have embraced Jewish culture and are working to bring it to the Polish masses through Jewish music and film festivals and Jewish organizations. Just try to make it out of a major Polish city without seeing posters for a klezmer concert (where often the audience and even performers are strictly of the Gentile variety). Perhaps the most famous Jewish cultural event is the International Festival of Jewish Culture, held annually in Krakow's "Jewish Quarter," Kazimierz. The event is attended each year by 20,000 or so, most of them non-Jewish Poles.

Poland, once seen as nothing more than a Jewish graveyard, is discovering an active Jewish community again. Today, the sites that were once death camps function as museums, the most famous and most visited of which is Auschwitz-Birkenau, which over a million people visit annually. The walls of the former Jewish Ghetto in Krakow now hold plaques, while a memorial stands on the site where the Warsaw Ghetto once was. The synagogues that survived the war are being restored along with their respective cemeteries, and some of those that have not been turned into museums are actually functioning as synagogues once again. These are just a few of hundreds of testimonials to Poland's Jewish history, and their existence serves both as its reminder and a hope for a continued shared history.

A.S.

FURTHER READING:

Irena Sendler: Mother of the Children of the Holocaust by Anna Mieszkowska. Praeger, 2010.

The Jews in Poland and Russia, vol. 1-3 by Antony Polonsky. Littman Library Of Jewish Civilization, 2010.

Neighbors: The Destruction of the Jewish Community in Jedwabne, Poland by Jan Gross. Princeton University, 2001.

In the Shadow of the Polish Eagle: The Poles, the Holocaust and Beyond by Leo Cooper. Palgrave, 2000.

This Way for the Gas, Ladies and Gentlemen by Tadeusz Borowski. Penguin, 1976.

The Jews of Warsaw 1939-1943: Ghetto, Underground, Revolt by Visrael Gutman. Indiana University Press, 1982.

CHAPTER 9

POLES AT WAR

"I belong to a nation that over the past centuries has experienced many hardships and reversals. The world reacted with silence or with mere sympathy when Polish frontiers were crossed by invading armies and the sovereign state had to succumb to brutal force."
–Lech Wałęsa

Many visitors to Poland make a similar observation: Poles are unusually obsessed with wars, particularly when it comes to World War II. It takes different forms than in other cultures (there are no World War II reenactors getting together every VE Day as far as I know), but the war is always present in Poles' consciousness, just under the surface of everyday life.

So why this obsession with the traumatic events of the past? Partly because World War II is still a recent historical event, and thus has a direct influence on present-day Poland, as it was because of the outcome of the war that Poland suffered decades of communism, which it is still recovering from. Partly because many Poles feel that their contribution to the war effort and its suffering has been overshadowed or ignored by the West—and for good reason: how many blockbusters have been made about the British, French, or American forces in the war compared to the significant Polish contribution?

We will return to World War II. However, before that great war, there were many others of significance, as Poland has never particularly gotten along well with her neighbors. From insurgencies and uprisings to full-scale battles, Polish lands have long served as theaters for warfare. Of course, listing all of them is a job for the history books, so below are only the most significant wars, with a focus on the ones that are still frequently discussed today.

THE SWEDISH WARS AND THE DELUGE

Though Poland had been in conflict with its neighbors since its founding, one of the country's first decisive clashes was a series of wars with Sweden between 1558 and 1660. Besides loses of land and lives, these wars would ultimately begin the decline of the Polish-Lithuanian Commonwealth that ended with Poland's disappearance from the map (see Chapter 42).

The Commonwealth's troublesome relationship with the Kingdom of Sweden actually began with a conflict over the throne between Sigismund III Vasa, king of Sweden and Poland, and Duke Charles of Sweden, Sigismund's uncle who aspired to, and soon gained, the Swedish throne. The rest of Sigismund's career would be spent trying to get back what he lost, and leading his overconfident forces in a game of thrones. In addition, the Commonwealth was simultaneously fighting the Muscovites (Russians), Tatars, and Moldavia while also squashing rebellions begun by the nobility.

Between 1600 and 1660, Poland would fight Sweden in three wars followed by the disastrous Deluge, a series of campaigns between 1648 and 1667 during the Russo-Polish and Second Northern Wars. This would prove to be the beginning of the end of the Polish-Lithuanian Commonwealth, as the nation lost a significant part of its population and its status as a major European power. In the Deluge, Warsaw was completely destroyed by the Swedish forces and ninety percent of its population was killed or dispersed, while the Commonwealth's riches and art were stolen, most never to return.

POLISH–OTTOMAN WARS

When asked to name a Polish military victory, most Poles will immediately point to the defeat of the Ottoman Turks at the Battle of Vienna and the heroism of Polish King John III Sobieski. Numerous paintings by national icons Jan Matejko and Juliusz Kossak depict the 1683 victory of the Poles that kept the Ottoman menace from conquering the rest of Europe and drove them back to the east.

Though the Poles (together with the Holy Roman Empire) did prove victorious in that battle, it was at a great cost. By saving Vienna after it had been under siege for two months by the Ottoman Empire, Sobieski helped the ruling Habsburgs to recover Hungary and rise to become a great power, which would later reward Poland by taking a slice of it during the Partitions. Meanwhile, as the Polish-Ottoman wars raged on between 1672 and 1699, the Commonwealth also ignored the rising Prussian threat, and lost Ukraine to the Muscovites, which would soon become part of the Russian Empire. Thus, the Commonwealth sealed its fate as it allowed its neighbors to grow powerful until they decided to take Poland, weakened by its wars and economic mismanagement, for themselves. Ironically, Sobieski would be the last truly free ruler of Poland for over two hundred years.

REBELLIONS UNDER THE PARTITIONS

By 1795, Poland as a nation had ceased to exist, its land divided between the overwhelming forces of Russia, Prussia, and Austria. There were two significant rebellions in the following half century: the November and January Uprisings.

The first one began in November 1830 and was the only one with any hope of success, though the Polish forces were outnumbered 70,000 to Russia's 180,000. What began as a revolt of young Polish army officers in Warsaw soon spread to Lithuania, Belarus, and Ukraine, though the Polish government went through alternating phases of support and acquiescence to Russia in the following eight months of fighting. They were hoping for foreign intervention from France or England but it never came, and by September 1831 the Russian army had taken Warsaw, and the Polish forces surrendered in October. As a consequence, the Polish constitution was suspended and about 80,000 Poles were sent to Siberia while many soldiers were drafted into the Russian Army. A huge wave of emigration also followed (see Chapter 43).

The second failed uprising began in January 1863, with even greater odds against the Poles. Having no organized army this time, the Poles fought a guerrilla war for sixteen months against the far larger and better-trained Russian forces. After the rebellion was crushed, a second wave of deportations to Siberia began, along with waves of emigration, at least for those lucky enough to not find themselves publicly hanged.

WORLD WAR I AND THE POLISH-SOVIET WAR

Poland still did not exist as a nation at the start of World War I in 1914, but that did not stop its three occupiers from wooing its people to join their causes. About two million Poles were conscripted into Prussian, Russian, and Austrian armies, but as much of the actual fighting would take place on historically Polish lands, all three nations declared promises of independence or nationhood to gain the support of the Polish locals living there. By November 1918, with the Allies declaring victory and all three occupiers on the retreat, Poland once again became a nation with a state, headed by Chief of State Józef Piłsudski—though not without great cost. Polish soldiers had over a million casualties, and civilian casualties were even higher, with devastating damage to Polish lands thanks to the destructive battles the German, Russian, and Austro-Hungarian armies had fought there.

Between 1918 and 1921, the newly created country would fight Ukraine, Germany, Czechoslovakia, and Lithuania as well as several non-state players over territory, generally successfully. However, the most significant conflict was between Poland and the Soviet Union in the Polish-Soviet War of 1919–1921. After the formal conclusion of World War I, Lenin still had plans to take control of all of the lands up to Germany and create a Socialist bloc. Meanwhile, Piłsudski's own plan was to create a federation of states opposed to Russia on Poland's eastern border. Neither plan came to fruition, though the Polish army did take advantage of Russia's preoccupation with its civil war to take much of Lithuania, Belarus, and Ukraine as far as Kiev. They were driven back by the Red Army to the edge of Warsaw, and just when it looked like Poland would fall once again to greater Russian forces, the Poles beat the Red Army back in the Battle of Warsaw and kept most of the land gains they had made. Poles today still refer to this battle as the "Miracle on the Vistula," and it is considered to be one of the most important as this Polish victory saved Europe from the advancing bolshevism.

Soldiers of Batalion Zośka of Polish Home Army during the Warsaw Uprising on August 5, 1944. They are in confiscated German uniforms and armed with German weapons.

WORLD WAR II: THE UNTOLD STORIES

The most devastating war in Polish history was undoubtedly World War II, the effects of which are still felt today. Poland's once thriving Jewish population is only now showing signs of revival, though on a much smaller scale (see Chapter 8). There are still plenty of Poles alive from the generation that lived through the war, and even a few that fought in it. And from popular history books to popular culture, the war is ever present in the Polish consciousness.

On September 1, 1939, Hitler's forces crossed the Polish border and war officially broke out. Most people know that part of the history. Yet aside from that, most histories focus on the French and British theaters, or the American entry in 1941, with little mention of the significant Polish contribution. While the Allies concentrated on the defeat of Nazi Germany and Imperial Japan, for Poland it was a fight for its very existence.

Poland had the fourth largest armed forces of the Allies, and the country suffered more damage to its territory and population in proportion to its size than any other nation involved in WWII. In total, over six million Polish citizens perished, or about 18 percent of the prewar population. For comparison, Germany lost 7.4 percent, the USSR, with the most total casualties, lost 11.2 percent, and the United States only lost 0.2 percent of its citizens.

Both the Nazis and the Soviets strove to eliminate the educated Polish upper and middle classes, leaving a poor and uneducated populace that would offer no resistance to either occupying force. Those who weren't killed outright in the streets and in the woods were sent to Siberian gulags by the Soviets or labor camps by the Nazis. From 1940, the nefarious Auschwitz concentration camp first served as a work camp for Polish prisoners of war and conscience.

In Poland, the war lasted from September 1939 until the summer of 1947, and proceeded in three stages: the initial attack and occupation by both the Nazis and the Soviets from 1939 to 1941; Hitler's betrayal and the push of the Allied resistance, now with American and Soviet help, from 1941 to 1943; and the driving out of Nazi forces and the fight for Poland's liberation from 1943 to the end of the war. Though Poland officially fell on October 6, 1939, its people never stopped fighting, creating a vast underground society and military force.

The civilian branch of the Polish resistance consisted of the Polish Government-in-Exile, first based in France and then in London. In occupied Poland, it created the most complex underground state of any country in the war. The underground government organized the education, intelligence gathering, press, and propaganda activities of the nation right under the noses of the occupying forces.

The military branch of the resistance was active as early as in the fall of 1939. By 1942, most of the different resistance groups had joined the Home Army (Armia Krajowa or AK in Polish), a force of about 400,000 soldiers. The Home Army engaged in acts of sabotage and guerilla campaigns as well as outright warfare against Nazi forces in the countryside of Poland. However, after Poland's initial defeat, a significant part of its military traveled to France and fought in the French Campaign of May–June 1940. After the fall of that country, the forces were split, with a large part joining the British military. In the Battle of Britain that followed in the fall, the Royal Air Force included some 145 Polish pilots, who had the best kill ratios of any squadrons by far.

With the USSR changing sides to join the Allies in 1941, Poland and Soviet Russia officially resumed diplomatic relations. This allowed the formation of a Polish Army in Russia made up of now released Polish prisoners of war, who would follow General Władysław Anders from Siberia to Persia, train in Palestine, and then join the British Army in North Africa. One of the most famous battles in the Polish conscious-ness is the Battle of Monte Cassino in the first half of 1944. Led by

General Anders, the Second Polish Corps succeeded in capturing the strategic target after numerous Allied failures, changing the course of the battle over Italy.

The Polish troops at Monte Cassino had an unusual ally helping them—a bear (yes, as in an actual brown bear) by the name of Wojtek the Soldier Bear. Orphaned as a cub, this curious bear was adopted by the Polish soldiers of the twenty-second Artillery Supply Company of the previously mentioned Second Polish Corps while they were stationed in Iran. The bear became an official enlisted soldier, documents and all, and would spend evenings drinking, dancing, wrestling, and even smoking—well, eating—cigarettes with the men, and then help them in battle by carrying heavy artillery crates. Following the war, Wojtek was demobilized and spent the remainder of his life as a beloved member of the Edinburgh Zoo.

Meanwhile, by 1944 the eastern offensive, led by the Red Army, was sweeping its way west, driving out the Nazis and "liberating" Poland. However, this liberation was more of a reoccupation. Stalin had denounced the independent Polish Government-in-Exile as well as its military branch, the AK, and began promoting the other Polish Army organized by both the Soviets and the puppet government made up of communist sympathizers. In many cases, the Red Army would drive back the Nazi forces in Poland together with the AK; afterward, AK members would be arrested by the Soviets as rebels—as they were not members of the Soviet-recognized Polish Army—and sent to Siberia or executed outright. In this way, as the Red Army marched west and "liberated" Polish cities, they would deport or kill AK members, intelligentsia, and anyone else who resisted or was deemed bourgeois, confiscate their possessions, and install their own people in positions of power.

As this strategy became more widespread, it became apparent that Warsaw was the last hope for a free Poland. If the Polish forces could liberate the city from the Nazis themselves and hold it from the Soviet forces, the Government-in-Exile could return as the legitimate ruling power. This was the motivation behind the ultimately disastrous Warsaw Uprising.

On August 1, 1944, with the Red Army stationed just across the Vistula River from Warsaw's center and well-equipped Nazi forces garrisoned in the city, the uprising began. It would last for sixty-three bloody days. While the initial battles resulted in Polish victories, the poorly armed Poles were ultimately no match for the Nazis, who received regular reinforcements. The Poles had been hoping for Allied assistance, but other than a handful of airdrops from the British and a few dozen soldiers from the communist-led Polish Army, they were on their own. An estimated 250,000 Polish civilians died in the course of the fighting, with tens of thousands of additional military casualties. Upon capitulation, Hitler ordered the complete destruction of Warsaw. By the time the Soviets entered the city in January 1945, over eighty-five percent of it had been leveled.

With Poland largely in Soviet hands, the results of the Yalta Conference were no surprise. Churchill and Roosevelt acceded to Stalin's will and Poland—now with its borders shifted west—would remain under Soviet control for the next forty-five years.

POLAND IN THE WAR ON TERROR

Although Poland has been at peace since 1968, recent events have resulted in Polish troops once again entering conflict zones, though not on its own soil for once. Following the attacks on the United States on September 11, 2001, Polish soldiers became involved in the War on Terror in both Afghanistan and Iraq, as well as serving in NATO and UN peacekeeping forces, mainly in the Middle East and Africa. Poland was one of the four countries that took part in the 2003 Invasion of Iraq, and lost twenty-three soldiers in that country between 2003 and its withdrawal in 2008.

Today's Polish Armed Forces include the Army (Wojska Lądowe), Navy (Marynarka Wojenna), Air Force (Siły Powietrzne), and Special Forces (Wojska Specjalne), and number some 100,000 active duty soldiers and 20,000 reserves. As military conscription ended in 2010, the country has transitioned to a professional army and is still in the process of modernizing its military equipment and downgrading its forces after pulling out of Iraq. Still somewhat wary of its neighbors, Poland has placed its hopes in its NATO allies, and with any luck has seen the last of its days as a battlefield for European conflicts.

A.S.

FURTHER READING

The Deluge by Henryk Sienkiewicz. 1886.

Forgotten Holocaust: The Poles Under German Occupation, 1939-1944 by Richard C. Lukas. Hippocrene Books, 2001.

Jan Sobieski: The King Who Saved Europe by Miltiades Varvounis. Xlibris, 2012.

No Greater Ally: The Untold Story of Poland's Forces in World War II by Kenneth K. Koskoda. Osprey Publishing, 2011.

A Question of Honor: The Kosciuszko Squadron: Forgotten Heroes of World War II by Lynne Olson and Stanley Cloud. Vintage, 2004.

Rising '44: The Battle for Warsaw by Norman Davies. Penguin, 2005.

Unvanquished: Joseph Pilsudski, Resurrected Poland, and the Struggle for Eastern Europe by Peter Hetherington. Pingora Press, 2012.

Warsaw 1920: Lenin's Failed Conquest of Europe by Adam Zamoyski. Harper Collins UK, 2008.

White Eagle, Red Star: The Polish-Soviet War 1919-1920 and The Miracle on the Vistula by Norman Davies. Random House UK, 2003.

CHAPTER 10

THE PEOPLE'S REPUBLIC

*"What a magical ballot box! You vote Mikołajczyk
and Gomułka comes out!"*
(popular joke during the 1947 elections)

Several years ago, at a talk I attended at the Jagiellonian University, historian Norman Davies proposed a rather radical thesis: World War II did not end in 1945 like all the history books tell you. In fact, World War II actually ended in 1989. After all, if the goal of World War II was the freeing of Poland and other sovereign states invaded by the Nazis and the USSR, this objective was not achieved until the fall of the various Soviet regimes between 1989 and 1992.

While some may see this as a radical revision of twentieth century history, the fact remains that Poland was under de facto Soviet control for fifty years. However, the actual fighting of World War II did end in 1945, and life behind the Iron Curtain went on, often in the most surprisingly absurd ways.

THE RED ARMY MARCHES IN

If the end of Poland's Soviet enslavement did not come until 1989, it began in earnest in 1944, when the Red Army set up camp on Polish soil (see Chapter 9). The country's fate was further sealed in 1945 when Roosevelt and Churchill met Stalin at Yalta and conceded the territories the Red Army had "liberated." To this day, many Poles view the Yalta agreement as a betrayal of Poland by the Allied Forces. After all, Poland had the fourth largest armed force of the Allies and lost one fifth of its territory and one third of its population in the fight—just to be occupied all over again.

However, before Stalin could take over Poland in earnest, he had to eliminate all opposition, which would largely come from the landowning middle and upper classes and intelligentsia. Part of this was achieved proactively, like during the Katyn massacre. Part of this was achieved from the sidelines, like when the Red Army sat back and watched the Nazis destroy Poland's capital city following the failed Warsaw Uprising. Polish institutions had to be delegitimized as well, especially the Government-in-Exile in London and the Home Army (AK). This led to the creation of the Polish Workers' Party, which established the Provisional Government of National Unity, a communist-backed alternative to the Polish Government-in-Exile, as well as the Polish People's Army, the communist version of the AK. In July 1945, the United States recognized the communist-backed government as the legitimate Polish ruler, and the Soviet takeover was finalized in 1948 with the establishment of the Polish United Workers' Party and de facto elimination of any competing political parties for the next forty years.

THE PEOPLE'S REPUBLIC

Of all the Soviet-ruled states established at the end of World War II, the Peoples' Republic of Poland (PRL) was a unique case in several ways. First, it had the most active underground civil society of any country, due mostly to the Nazi invasion in 1939. Poles under Nazi occupation established underground universities, governments, armies, printing presses, and other basic institutions, including an entire underground economy. When the Nazis left and the Soviets took over, these networks remained. Second, because there was no significant presence of a Polish Communist Party before the war, communism was viewed as a system forced onto the Poles from without, with almost no grassroots support. Not everyone actively opposed the communist regime, however—many simply accepted it as inevitable and went along with it when it benefited them. This went hand in hand with the Polish attitude toward invading forces and its traditional hatred of the Russians. Finally, the Catholic Church was uniquely strong in Poland, and due to the death of most of Poland's Jewish population and the expulsion of Germans from Polish territories, the Polish population was almost homogenously Catholic. And with the appointment of a Polish Pope in 1978, the Church's influence (and sympathy) would increase tenfold. All of these factors led to a slightly different, more liberal brand of communism in Poland. For example, it was the only country where agriculture was never collectivized (though not for lack of trying).

(marekuliasz / Shutterstock.com)

Nonetheless, the early communist era in Poland was a time of terror and paranoia: one of the first institutions to be established was the much-dreaded secret police (Urząd Bezpieczeństwa or simply UB). At its height, there was one UB agent for every 800 Polish citizens. That meant that there was a good chance your neighbor was either an agent or an informant, and even if this was not the case, it was safer to assume it was. And just to keep things interesting, the definitions of a crime or who was and was not a "public enemy" remained ever fluid.

Shortages of goods created a second economy, and everyone knew that if you needed anything from a clerk or bureaucrat, you had better bring a "gift" like stockings, chocolates, or vodka. There was even a special word for the lengths one had to go to to get anything done, which remains in use to this day: *kombinować*. While there is no good English translation, the closest might be to "make do with" or "make something happen" or the more modern "hustle." Getting something from a shop was a last resort; if you needed an item, first you would try to *kombinować* it through a friend or acquaintance. Everyone had an uncle whose second cousin's mother-in-law knew a guy. While today *kombinowanie* is generally looked down upon, in communist Poland it was *kombinuj* or starve.

It was also a time of absurdity, often comically so—humor was found in the spaces between reality and government propaganda. Whole anthologies of PRL-era jokes have been published in the decades since. Here's a sampling:

A Soviet officer is addressing a Polish recruit:

> *- Who is your father?*
>
> *- Comrade Stalin!*
>
> *- How do you mean?*
>
> *- Why, is not Comrade Stalin father to us all?*

The surprised officer admits the young man is correct and continues:

> *- And who is your mother?*
>
> *- The Soviet Union!*
>
> *- How do you mean?*
>
> *- Because they say that the Soviet Union is the mother of all nations...*

The officer likes the recruit's answers, and with hope in his voice he asks one more question:

> *- And what would you like to become?*
>
> *- An orphan...*

However, life under the communist regime was not all queuing and spying on your neighbor—the new government also introduced some much needed policies, not least of all the physical rebuilding of a country largely destroyed by war. In addition, the communist system brought free universal health care, free and compulsory education for all, free university education, and funding for the arts. Of course, all of this came with a caveat: revised histories were taught in schools, and only art that was deemed "socialist" was allowed. Students that came from working-class or Party families were more easily accepted to the best universities. Censorship was all-pervasive in the state-run outlets, and the state-sanctioned press only gave an "official" account of events that seldom resembled reality. This naturally led to the widespread propagation of the underground press, called *bibuła* (the Polish version of Russian *samizdat*).

Between 1948 and 1989, Poles would rebel against the system en masse five times: in 1956, 1968, 1970, 1976, and 1980. While in principle the protests were against communism, it was the dire economic situation that drove desperate workers to strike and angry students to the streets. Despite the state's best efforts, common people had access to Western media and underground newspapers and could see the disparity between reality and propaganda on the empty store shelves. Nonetheless, each protest was followed by a crackdown from the authorities, the most severe of which would follow the first taste of freedom many Poles would experience: the rise of Solidarity.

SOLIDARITY

If one were to trace the fall of the Berlin Wall in November 1989 and the eventual collapse of the Soviet system to one solitary event, the most likely candidate would be the firing of a woman named Anna Walentynowicz on August 7, 1980. Walentynowicz, an outspoken organizer, underground *bibuła* editor, and general troublemaker in the eyes of the authorities, also happened to be a crane operator at the very shipyard where Lech Wałęsa, future president of a free Poland, had been an electrician. So how did the firing of one woman lead to the collapse of an entire political system?

The first part of the domino fell on August 14, 1980 at the Lenin Shipyards in Gdańsk. After Walentynowicz was fired just five months shy of retirement, her fellow workers demanded that she and Lech Wałęsa, who had been fired in 1976, be rehired, and sought greater rights for all shipyard workers. Despite the communist authorities' efforts in suppressing all news of the strikes (even going as far as cutting phone connections between Gdańsk and the rest of Poland), word of the strike spread quickly, and strike committees from around the country began to arrive and organize their demands. They were soon joined by the Workers' Defense Committee (Komitet Obrony Robotników, or KOR), a group of intellectuals fighting for workers' rights. Within days, over two hundred shipyards, factories, and other industries and their over one million workers were on strike. The demands were now bigger than local issues: Wałęsa and the others were calling for the right to form an independent trade union.

On September 17, the Solidarity Independent Self-governing Trade Union (NSZZ "Solidarność") was formed and officially sanctioned by the government. However, Solidarity was much more than just the first independent trade union in the Soviet bloc—it was the first democratic crack in the communist glass house. The most significant victory was the union's legal right to strike, which gave workers unprecedented powers against the state. Over the course of the next year, Solidarity would transform from a trade union into a social movement and political party precursor, with nearly ten million members—one third of Poland's population—at its peak in late 1981. The movement fought for freedom and against corruption, but was careful to remain non-violent, so as to not give the authorities an excuse to shut it down.

Despite this, the situation in Poland in 1980–81 was becoming increasingly unacceptable to Moscow. In October 1981, General Wojciech Jaruzelski was appointed First Secretary, and on December 13, he declared martial law. Solidarity was deemed illegal, and most of its leadership was arrested that night, when about 10,000 activists were rounded up, many of whom would remain in prison for years. Tanks rolled down the streets of major cities as curfews were imposed, airports were closed and lines of communication and transport were cut. The military proceeded to take charge of all major government institutions indefinitely, and all press outlets other than the official one were banned. It looked like curtains for the revolutionary labor union, and yet it would re-emerge in 1988, stronger than ever.

So who ran Solidarity in the eight years between martial law and independence? Many people might be surprised to hear that it was a group of women based in Warsaw who began and ran the underground newspaper *Tygodnik Mazowsze* (Regional Weekly), and thus kept Solidarity going while the male leadership was locked away or in hiding. Led by editor Helena Łuczywo, they planned meetings, organized hundreds of thousands of Solidarity supporters and distributed the weekly throughout all of Poland. The free press served as the main means of communication between the three pillars of the Polish opposition: the workers (represented by Wałęsa), the intellectuals and students (represented by Adam Michnik and Jacek Kuroń), and the Catholic Church (represented by activist priest Jerzy Popiełuszko and Pope John Paul II). It was the press that allowed the three other factions to communicate with each other as well as with the Western world, whose support would be crucial when it was finally time to bring down the regime.

THE WALLS COME CRASHING DOWN

That moment came ever closer when Mikhail Gorbachev became the leader of the USSR in 1985. Gorbachev would soon abandon the only real argument Poland's authorities had for preserving the communist system—the Brezhnev Doctrine, which promised Soviet military intervention in any state that tried to abandon communism.

Meanwhile, the economic situation in Poland was growing increasingly worse. While Poles had experienced a taste of prosperity in the 70s, when the government borrowed well over its limit, the 80s saw a return to food rations and empty shelves. The infamous Pewex shops, which took U.S. dollars and stocked Western goods, became the only place to buy even basic items like toilet paper. Those who could, fled to the West in droves, while the Polish Communist Party, losing members and ever more in debt, faced the inevitable: they would have to make a deal with the opposition.

Following a renewed wave of strikes, in September 1988 the authorities secretly met with Wałęsa and planned the Round Table Talks that would take place in Warsaw from February to April 1989. The result was the Round Table Agreement of April 4, which made independent trade unions legal again, created an independent legislative body, the Senate, and allowed the election of a president. Solidarity became a political party, and its members were overwhelmingly elected to the new Senate (99% of seats) in the June 4 election. Though the election was only partially free (two-thirds of the seats of the lower house were reserved for Communist Party members), it was the first such election in the entire Soviet Bloc, and the last one in which the communists would hold any real power. Above all, the election showed the overwhelming unpopularity of the Polish Communist Party, and delegitimized its rule. That August, a Solidarity member became prime minister, and the final domino fell in December 1990, when Lech Wałęsa became the first freely elected president of Poland in sixty years.

A.S.

FURTHER READING

The Captive Mind by Czesław Miłosz. Vintage, 1990.

Countdown: The Polish Upheavals of 1956, 1968, 1970, 1976, 1980 by Jakub Karpiński. Karz-Cohl Publishers, 1982.

The Church and the Left by Adam Michnik. University Of Chicago Press, 1993.

Iron Curtain: The Crushing of Eastern Europe, 1944–1956 by Anne Applebaum. Doubleday, 2012.

Solidarity's Secret: The Women Who Defeated Communism in Poland by Shana Penn. University of Michigan Press, 2005.

Solidarity: Poland in the Season of its Passion by Lawrence Weschler. Simon and Schuster, 1982.

CHAPTER 11

POSTCOMMUNISM: NOW WHAT?

"I began to realize why the Poles were so dour and icy: they had been several times through hell, and war had steeled their hearts against everything. They had become so hard that nothing now could hurt them again."
–James Kirkup, *One Man's Russia*

It's the summer of 1989. Poland has just held its first election where popular votes actually mattered since the 1930s. The anticommunist opposition (i.e. most of the Polish population, there and abroad) is elated. The freedom they've been fighting for over the decades is finally within reach! Except . . . now what?

That was exactly the situation Poland's opposition leadership found itself in the early 1990s. Yes, capitalism had triumphed over communism . . . but how does a country that hasn't had a market economy for half a century make the transition? How do you go from empty store shelves and riot police to shopping malls and MTV? The answer was quickly and painfully, with a lot of learning along the way. Poland went through a period called "shock therapy" during which just about everyone in Poland cursed the name Leszek Balcerowicz for a few years (see Chapter 12). Balcerowicz was Poland's new finance minister and the architect of the neo-liberal plan to end the country's spiraling inflation and balance its budget while opening its market to imports and exports. While he did accomplish those goals eventually, the "shock" part of the plan included wage freezes, massive price hikes, political instability, and a decade of general discontent, economic emigration, and crushing poverty for many.

In other words, the 1990s were not a pretty time for Poland, financially. But the country did emerge with one of the highest growth rates in the region, and would go on to join the European Union in May of 2004, just shy of fifteen years since the 1989 elections. It would even go on to beat the odds in the recent recession, becoming the only EU country with positive growth by 2009. Not bad for a relative newcomer to the free market.

So what is modern Polish society like today? Increasingly diverse, capitalistic, concerned with growth, jobs, and football scores more than with politics—in other words, European. But it still carries the legacy of its history and desperately wants to prove itself as a proper European nation with a seat at the foreign policy table.

COMMUNISM: A LEGACY

One particularly popular Polish hobby is complaining about bureaucracy. However, Poles are often justified in doing so, as any foreigner who has had to experience Polish red tape will tell you. Few processes are automated, even fewer are done online, and queuing still remains the national pastime as far as government offices are concerned. The process of getting a government ID card or registering a business often takes months, half a forest of paperwork and requires submitting forms at different windows in the same building at best, and in completely different buildings across town from each other at worst.

It's true that you no longer need to bring a bottle of vodka to be seen at the doctor's office, but some relics of the system remain. For example, in theory, all working Poles are covered for health care by the government; in reality, many pay out of pocket for better or faster service at private clinics. The same is true of education: while those accepted to public universities are free to study without accruing crippling debt, the demand far outnumbers the number of spots open to new students, and many end up studying at expensive (and often inferior) private colleges, or studying *zaocznie*, which means taking paid night and weekend courses while working during the week—if they can find a job that doesn't require a degree.

Most Poles have seen little improvement in this until very recent years, and agree that little will change until a new generation—one that doesn't remember the communist way of doing things—enters into politics and the government workforce.

FROM INEQUALITY TO INEQUALITY

Under communism, everyone was equal—except some were more equal than others. In the free market, inequality is built into the equation, and Poland is no exception in this regard. It's enough to contrast two streets—one on which the Western visitor will feel right at home, and one that seems right out of a Third World country. The first one is Warsaw's Nowy Świat ("New World") Street, where you will find a Starbucks, an H&M, a Ferrari salon, an art house cinema, and a mix of Poland's yuppies and students as well as a plethora of tourists from around the world. The second is any street in an eastern Polish town, where you'll be lucky to find paved roads without potholes the size of small ponds, a few small groceries, the obligatory liquor store, and a bunch of young people hanging around with nothing better to do.

In fact, right before Poland's accession into the EU, the unemployment rate was a stark twenty percent, with the figure double for those under twenty-five. As the borders opened up, the unemployment figures went down as about two million Poles emigrated to the UK and Ireland to take on menial work for much higher pay. While official unemployment figures have reached ten percent, these are deceptive as the numbers are much lower in the major cities and much higher in rural areas or former mining or manufacturing towns, many of them now nearly empty as factories closed and former workers emigrated to other countries in the EU. Meanwhile, the risk of poverty rate is much higher in Poland than the European average, and has been increasing since 2000. Job insecurity, nearly non-existent under communism, has also significantly increased.

In short, the years after communism opened Poland to foreign investment and a free market, which brought wealth for a few, a much higher standard of living for the majority, an abundance of new goods and services for those who can afford them, and a wave of economic emigration, together with greater job insecurity and poverty in general.

EVERYTHING YOU NEED TO KNOW ABOUT MODERN POLISH POLITICS TO HOLD A CONVERSATION OVER COCKTAILS

In the sphere of politics, modern Poland has become truly European. Between 1990 and 2007, Poles changed their minds more often about their political leaders than they changed the oil in their imported cars. Amidst the chaos, few figures that emerged were qualified to lead, and even fewer had a solid plan about how to govern the newly free nation. As it turns out, it's much easier to be opposed to an ideology than to have one of your own. The earliest political battles focused primarily on getting the communists (or anyone thought to have communist ties or sympathies) out of power.

Today, Poland is governed by two legislative bodies, the Sejm (lower house) and the Senate (upper house), the Council of Ministers (the executive), an independent judiciary, and has both a prime minister (head of government, the leader of the party with a legislative majority) and a president (head of state, elected by popular vote). The president's powers are largely counterbalanced by the prime minister and the legislature, which means that should the two come from opposing parties (which has happened), more political bickering than governing is likely to take place. Because Poland is a multi-party legislative democracy, fringe parties elected to the legislature by popular vote have often ended up in positions of real power when governing coalitions were formed. While this led to entertaining fodder for the press, it also resulted in frequent changes in government as the population liked to punish incompetence, whether real or perceived, by voting for the exact opposite candidate.

Any mention of twins in reference to Polish politics is likely to allude to Lech and Jarosław Kaczyński, identical twins who began their public careers as child actors and went on to found the center-right Law and Justice (Prawo i Sprawiedliwość or PiS) political party. For a time, Lech served as president while his brother served as prime minister of Poland, resulting in a heyday for comedians and political cartoonists alike. The politics of the brothers were often nationalist and even anti-EU, though not as extreme as those of some of their supporters.

As of this writing, Poland is governed by the center-left Civic Platform (Platforma Obywatelska or PO) political party, led by Prime Minister Donald Tusk, who won the job in 2007 and was re-elected in 2011, making him the longest serving prime minister of postcommunist Poland. The presidency is held by Bronisław Komorowski, also of Civic Platform, who took over following the death of President Lech Kaczyński in a plane crash that killed ninety-six people, including many government and military leaders, on April 10, 2010. Though that accident sent shock waves throughout Poland and the world, perhaps the biggest testament to Polish stability since 2007 is the fact that despite such a quick and tragic loss of a large part of the government, the country's institutions continued to function without so much as a hiccup.

Warsaw: mourning the victims of the plane crash that killed President Lech Kaczynski and nearly 100 others, April 15, 2010 (Tomasz Bidermann / Shutterstock.com)

One important distinction that should be noted is the concepts of right wing and left wing as they apply to Poland, which are significantly different than in the United States and most other Western countries. To Westerners, Poland seems to lean predominantly right. However, while extreme right wing parties may get more media attention, their actual popularity is just as marginal as in most other democracies. As a whole, Poland is more left wing and less religious than it is portrayed in Western media. As an example, between seventy to eighty percent of Poles opposed the invasion of Iraq in 2003, and a majority supports government healthcare and welfare services.

However, many citizens of the older generation identify themselves as right wing more as a statement of their opposition to the old communist regime than as a reflection of their views. In such issues as the support of unions, welfare, and opposition to privatization, their views would be considered left wing in other countries. The largest difficulty for the popularization of modern left wing parties in Poland is this stigma of being associated with communism.

In addition, supporters of different Polish political parties today are divided by geography as much as they are by age. Though in recent times Civic Platform has enjoyed a majority and the general support of the urban population, Law and Justice, the second largest and more conservative party, enjoys overwhelming support in the rural and eastern parts of Poland, as well as with older voters. Meanwhile, the Catholic Church in Poland has largely thrown their weight behind the ultraconservative populist League of Polish Families (Liga Polskich Rodzin or LPR), while the populist party and farmers' union Self Defense (Samoobrona) enjoyed a brief surge in the early 2000s but has since lost popularity. Above all, Poles' enthusiasm for democracy has decidedly waned to a European level since the first election in 1989, with voter turnout hovering between forty and fifty percent since 1991.

POLAND TODAY

The end of communism brought freedom—in the form of multiparty elections, freedom of speech, and a free market—but real freedom in today's Poland is largely dependent on one's financial and physical well being. Poland is still very much a nation under construction, both literally (as its new train stations and roads will attest to) and figuratively, as it searches for its place within the European framework and a proper balance between the state and the free market, between Polish and global aspirations. In this sense, while it is still catching up materially to the West, it is already there in spirit, and few visitors will feel out of place walking down the streets of its major cities.

A.S.

FURTHER READING

Central and East European Politics: From Communism to Democracy by Sharon L. Wolchik and Jane L. Curry, ed. Roman & Littlefield Publishers, Inc., 2011.

Contemporary Poland by Grzegorz Węcławowicz. Westview Press, 1996.

The Ghosts of Europe by Anna Porter. Thomas Dunne Books, 2010.

Poland Beyond Communism: "Transition" in Critical Perspective by Michał Buchowski et al. University Press Fribourg Switzerland, 2001.

Poland's New Capitalism by Jane Hardy. Pluto Press, 2009.

CHAPTER 12

POLAND GETS DOWN TO BUSINESS

*"It is a historical given that the recovery of independence brings with it
problems those struggling to achieve it had never foreseen or even believed
possible."*
–Adam Zamoyski

Though economists are very fond of numbers, when you consider the
state of the Polish economy, the actual figures are only the tip of the
góra lodowa. Beneath the surface, there's history, national complexes,
pride and a dash of EU funds all working in tangent to determine
Poland's economic present and future.

THE ECONOMIC LEGACY OF COMMUNISM

In order to understand Poland's present economic status, including its recent "miraculous" growth when the rest of Europe was in
recession, we need to look back at least to the 1970s. Communism left
an economic as well as a social legacy in Poland, from the culture of
kombinowanie and bureaucracy (see Chapter 10), to a devastated and
indebted national economy. In fact, almost every aspect of the Polish
economy today can be traced back to the changes that occurred in the
70s and 90s as well as the most recent recession.

In the 50s and 60s, the giant state owned companies were not
designed to be motivated by profit or efficiency like in capitalist economies, and they employed workers whether they made money or not.
Goods were exported to the USSR and other Warsaw Pact nations,
while few products made it in from the West. Management was also

not held responsible for losses, as there was no competition and only quotas mattered. In turn, the workers had most of their basic needs met by their employers, from housing and clothing to healthcare and even social and cultural welfare—including the prevalence of cinemas, theaters, choirs, and sports teams on factory campuses—though their pay was incredibly low. While workers lost some of these benefits due to the economic crisis of the 70s, many social programs were still in place by the time the transition to the market economy began.

THE 1990S: PRIVATIZATION AND TRANSITION

In 1990, Poland's Minister of Finance Leszek Balcerowicz instituted the "shock therapy" series of reforms, which were designed to rapidly transform Poland's socialist economy into a capitalist one. While it did end hyperinflation and resulted in much higher growth in the long run for Poland than other postcommunist countries, in the short term it meant over a million layoffs, sustained high unemployment, and the bankruptcies of many firms.

One of the first priorities for the Polish economy was also the privatization of its state-owned enterprises. While necessary, this process was often riddled with corruption and nepotism. For one, it led to much capital landing in the hands of the *nomenklatura*, an economic class created in the 70s when the Polish market opened to Western imports. These were the people who had access to foreign networks and were best positioned in 1989 to "spontaneously privatize" the companies that they were already operating, if not out in the open. Since there were very few regulations to prohibit corruption at the time, the *nomenklatura* were often the gatekeepers between Western aid organizations and Polish industry, and had access to loans at a time when Polish companies were being sold at bargain basement prices. Significantly, this new elite was not necessarily the same as the communist elite, as well-positioned members of Solidarity benefited too. While the *nomenklatura* did not become as rampantly wealthy as the oligarchs in Russia, the comparison is not without merit.

The opening of the Polish market also resulted in a surge of foreign investment. On the one hand, this brought much needed new technologies and business practices to a nation that had been closed to both. On the other, the biggest problem with foreign investors in

Poland was their tendency to buy up the most profitable enterprises, while leaving the deadbeats to the state or Polish companies. Workers were also often cherry-picked, with older and problematic employees quickly laid off for the state to take care of. Thus, in the decade or so following the end of communism, Polish industry was concentrated into very few hands, most of them foreign.

This rapid buy-out of former state-owned companies led many citizens feeling that Poland is not owned by Poles, a sentiment that is as strong as ever today, and not without reason. For example, ten of the twelve largest commercial banks in Poland are owned by foreign institutions, mostly from the UK or U.S. This trend is even more obvious in the housing market, where the properties in the old towns of major Polish cities are mainly owned by hotel chains or foreign landlords, primarily from the UK, Germany, and increasingly from Russia.

Ironically, though the process of Polish freedom began with the trade unions that fought for the rights of their workers, it was the ordinary Polish workers that lost out the most in the transformation to a market economy. As a result, the importance of trade unions faded during the turbulent times of the 90s, though since 2006 they have seen a resurgence, mainly due to the mass migration of many workers and thus greater bargaining power of those who remained.

1999–2004: GROWING PAINS

After 1990, full employment and benefits were regarded as communist relics. In 1999, a restructuring of the social services system began, most noticeably in the privatization of pensions and the healthcare system. As a condition of foreign aid and entry into the European Union, public spending was drastically reduced, leading to cutbacks in education, health services, and the social safety net and increases in GDP and wages as well as unemployment.

One of the most noticeable changes was in job security. More and more employers, both Polish and foreign, stopped hiring regular employees and instead either issued temporary contracts or required workers to be registered as self-employed, so that they would take on the burden of paying taxes and benefits. Young workers, meanwhile, experienced successive stints as unpaid "interns" who never received the employment contracts they were promised after months of free labor.

In 2003, unemployment was at twenty percent nationwide, with the number double for workers under twenty-five or in many rural areas. The Polish economy could not sustain such high figures, and with Polish entry to the EU in 2004, the floodgates opened.

2005–2008: EXODUS, CRISIS, RETURN

On May 1, 2004, when Poland joined the European Union, the UK, Ireland, and Sweden opened their doors to workers from the new Member States, expecting a trickle of migrants in the low hundreds of thousands. What they got instead was an estimated two million economic immigrants from Poland alone flooding in, with over half going to the UK for work. Poles took jobs in agriculture, construction, healthcare, and overwhelmingly in the service industry. Higher wages and the chance to learn English and new skills attracted many young workers with college degrees, who took jobs far below their education level, leading to a temporary brain drain for the Polish economy. In EU countries that delayed employment to citizens of postcommunist countries, fears of the "Polish plumber" taking jobs away from locals were widespread, though these later proved to be ill founded.

The dark side of the economic migration story has been the prevalence of exploitation. Particularly in the early years, few migrant workers had contracts or union protection, and they were often overcharged by newly created employment agencies promising lucrative jobs and rarely delivering. In addition, wages were regularly withheld and there were frequent cases of forced or unpaid overtime, especially when employers provided housing as well. Worker accommodations were often crowded and unsanitary, though those who lost their jobs were even worse off, as homeless Poles began sleeping in British train stations because they couldn't afford the journey home.

Meanwhile in Poland, the country's entry into the EU also brought a new wave of transnational corporations, primarily in the telecommunications, transportation, and postal segments. The service and real estate sectors expanded as well, and business practices such as marketing, quality control, human resource management, and the use of computer networks were rapidly introduced and propagated. The entry of so many foreign companies since the fall of communism brought technological and managerial knowhow as well as an injection of capital, so towns and regions in Poland began to compete to attract foreign investment, producing scores of glossy brochures from newly created marketing departments.

As the global economic crisis hit in 2008, the pound and euro began losing their value in comparison with the Polish złoty, and suddenly Poland looked attractive to migrant workers once again. Between 2004 and 2008, the Polish economy improved significantly, with unemployment dropping down to seven percent, thanks to emigration and foreign investment. Thus, many who had left began returning home to newly created jobs, bringing with them new language and customer service skills. And while Poles had left to work menial jobs throughout Europe, those same menial jobs in Poland were now being filled by Ukrainians, Belarusians, Indians, North Koreans, and Southeast Asians.

2008–THE FUTURE: GROWTH AND A LOOK AHEAD

So what does Poland's economy look like today? Its largest industries are services, manufacturing, construction, and agriculture, and its predominant trade partner is Germany. Unemployment has been hovering around ten percent since 2010, though the figure is much lower in urban areas and higher in the rural east of the country. Meanwhile, Poles continue to place a heavy emphasis on education, primarily in high-tech and knowledge industries. Cities such as Krakow have ambitions of becoming the Silicon Valley of Central Europe (and are succeeding in attracting companies like Google and Dell to their doorstep). Except for Russia, Poland is the largest of the postcommunist economies, and has attracted the most foreign investment. In the midst of the global recession in 2009, it had the only positive growth (1.6%) of the entire EU, and continues to top the charts.

However, GDP per capita is still quite below the EU average while unemployment and inflation are higher than average. This translates to sparkling new shopping malls stocked full of goods from around the world, with few shoppers who can afford to buy them. Though recent years have seen a surge in Polish entrepreneurship, barriers of entry for businesses, primarily small companies, are very high, and the tax codes are unnecessarily complicated.

(Aquir / Shutterstock.com)

Western economies have had half a century or more to develop the social mechanisms of capitalism along with new technologies and business practices, while Poland and the other countries of Central and Eastern Europe found themselves plunging into the deep end of a capitalist market in 1990. Poland may have managed to stay afloat, but it will take some time before the country can do a graceful backstroke.

A.S.

FURTHER READING

From Solidarity to Sellout by Tadeusz Kowalik. Monthly Review Press, 2012.

Poland's Jump to the Market Economy by Jeffrey Sachs. MIT Press, 1994.

Poland's New Capitalism by Jane Hardy. Pluto Press, 2009.

CHAPTER 13

LANGUAGE: LOGIC HAS NOTHING TO DO WITH IT

Stół z powyłamywanymi nogami.
A table with its legs broken off.

Chrząszcz brzmi w trzcinie w Szczebrzeszynie.
The beetle buzzes in the reed in (the town of) Szczebrzeszyn.

Karol kupił Karoli korale koloru koralowego.
Charles bought Carol a coral-colored strand of beads.
(Polish tongue twisters)

An American living in Poland for some time decided to have a second go at learning Polish. The first time had ended in failure because Polish was, quote, "too hard." He had decided to give the language a second try, was already making some progress, and was enthusiastic about how much he had learned when, woe and behold, he decided to go to the local butcher's.

"Poproszę pięć parówki," he said in what seemed like perfect Polish, albeit with a very American accent.

"Co?" asked the middle-aged, typically impatient sales lady behind the counter.

"Po-pro-szę pi-ęć pa-rów-KI," repeated our American, this time feeling just slightly less confident about his seemingly perfect, newly created sentence in Polish.

"Aaahhh . . . !" the sales clerk smiled conspicuously, "pięć parów-EK!" and she went on to weigh and pack five hot-dog sausages for him.

Now our American was in utter shock. "How is it," he said when recounting this story, "that from one to four the plural noun ending is 'ki,' and then starting from five it changes to 'ek'? And that's only for plural *feminine* nouns. . . . It just isn't logical!" After this linguistic epiphany at the meat store our American gave up learning Polish once and for all. "Besides," he summed up his second short-lived adventure of trying to learn the Polish language, "most Poles speak *English* anyway."

Whether the language is logical or illogical will not be disputed here, but what is it about the Polish language that supposedly makes it so . . . *difficult*?

Let us take a quick look at language in Poland, followed by some of the technical intricacies of the Polish tongue, for those brave souls who want to give it a shot.

THE POLISH LANGUAGE

It is interesting to note that Polish uses the Latin alphabet instead of the Greek-derived Cyrillic alphabet, which is used in some of the other Slavonic tongues. This is a historical and cultural consequence of Poland's accepting Christianity in the year 966, when Latin was used as the official language of administration and the Roman Catholic Church. Polish had a variety of sounds that had to be reflected in its newly acquired Latin-based spelling system, which is why you will see certain diacritical marks on vowels (ą, ę, ó) and consonants (ć, ł, ń, ś, ź, ż) that might look strange but basically tell you how the letter should be pronounced.

The Polish language belongs to the group of West Slavonic languages, and in that sense might sound fairly similar to Czech or Slovak, although the average Pole will not understand too much of either of those languages. Polish is the official language of Poland and is spoken by practically 99% of the population. There are also regional dialects that are spoken in some of the more rural areas roughly covering the administrative provinces, such as the Lesser Polish, Mazovian, Silesian or Greater Polish dialects. As far as dialects go, the most well known, and most different-sounding from standard Polish are Kashubian, now officially bearing the status of a regional language, which is spoken in and around the rural areas of Gdańsk and Gdynia, and the dialect of the Tatra highlanders, popularly known as *góralski*; for more about the highlanders (*górale*), see Chapter 32. In the past, Poles could often differentiate between Polish that was spoken in sparsely populated areas far from the larger urban areas and that which was spoken in bigger towns and cities. These slight differences heard in everyday speech were usually the result of a basic education, lack of access to popular culture and specific language patterns that had been passed on for several generations. Currently, even the younger generations of Poles coming from rural areas are very much aware of any potential linguistic differences and, with much greater access to education as well as mass media, these differences have been almost entirely eliminated.

Other languages in Poland are those spoken by the minority populations, such as German in the southwestern regions and Belarusian and Ukrainian in the remote eastern parts of Poland. Russian was once taught as a mandatory foreign language in schools until 1990 and is more or less understood by members of the older generations, though if it is spoken at all, it is very reluctantly and under protest. Although Poles have generally had a bad reputation for not knowing English, this has drastically changed over the last decade, with more and more Poles moving and traveling abroad, and with the large number of foreign language courses being offered in all major cities, small towns, and even rural villages.

ON BORROWED ENGLISH WORDS IN POLISH

Although some purists of the Polish language might not want to admit it, Polish has shamelessly borrowed, and continues to borrow, words from other languages, and currently especially from English. Anglicisms, as they are called, starting pervading into the Polish maritime language in the eighteenth century. These were followed by words denoting terms connected with trade, clothing, food, sports, finance, and religion in the next century, with the twentieth century seeing a steady rise in the number of English words entering both more technical as well as more colloquial Polish. What was the source of these new words? Traders, visitors and Polish emigrants coming back to Poland as well as new technologies, imported goods, literature, and the media. A study from 1938 on the Polish language that was spoken in the U.S. gives examples of American words that were assimilated by Poles; some instances of this "Polglish" include: *kendy* (candy), *oldfasziond* (old-fashioned), *lunczrum* (lunch room), *absolutnie* (absolutely), and *beć ju lajf* (bet your life). Today, Polish is seeing an influx of loanwords coming from technology (especially the IT industry), politics, and economics. Perhaps one of the funniest examples of Ponglish is the word *ksero*, which means "photocopy," but is taken from the American brand name Xerox. Borrowed words from English are heard quite often in colloquial speech, especially among children and teenagers. These include *słitaśny* (sweet), *uploadować* (to upload), *hejter* (hater), *celebryta* (M)/*celebrytka* (F) (celebrity), *meetnąć się* (to meet up), and *walnąć komenta* (to make a comment). These are also often used by adults as remarks on blogs, Facebook and other social networking services—and sometimes just for fun. Try this one on for size: "*Luknij przez windows'a na mojego nowego car'a*" (Look out the window at my new car).

DIVING INTO POLISH: NOUNS

In Polish, nouns have genders. Three, actually, which means a noun can technically be a "he" – *on* (masculine), "she" – *ona* (feminine), or "it" – *ono* (neuter). This is mainly due to grammatical reasons (you'll see what those are a little further down), so most nouns have, unfortunately, been assigned a gender entirely arbitrarily. How, you may ask, is a hapless person learning Polish to know whether a table is a he, she, or it? You can check by adding a demonstrative pronoun, that is, the word "this," to see if it is **"ten** stół" for masculine, "**ta** stół" for feminine or "**to** stół" for neuter. The last two options will make a Polish person cringe, so you know that "stół" is a "he"—*on*—a masculine noun, because in Polish you always say "ten stół." Then you just have to remember that fact forever because a noun will (usually) never change its gender. For example, a shirt (*koszula*) will always be feminine, and a child (*dziecko*) will always be a neuter "it," just as in English. Thus, we have *ta koszula*, meaning "this shirt," and *to dziecko*, meaning "this child." No problem, right?

How a noun ends will sometimes suggest just what gender it might be; for example, very many feminine nouns end in "-a," as in *koszula* (shirt), *dziewczyna* (girl), or *trawa* (grass); but don't be fooled— Polish, like any other language, is full of exceptions to the general grammatical rule. This keeps things interesting, after all. Why on earth does the word for man, *mężczyzna*, also end with an "-a," when it is clearly masculine? And then *osoba* (person) is a feminine noun regardless of whether it refers to a woman or a man . . . is that not what one would call gender equality in a language?

The plural endings of nouns also add more linguistic spice. The plural forms are different for the various genders, and in many cases the singular form of a given noun may change so much that its plural form looks like a whole new word altogether. Some examples of plural forms:

Masculine nouns

stół – stoły	(table – tables)
lek – leki	(medicine – medicines)
chłopiec – chłopcy	(boy – boys)
wujek – wujkowie	(uncle – uncles)
mąż – mężowie	(husband – husbands)
student – studenci	(student – students)

Feminine nouns

kobieta – kobiety	(woman – women)
noga – nogi	(leg – legs)
twarz – twarze	(face – faces)

Neuter nouns

oko – oczy	(eye – eyes)
dziecko – dzieci	(child – children)
piwo – piwa	(beer – beers)
zwierzę – zwierzęta	(animal – animals)

Beautiful, as the linguists say, but obviously not much fun for the average Polish-language student trying to wrap his or her head around it all.

ADJECTIVES

Adding an adjective to modify a noun makes things even more interesting (read: difficult) because the adjective's ending has to reflect the gender of the noun as well as whether it is singular or plural—e.g. *stół – stoły* or *dziecko – dzieci*. So, if you have an adjective like "big," which is *duży* in Polish, then you get *duży stół, duża koszula,* and *duże dziecko,* or *duże stoły, duże koszule,* and *duże dzieci* for the plural nouns.

Interestingly enough, Polish doesn't have articles such as "a," "an" or "the." So, "sklep" can mean either "a store" or "the store." *Which* store someone is talking about is deduced from the context of the whole sentence. Doesn't that just sound dandy?

CASES

Most importantly (and undoubtedly the source of many headaches), Polish is a highly inflected language. What does that even mean? In general, that the nouns (and also adjectives, quite unfortunately) are inflected for **grammatical case** and, as Grzegorz Krynicki, an assistant professor at Adam Mickiewicz University notes, in Polish we "tend to think by means of relations between nouns." The different grammatical cases express the relationships between the nouns (and their adjectives) and the other parts of speech in the sentence. There are seven possible cases. The seventh case (the Vocative) is most often used when directly addressing someone and always ends with an exclamation point. So when you hear someone yell out "Kasiu!" on the street, think of it as the equivalent of informally shouting "Yo, Kasia!" But if you take into consideration the fact that you have both singular and plural nouns, you end up with a whopping fourteen possible noun endings!

The endings, also called declensions, might overlap in form for the different cases. This is called syncretism, as in, the declensions of masculine nouns might look the same in the Nominative and the Accusative. Luckily, every case has a name and a set of pronominal questions in the form of "what?" ("co?") and "who?" ("kto?") to help inflect a given noun. Although Polish children can obviously speak Polish quite well by the time they go to school, every Polish child has to learn the different case names, their corresponding pronominal questions and the declensions of different nouns in all of the cases. Let us have a quick look at these cases and their endings.

"Moja mała siostra," which means "my little sister," will serve as an example of what these endings, or declensions, look like. As you can see, all of the parts of speech have to agree with the noun (*siostra*) they modify in gender, number, and case.

I. Nominative (kto? co?)
Moja mała siostra ma 25 lat.
My little sister is 25 years old. (Literally, "has 25 years")

The nominative usually corresponds to the English subject. It answers the pronominal question "who" or "what" something is in a sentence.

II. Genitive (kogo? czego?)
To jest rower **mojej małej siostry**.
This is my little sister's bike.

The Genitive most often expresses possession and answers the question "of whom/of what?."

III. Dative (komu? czemu?)
Dam to **mojej małej siostrze**.
I will give this to my little sister.

The Dative expresses the indirect object in a sentence. It answers the pronominal question of "to whom/what something is done."

IV. Accusative (kogo? co?)
Kocham **moją małą siostrę**.
I love my little sister.

The Accusative corresponds to the direct object and is most often chosen as the complement of a verb. It answers the pronominal question of "whom/what"?

V. Instrumental (kim? czym?)
Idę z moją małą siostrą.
I am going with my little sister.

This is a tough one. It answers the pronominal question of "whom" after verbs like "be" (być) or "become" (zostać). Its pronominal question is "with whom?/with what?," and the Instrumental is used to express "the means by which" something is done.

VI. Locative (o kim? o czym?)
Mówię o **mojej małej siostrze.**
I am talking about my little sister.

The Locative answers the pronominal question "about whom/what?" and comes after certain prepositions, the most common ones being: "o" (about), "w" (in), "po" (after), "na" (on, at), and "przy" (near, during, while).

VII. Vocative
Moja mała siostro! Jesteś wspaniała!
Oh, my little sister! You are wonderful!

The Vocative is used most often when directly addressing someone, thus calling for his/her undivided attention, and is often used together with professional titles or for the affectionate, diminutive forms of first names, e.g. "Kasiu!" instead of "Katarzyno!"

Note how the endings change in every part of speech and for every case. In the example above, syncretism takes place in the Dative and Locative, so the declension looks the same although the case forms fulfill different roles in the sentences. All of this probably looks out of this world . . . and coming up with these case endings comes naturally to a Polish person in everyday speech! So even a simple sentence such as "I watch TV" is "Oglądam telewizję"—the direct object (TV) is marked for the Accusative in an affirmative sentence, but when negated the sentence "I don't watch TV" changes to "Nie oglądam *telewizji*," and the direct object is Genitive-marked. This exception is called, for those who might like to know, the "Genitive of Negation."

The grammatical case is, again, hidden in the noun's form. Oh, those wonderful exceptions to all those rules!

NEGATION

While we're on the topic of negating sentences, you should know that Polish language can have constructions that look like a double negation to the English eye, such as "Nic nie wiem," which can literally be translated into "I don't know nothing." Here is another great example: "Nikt nic nikomu nie mówi." How many "no's" are in that one? It literally means, "No one doesn't say nothing to nobody" and is grammatically correct not just for members of the Polish mafia. Logic and grammar have nothing in common at this point. Obviously.

VERBS

Polish verbs are a whole 'nother story, as they say. The infinitive, or basic form of the verb, usually ends with a "ć," less commonly a "ść"/"źć" or, rarely a "c." Thus we have, for example, *szukać* (search), *iść* (go), *znaleźć* (find), or *piec* (bake). The system that Polish verbs are based on is understood as that of a basic stem to which different grammatical endings are added according to certain rules, which then make up the entire verbal paradigm. This is called conjugation. Let us take three verbs in the present tense, conjugate them in the singular and plural forms for the first, second and third person and compare the endings.

PRESENT TENSE

Pronoun/Verb	*pisać* – to write	*widzieć* – to see	*czytać* – to read
I ja	piszę	widzę	czytam
you ty	piszesz	widzisz	czytasz
she/he/it ona/on/ono	pisze	widzi	czyta
we my	piszemy	widzimy	czytamy
you wy	piszecie	widzicie	czytacie
they oni/one	piszą	widzą	czytają

The verbs are conjugated in the present tense according to three major sets of endings (in bold) added to the stem. So, the lucky Polish-language student will always have to know exactly which ending goes with the verb he or she wants to use at that exact moment. Also, with some minor exceptions, Polish doesn't make use of helping verbs, such as the Polish equivalents of be, have, do or used to, in its tenses. Therefore, *ja piszę* can mean "I write," "I'm writing," or "I have been writing." If that makes learning the verbal paradigms any easier, let it be so.

The past tense is generally more regular for all verbs, with the exception that there is a marked difference in the ending because it depends on whether the pronoun is feminine (F), masculine (M) or neuter (N). We will take just one verb, *pisać*, and see how it conjugates in the past tense.

PAST TENSE

Pronoun (M/F/N)		*pisać* – to write
I ja		pisałem/pisałam
you ty		pisałeś/pisałaś
he/she/it	on/ona/ono	pisał/pisała/pisało
we	my	pisaliśmy/pisałyśmy
you	wy	pisaliście/pisałyście
they	oni/one	pisali/pisały

Again, there are no helping verbs to reflect the sense of continuity in the past, thus *ja pisałem/pisałam* can either mean "I wrote," "I was writing," "I used to write," or "I have been writing." The context will determine just what nuance of the verb is meant.

For the concept of the future, Polish differentiates between something that will be in the process of being done (imperfective) and will already be done (perfective), and most verbs will be conjugated according to that differentiation.

FUTURE TENSE

Pronoun (M/F/N)		*czytać* – to read (imperfective)	*czytać* – to read (perfective)
I	ja	będę czytał/czytała/*czytało	przeczytam
you	ty	będziesz czytał/ czytała/*czytało	przeczytasz
he/she/it	on/ona/ono	będzie czytał/czytała/ czytało	przeczyta
we	my	będziemy czytali/czytały	przeczytamy
you	wy	będziecie czytali/czytały	przeczytacie
they	oni/one	będą czytali/czytały	przeczytają

The future neuter form in first and second person singular (marked by *) sounds so strange to a Polish person that many would say it is even ungrammatical. But no, it is perfectly correct, although you would probably only see that form being used by, for example, an egg (*jajko*), such as Humpty Dumpty, that was talking about itself: "Ja będę pisało na tej ścianie" ("I will write on this wall"). The imperfective form corresponds to the English future form, suggesting a continuous action: "I will be reading," whereas the perfective form means "I will have read." Also, Polish accepts an alternate form to denote the future tense that consists of the helping verb (*być*) and the infinitive of the main verb (*czytać*), which is uniform for all persons, singular and plural—e.g. "Ja będę czytać, ty będziesz czytać, etc." And that is just the tip of the iceberg when it comes to verbs in Polish.

WORD ORDER

Because Polish is such an inflected language, it allows for words to be jumbled around in a sentence without changing the meaning of that sentence. Thus, in Polish the word order is less ordered than in English because the grammatical case (meaning) is hidden in the words themselves, which means it doesn't matter as much where those words are in the sentence. Although, on the other hand, you can't just throw them around anywhere!

English prefers sentences with the SVO (subject-verb-object) word order. Thus, English must always have an explicit subject. In Polish, however, the form of the verb implies who, or what, the subject is. Let's look at a simple sentence in English: *I* (S) *read* (V) *books* (O). In Polish that would be: *Ja* (S) *czytam* (V) *książki* (O). But you can drop the *Ja* part, the *I* that is the subject, because the form of the verb *czytam* already tells you it's first person singular. So then you have a perfectly grammatical, albeit shorter, sentence: *Czytam* (V) *książki* (O). Hemingway would be proud. Now comes the fun part: you can shift things around a little more and you get: *Książki* (O) *czytam* (V) *bardzo chętnie* (adverbial phrase), meaning, literally: "Books I read very eagerly." More Yoda than English, it seems.

FORMAL/INFORMAL

One of the first things many Polish students notice is that you cannot address any person with a simple "you" without being aware of the level of formality between that person and yourself. Polish is quite a formal language in terms of addressing other people, but once you get the hang of it, trying to talk to your wonderful next-door neighbor or overly suspicious potential future mother-in-law will be a cinch.

To show respect and distance, and to sound polite and formal, you will use *Pan* (Mr., sir) *Pani* (Ms., Mrs., Miss, madam), *Państwo* (Mr. and Mrs., ladies and gentlemen, also used when addressing a married couple), *Panowie* (sirs, gentlemen) or *Panie* (ladies). This is how you address people older than yourself, strangers, casual acquaintances, people you do not know very well (or like for that matter), people of authority or those holding a higher position than you, such as a superior or the boss at work. Originally, Pan/Pani meant "master/ lady," as in "master of the house/lady of the house" to distinguish the aristocratic gentry (*szlachta*) from the common peasants who tilled the land. *Panna* (Miss) was used to specifically address a (usually young) unmarried woman, but currently sounds archaic and outdated, and is rarely used in everyday speech.

If you're lucky, you may get a chance to witness an argument between two Polish people, for example two elderly ladies arguing about their place in a line at the local post office, who will most likely address themselves per the formal *Pani*. Despite the heated debate about who was first, and quite probably the employment of a few stronger adjectives to describe the person, you just might hear one of the ladies say: "*Proszę Pani, jest Pani skończoną idiotką!*"—"Madam, you are most definitely an idiot!" So much for politeness.

To be polite, sound slightly less formal but still show respect for the person being addressed, you might hear a Polish person saying *"Panie Włodku"* to a man by the name of Włodzimierz, or *"Pani Zosiu"* when addressing a woman whose name is Zofia. This is a combination of the formal "titled address" of *Pan* or *Pani* and the person's name used in the diminutive. In English this would sound quite strange, like saying "Mr. Bob" or "Ms. Cathy."

"Ty," the equivalent of English's ubiquitous "you," implies an informal, equal position and is used to address friends, close family members, and people who have explicitly agreed to be on informal "you" terms with your humble person.

As one person on an Internet forum stated blatantly: "when in doubt, treat every Pole as a master."

PRONUNCIATION AND SPELLING

We will not even attempt to delve into the intrinsic features of Polish pronunciation or spelling, although I will mention several of their aspects. If you have ever heard the "Our Father" ("Ojcze nasz") prayer recited in Polish, it might have sounded like a whole bunch of "sh," "ch," and "dge" sounds, known to linguists as fricatives and affricates, all jumbled up together in that one prayer. And if you think *Szczebrzeszyn* looks, and sounds, cosmic, you're not alone. But there is a way to explain all of this. In Polish, spelling and pronunciation go hand-in-hand because Polish is a phonetic language, which means that letters or certain combinations of letters will always be pronounced the same way. So, although some words look like a bunch of consonants that have been randomly combined to deliberately hurt your eyes and break your tongue, once you have an understanding of how those letter combinations work, pronouncing a specific word will actually not be that hard. Although the "szcz" in *Szczebrzeszyn* looks like it could get no worse pronunciation-wise, do not despair—it is simply the two English sounds of "shch" put together. Plus you get a whole *three* vowels in that word!

Another regularity is stress (how loud or emphasized a syllable sounds when pronounced out loud), which almost always falls on the penultimate (second-to-last) syllable of a word.

As a final word, many Poles, in turn, still find English "hard to speak, difficult to write, and impossible to read." Go figure.

M.T.

FURTHER READING

Grammar of Contemporary Polish by Oscar E. Swan. Slavica Pub, 2003.

CHAPTER 14

(THE POLITICS OF) RELIGION

"Let Thy Spirit descend and renew the face of the land, this land!"
–Pope John Paul II

Poland's first official ruler, Mieszko I, knew that one monotheistic, organized and hierarchical religion, Christianity, would politically unify the people of his land; the only choice to be made was where to turn to for intermediary religious and political support. The land he ruled covered roughly 250,000 km^2 and was populated by over one million people, all of whom were pagan—they had their own local deities and places of cult worship. The neighboring Holy Roman Empire, although seemingly a logical choice, was in fact a German kingdom ruled by German emperors who were intent on subordinating their Slavonic neighbors, and if that did not work, then on eliminating them along with their language and culture. So instead, Mieszko I sought the cultural and political benefits that Christendom would bring via the Czech Bohemians, marrying their princess and adopting Christianity for himself and all of his people. Mieszko further emphasized Poland's unity and independence by officially placing it in the care of the Roman Catholic Pope, which resulted in Poland always siding with the Vatican throughout Europe's turbulent religious history, thus rousing even more antagonism with the German Holy Roman Emperors.

THE CATHOLIC CHURCH
Catholicism is an essential feature of Polishness, but at the same time there would be no Polishness without Catholicism. The Church has

played a significant role in relation to Polish patriotism because it always constituted an alternative to the surrounding political system. If that system was not tolerated, the Catholic faith provided a sense of national identity, and its rites and symbols were extremely emotionally charged. Thus the Catholic Church has always stood as a steadfast bulwark against any type of attack, be it religious or political, or both, and the historical periods of such attacks against the Catholic Church in Poland only drew Poles to it more strongly. In this context, a Catholic Poland played the important role of the main defender of Christianity during the period of constant assaults from Muslim Turks and Tatars in the fifteenth century, keeping the religion of Islam at bay in this area of Europe.

Likewise, Poles' national aspirations were identified with the Catholic faith when Poland as a nation was totally erased from the maps of Europe during the Partitions (see Chapter 42), and the Church was subject to Russian Orthodox or German Protestant rule. This faith was all the more important when Catholic priests became the staunchest and most trusted supporters of national morale during those hard times, and Catholics were able to uphold a Polish national identity despite fierce Austrian, Prussian, and Russian attempts to utterly oust it. The Poles' sense of national unity in this religion was also unyielding when the German occupation tried to obliterate it during World War II.

Polish Catholicism has been described as more mystical and traditional than intellectually orientated, with its chief features being emotionality, emphasis on tradition, religious rites and customs as well as the Marian cult (see Chapter 16). More than feeling bound by doctrine and practice, and somewhat lax about certain religious obligations, is the Poles' deep faith in an understanding, merciful, and always helpful God.

Today, over 90% of Poles declare themselves Roman Catholic, though the number of actual practicing Catholics is closer to 60%. Poland is said to have been the only country in Europe whose ethnic makeup was drastically altered as a result of the aftermath of World War II. The Nazis' tragic elimination of the Jews, for whom Poland had been a religious haven for many centuries, the change of borders and subsequent massive forced resettlement turned it into an ethnically homogeneous country, with many of its minority groups assimilating the Polish language, culture, and Roman Catholic religion over the years. Before

WWII, 67% of the population was Polish, while the rest were Ukrainians (14%), Jews (9%), Belarusians (3%), and Germans (2.5%), among others. Today these ethnic groups comprise only about 1–1.5% of the country's entire population of thirty-eight million (as of 2010), and of these it is the German minority group that is the largest (ca. 0.4%). The Roman Catholic Church (*Kościół Rzymsko-Katolicki*) thus also has adherents among the German, Lithuanian, Slovak, and Roma minority groups.

OTHER RELIGIONS

An interesting split from the Roman Catholic Church is the Polish Catholic Church—a religious entity founded at the end of the nineteenth century by Polish immigrants in the U.S. that is not subject to the Pope in Rome and its clergy are not bound by celibacy. It has about 21,000 followers in Poland, most of whom live in Warsaw. Another is the Old Catholic Mariavite Church, with about 25,000 believers.

The second largest non-Catholic creed is the Eastern Orthodox Church (*Kościół Prawosławny*), which uses Old Church Slavonic as its liturgical language. Its main followers are mostly Belarusians or Ukrainians living along Poland's eastern border, mainly in the Podlasie region. Sermons are given in those national languages.

A large part of the Belarusian minority group and part of the Ukrainian and Lemko minority groups also belong to the Polish Autocephalous Orthodox Church, the liturgical language of which is also Old Church Slavonic.

The Uniate Church, also called the Greek-Catholic Church (*Kościół Grecko-Katolicki*), which split off from the Eastern Orthodox Church with the Union in Brest (1596) and accepted the supremacy of the Pope in Rome but retained its Eastern rites, the liturgical language of Old Church Slavonic and traditional practices, has followers among the Ukrainian and Lemko minority groups as well.

There are several Protestant churches in Poland, with the large German minority group having many followers in the Lutheran Church of the Augsburg Confession, but using Polish in its liturgical services. Other Protestant churches include the Methodist and Baptist churches, the United Evangelical Church (including Pentecostals), the Church of Jesus Christ of Latter-day Saints (Mormons), and missionary groups such as Seventh Day Adventists.

Poland also has small minority groups of Muslims, Jews, and Karaites (as distinguished from Rabbinic Judaism).

Most of the various churches are affiliated with the Polish Ecumenical Council, the work of which was strongly supported by Pope John Paul II, whose first meeting with its representatives took place during his second pilgrimage to Poland in 1983. This "pilgrim Pope," called so because of the many various countries he would visit worldwide with his evangelical message, was elected by the Vatican's College of Cardinals on October 16, 1978. The famous words of *"Habemus Papam!"* (We have a Pope!) filling St. Peter's Square came as a great surprise when the entire Christian world welcomed a new Pope who was from Poland—after over 500 years of nothing but Italian Popes!

THE POLISH POPE

Cardinal Karol Wojtyła, now Pope John Paul II, was also a patriotic Pole who was deeply aware of his homeland's tribulations, particularly following countrywide spurts of organized opposition and protest of the political and economic system in Poland, which was very much in an internal crisis by 1979. That year, the Pope made his first

Statue of Pope John Paul II, Krakow
(Brasiliao / Shutterstock.com)

historic pilgrimage to communist Poland, and during his very first homily he addressed Poles with the now-famous words, "Let Thy Spirit descend and renew the face of the land, this land!"—a profound statement that was, ironically, spoken on Warsaw's Victory Square to over 300,000 people. The theme for that first visit had been Christ's message from the Scripture—"Do not be afraid!"—and the religious occasion was the 900th anniversary of the martyrdom of St. Stanisław, Poland's patron saint and symbol of religious insubordination to secular authority. This was an implicit call for all Poles to stand together and fearless against their burgeoning fight with a totalitarian regime. Thus the Pope's implicit message, encouraging Poles to voice their dissatisfactions and aspirations and to openly question the relationship between worldly authority and human morality, led to a general awakening of national pride, a sense of togetherness and renewal of the Polish collective identity that foreshadowed everything that was to come in the following two decades. His words expressly articulated, confirmed and gave uniform direction to what the Polish people had intuitively been sensing in their troubled hearts.

John Paul II made seven pilgrimages to Poland. The first three took place during the communist period: the first, in 1979, carried the concept of "renewal" as its major theme; the ones in 1983, when Poles were dealing with the hardships of martial law, and in 1987, at the eve of the country's political change, both implied the theme of "hope." The following pilgrimages took place in a "new" Poland in the years 1991, 1995, 1997, and 1999. The Pope always addressed and responded to Poland's socio-political situation in his homilies, which were publicly broadcast during Mass, and attended by thousands or even hundreds of thousands of Poles.

The pilgrimage in 1999 marked another occasion, that of the 1,000[th] anniversary of the creation of Gniezno as the first diocese and bishopric in Poland which, symbolically, was also the cradle of Polish Christianity. The Catholic Church in Poland had always served as a mainstay of tradition, a symbol of patriotism and human integrity, regardless the external circumstances. During Cardinal Wojtyła's first address to the crowd on St. Peter's Square, shortly after having been announced the new Pope, he solemnly stated about his person and his homeland: "They have summoned him from a far, distant country, but one which has always been close in the community of faith and the Christian tradition." Thus the Pope never failed to return to the source and significance of the great heritage of Poland's Christianity, which had started with the country's baptism thanks to the foresight of its first official ruler, Mieszko I.

During his visits to a postcommunist Poland of the 1990s, the Pope referred to his words spoken on Warsaw's Victory Square as ones expressing the main goal of his pilgrimages to Poland: to give this forcibly silenced nation a voice, to say what Poles could not say, and in their name, to those who would not speak with them—and for all the world to hear. This "godless" and "immoral" communism and its principles of totalitarianism would never last in a country founded on the principles of Christianity, a religious faith that had always been replete with symbols of struggle, hope and, ultimately, victory.

The Pope's pilgrimages were obviously never purely religious events, and they ultimately helped guide Poles through the struggles of the 80s. The political transformation from the fall of communism to democracy would soon encompass all countries of the Eastern bloc. It seems fair to state that the Pope's pilgrimages, visits, homilies and speeches were all part of a great plan to help overthrow totalitarian rule, and thus to lead to an eventual re-evangelization of Poland, Europe and, through them, the whole world, all of which he had helped carry into the new, third millennium.

Poland's part in European history calls for preserving its Roman Catholic cultural and religious heritage, both of which have constituted the essence of the country's national character. The Polish Pope always emphasized the ecumenical importance of unifying all people, Christians and non-Christians alike, and their inherent right to human dignity, integrity and morally responsible freedom, the importance and sacredness of the family as a unit, the value of human life, respect for human rights and solidarity, and the universality of Christianity regardless of geography, culture, skin color, wealth, status and, ultimately, religion.

John Paul II died on April 2, 2005. Six days later voices calling out "*Santo subito!*" would be heard on St. Peter's Square.

M.T.

FURTHER READING

John Paul II. The Pope from Poland by Tadeusz Karolak. Interpress Publishers, 1979.

Witness to Hope: The Biography of Pope John Paul II by George Weigel. Harper Perennial, 2005.

CHAPTER 15

ALL SAINTS' YEAR

Byli święci przed nami, będą i później.
There were saints before us, there will be after.

Jeden święty, drugi przeklęty.
One is a saint, the other damned.

Nikt nie jest świętym.
Nobody is a saint.
(Polish proverbs)

Saints seem larger than life—their unfathomable faith, boundless love for God and other mortals, superhuman courage and often incomprehensible suffering clearly hold a special place in the hearts of Poles. Most Polish people are named after a saint, and many Poles pray to the saints for intercession. Churches often carry the names of their patron saint, and saints are depicted in the crests of Polish towns and cities. The following are only a handful of the many devout men and women that Poles look up to with a sense of pride. Presented in chronological order, these are the short stories of their spiritually rich lives.

SAINT WOJCIECH
Wojciech came from a noble family. Born Vojtěch in 956, he probably would have become a knight, yet as a small boy he fell gravely ill and

his parents could do nothing more but to carry his limp body to the local church and promise to offer his worldly life to God. He miraculously recovered and, to fulfill his parents' promise, was bound for priesthood. Wojciech later became the Bishop of Prague, and tried to lead the pious life that he wanted his fellow clergymen to follow, much to his avail and to the growing aversion against him. He fled to Rome and, released by Pope John XV from his episcopal obligations, withdrew to a Benedictine monastery to find peace in carrying out the most humble of duties. He had to return, quite unwillingly, to fulfill the duties of the bishopric in Prague. A few years later his entire family was murdered, probably on orders of the Czech Prince Bolesław II, and Wojciech, again finding himself in conflict with the people, returned to Rome for the second time. There he was presented with the idea of working as a missionary to evangelize in the lands of the pagan peoples of Prussia. He worked closely with the Polish ruler, Bolesław the Brave, whose people were then just turning toward Christianity. Wojciech had preached among the Poles as a missionary, but the Prussians were irritated with his manner of commanding them to abandon their pagan ways. He was captured and murdered on April 23, 997; news of his martyr's death resounded all over Europe. Bolesław the Brave, later king of Poland, bought his deceased body for an equivalent weight in gold. Saint Wojciech is believed to be the author of the war song "Bogurodzica" (Mother of God), which Polish knights used to sing when going to battle. He was canonized in 999 by Pope Sylvester II and is the patron saint of Poland.

SAINT STANISŁAW OF SZCZEPANÓW

Stanisław, born in 1035, was the Bishop of Krakow and a loyal friend of the Polish King Bolesław the Bold (Bolesław II Śmiały). They saw it as their mutual mission to aid in the Christianization and unification of Poland. Over time, though, the king's cruel and often lawless ways of treating his knights and subjects greatly troubled Stanisław, who stood in their defense and finally excommunicated the king, thus himself becoming accused of being a traitor. The impulsive king wanted Stanisław dead, and sent his men to execute the bishop without trial. It is said that they dared not touch Stanisław, so the infuriated king decided to carry out the order himself in 1079. Stanisław is said to have been slain while celebrating mass. This ruthless murder stirred outrage throughout the land. The king was condemned for this atrocious act by his own people, forced to step down from the throne both he and the bishop had once worked so hard to attain and was banished. Stanisław was canonized by Pope Innocent IV in 1253. Pope John Paul II named him the patron saint of moral order. Stanisław is also the patron saint of Poland, Krakow, and many Polish parishes in Poland and abroad.

SAINT JADWIGA, CROWNED KING (YES, KING) OF POLAND

The fervently religious Jadwiga, born ca. 1373-1374, was only twelve years old and in love with another boy when she dispassionately agreed, upon the requests of the royal advisors, to marry the much older, pagan and entirely foreign Lithuanian ruler, Władysław Jagiełło. Her hand in marriage finalized Jagiełło's promise to accept Christianity and to establish an alliance with Poland, which guaranteed that both countries would experience, at least for some time, a period of relative peace and prosperity. Jadwiga had sacrificed her own happiness for the sake of her country, for which she was extremely admired and revered during her lifetime. She bore her first child, a daughter, nearly a decade later; Jagiełło was so overjoyed he invited almost all of Europe for the christening. Unfortunately, their daughter Elżbieta lived only three weeks, and Jadwiga died shortly after at the age of 25. She was known as a merciful queen who helped the poor, the needy and the sick. She had also financially supported many schools, and bequeathed most of her jewels and valuables to help fund the university in Krakow. Jadwiga was already considered a saint at the time of her death, and was beatified in 1987 and canonized in 1997 by Pope John Paul II.

SAINT STANISŁAW KOSTKA

Stanisław Kostka longed to become a monk, but when his father refused to grant him permission to enter a monastery, he decided to set out for Rome on foot. Two months and 2,500 kilometers later, he finally entered the city and was accepted by the Jesuit order. This was the year 1567. Kostka had wanted to go to India as a missionary, but came down with malaria (a disease rampant in those times as Rome was surrounded by marshland). He died on the eve of the Immaculate Conception, which he had stated would be a great act of grace on behalf of God. The sudden death of this extremely mature and religious Jesuit, at the tender age of only eighteen years old, and only ten months after having arrived in Rome, quickly led to a cult following. Stanisław Kostka was beatified in 1605 and canonized in 1726. He is the patron saint of Poland, young people, and altar boys.

Saint Andrzej Bobola

A group of Orthodox Cossacks came riding into the village of Janów Poleski early in May of 1657 to do two things: to plunder and to kill as many Catholics and Jews as they could find. Bobola, a Jesuit missionary and preacher, was captured and tortured mercilessly, but did not renounce his faith. He had come to live and preach in times of war and religious turmoil, especially in the lands along Poland's eastern border. He died, as a martyr, on May 16, 1657. In 1922 the Bolsheviks exhibited his remains as a curio that, after nearly 250 years, had remained fairly unchanged, and which convinced many that the Jesuit had truly been a man of God. His relics now lie in a sanctuary in Warsaw, whose Archdiocese he is the patron of. He was declared blessed by Pope Pius IX on October 30, 1853 and canonized by Pope Pius XI on April 17, 1938. Andrzej Bobola is also the patron saint of Warsaw and Poland.

Saint Adam Chmielowski

Adam Chmielowski would probably have become a famous Polish painter, just as his friends and renowned painters, Józef Chełmoński and Jacek Malczewski, if not for the fact that, apart from painting, he also wanted to dedicate his life to God. Initially a Jesuit, Chmielowski later founded a new order—the Albertines. He believed in living the secluded life of a hermit monk and began establishing hermitages in the Tatra Mountains. Chmielowski devoted the last thirty years of his life to helping the poor, the homeless and those stricken with alcoholism, for whom he founded a shelter in Krakow. He lived in the shelter and died in 1916 among those he had helped. Adam Chmielowski was beatified in 1983 and canonized in 1989 by Pope John Paul II. *Brat Naszego Boga* (Our God's Brother), a play about Chmielowski's life, written by the then Karol Wojtyła, was made into a movie in 1997 under the same title.

Saint Faustyna Kowalska

When the humble Helena Kowalska, very young, deeply spiritual and extremely poor, arrived in the small village of Kiekrz to help a nun in the everyday chores of the local convent, her only dream was to be faithful to God and to become a nun herself. She had had visions of Jesus long before, but did not have the resources to be accepted by the convent, and so it was decided that she would enter one through hard, physical work. After taking on the name of Faustyna, she experienced another revelation in which Jesus asked her that a painting be prepared according to His description and with the words "Jezu, ufam Tobie" ("Jesus, I trust Thee") inscribed at the bottom. Faustyna was often unsatisfied with the paintings that were prepared by the many artists who had been commissioned to depict the image. She wrote down her visions and mystical experiences in her diary, known as *Dzienniczek*, a written record which helped spread the message of Divine Mercy throughout the Catholic Church, establish observance of the Feast of Mercy (called Divine Mercy Sunday, celebrated on the first Sunday after Easter) and the Chaplet of the Divine Mercy prayer (*koronka*). In great physical pain and spiritual suffering, Faustyna died of tuberculosis in 1938 at the age of thirty-three. She was beatified in 1993 and canonized seven years later by John Paul II. A movie based on the visionary nun's life, entitled *Faustyna*, was made in 1994.

Saint Maksymilian Kolbe

Maksymilian Kolbe had a childhood vision of the Virgin Mary, who presented him with two crowns—one white, the other red. She asked him if he was willing to accept either of the crowns—the white one signifying perseverance in purity, the red one a symbol of martyrdom. Kolbe accepted both. A Franciscan avidly believing in the intercession of the Holy Virgin Mary, he provided shelter to refugees during World War II, including the 2,000 Jews he hid from Nazi persecution in his friary in Niepokalanów. He was arrested on February 17, 1941 by the Gestapo and imprisoned at the infamous Pawiak prison. Several months later Kolbe was sent to the Auschwitz concentration camp.

In the summer of 1941 several prisoners disappeared from the camp, which prompted the deputy commander to pick ten other male prisoners to be starved to death in an underground bunker as a measure against any further attempts of escape. Kolbe volunteered to take the place of a fellow prisoner who had cried out for his wife and children upon being chosen by the commander. After two weeks of dehydration, starvation and deep prayer, Kolbe was the only prisoner of the ten to remain alive. The bunker was to be emptied, so the guards were ordered to give Kolbe a lethal injection of phenol. Maksymilian Kolbe died on August 14, 1941. He was beatified by Pope Paul VI as a confessor (white vestments) in 1971 and canonized by Pope John Paul II as a martyr (red vestments) in 1982. Thus, Kolbe's dream of serving the Virgin Mary in a two-fold manner was fulfilled. The man, husband and father he had helped to save, Franciszek Gajowniczek, was in attendance at both ceremonies.

STANISŁAWA LESZCZYŃSKA

On a cold January day in 1970, a group of thirty people, all in their late twenties, arrived at the Grand Theater in Warsaw to meet with an elderly woman. They had come to pay their respects and to personally thank her for saving their lives—this was the only group of babies, out of the 3,000 born at the Auschwitz-Birkenau camp, that this nurse had been able to rescue, under inhumane conditions and risking her own life. All babies born in the camp were to be drowned in a barrel of water. She would, against the direct orders of Dr. Mengele and the German midwives, bring the newborns to their mothers, make diapers out of rags, and feed them whatever food she was able to smuggle in.

Stanisława Leszczyńska was born in 1896 in Łódź and was the wife of one of the city's best typesetters. In February 1943 her whole family was arrested by the Gestapo for helping Jews and preparing false documents for them. She was sent, along with her daughter, to the Auschwitz concentration camp as prisoner #41335 and worked as a midwife there until the end of the war. Leszczyńska's *Midwife's Report from Auschwitz*, first published in the late 1960s, describes the atrocities that befell babies born in the camp—the newborns received no food rations, making diapers for them was punishable by death and most slowly died of starvation, accompanied only by the great love of their helpless mothers. She wrote, "In the concentration camp all babies—against all odds—were born alive, beautiful and fat. Mother nature, as if opposing all hatred, was steadfast in fighting for her rights, with seemingly unlimited reserves of vitality." In June 1987, during a visit to Poland, Pope John Paul II pointed to Stanisława Leszczyńska as an example of Christian heroism. The process of her beatification was initiated in 1992.

POPE JOHN PAUL II

"Santo subito!" (A saint immediately!) chanted the people on St. Peter's Square, on the streets of Poland, and in countries all over the world. On April 2, 2005, at the hour of his death, and even before then, many had considered the humble Pope from Poland a saint; the one who had beatified and canonized hundreds before him was soon to enter into the same circle of blessed servants of God. Pope John Paul II's process of beatification was initiated shortly after his death on May 13, 2005, with the five-year waiting period, normally required by canon law before proceedings can begin, waived by Pope Benedict XVI. The miraculous healing of sister Marie Simon Pierre, a French nun who recovered from Parkinson's disease after fellow nuns sought John Paul II's intercession, is one of many documented cases of people touched by divine grace, either directly or through intercessory prayer to the late Pope. He was beatified on May 1, 2011 by Pope Benedict XVI (for more on Pope John Paul II, see Chapter 14).

M.T.

FURTHER READING

Faustina: The Apostle of Divine Mercy by Catherine M. Odell. Our Sunday Visitor, 1998.

St. Maximilian Kolbe: Apostle of Our Difficult Age by Antonio Ricciardi. Daughters of St. Paul, 1982.

CHAPTER 16

THE OL' WHITE AND RED

Poland has not yet perished,
So long as we still live.
What the alien force has taken from us,
We shall retrieve with a sabre.
–The first verse of *Mazurek Dąbrowskiego,*
the Polish national anthem, by Józef Wybicki

Poland's national symbol is at the heart of its coat of arms—the crowned white eagle. In the Middle Ages, the eagle, alongside the lion or griffin, symbolized the power of the monarchy, thus these three were mostly used as heraldic symbols on pennants and banners. Wild eagles were known for their predatory skills, and thus were associated with strength and agility, but it was especially the large, awe-inspiring white-tailed eagle flying over Polish lands that epitomized immense power and absolute freedom. The image of the eagle appeared on the coins of the first Piast rulers; the first to acknowledge it as a national symbol was Przemysł II, duke of Greater Poland who, when crowned king of Poland in 1295, desired to so commemorate the unity and strength of the Piast-ruled Polish kingdom of his predecessors.

One of the first historic settlements, known as Gniezno, was called such because, according to legend, it was there that Lech had seen a white eagle standing in its nest (*gniazdo*) against the red background of a setting sun (see Chapter 3). In medieval times a red, crimson background signified the color of the monarchy. Thus the heraldic emblem of a white, crowned eagle on a red background was officially approved during the reign of both Władysław I the Short and Casimir III the Great; it was then also introduced onto state seals.

THE POLISH FLAG

The colors of the Polish flag date back to the country's original coat of arms. It is also historically connected with the coat of arms of the Polish-Lithuanian Commonwealth, when the two colors of red and white were juxtaposed. White had always been the color of the Polish emblem's eagle, and this color was also used in the emblem of Lithuania's *Pogoń*— the charging knight on a steed. Both of these national emblems were then set against the red background of their respective heraldic shields. That is why white is positioned as the top horizontal stripe, in heraldic tradition, because the color of the emblem is more important than the color of the background—in this case the color red as the bottom horizontal stripe. Yet both stripes, or colors, are equal in size.

During the Partitions, state symbolism was almost entirely obliterated due to the notoriously anti-Polish policy of the partitioning powers of Russia, Prussia, and Austria. But white and red, symbolizing the nation's colors, continued to be used, despite heavy persecution, on insurgents' pennants, banners and standards. In 1918, when Poland was once again an independent and sovereign state, white and red were also revived as the official, national colors. In 1919, the Polish Sejm (Parliament) approved the national emblem of a rectangular red background with a silver eagle, its head facing toward the right, with its wings raised upwards, and its beak, claws, and crown in the color of gold. During World War II all political camps used the white and red color scheme, and after the war, Polish authorities again officially confirmed white and red as the national colors. These colors were used especially profusely during national holidays, such as on May 3, celebrating the declaration of Poland's first, and the world's second, constitution, or on November 11, National Independence Day, marking Poland's return to Europe as a sovereign state. The Polish flag was first raised in Paris during the Olympic Games of 1924 to symbolically honor the country.

The question of whether the eagle should have a crown or not later turned into a matter of ideology. It was the postwar communist

(Shutterstock.com)

authorities who were intent on taking the crown off the eagle's head, justifying this by stating that a crown was associated with landownership and, thus, exploitation. And so in 1945 the crown was removed from the national coat of arms, and this act was approved by a decree in 1955. But the socio-political changes after 1989 and emerging democracy also affected the state's symbols. The Republic of Poland placed the crown back on the eagle's head at the beginning of 1990.

THE NATIONAL ANTHEM

The first Polish hymn was actually a medieval prayer to the Virgin Mary called *Bogurodzica*. It also constitutes the earliest Polish vernacular verse to be found in written records, dating from the thirteenth century. Polish knights sang this most famous text for many centuries in the form of a prayer hymn as they marched into battle, such as during the great Battle of Grunwald in 1410. The first lines of the *Bogurodzica* were:

> *Bogurodzica dziewica, Bogiem sławiena Maryja,*
> *U twego syna Gospodzina Matko zwolena, Maryja!*
> *Zyszczy nam, spuści nam.*
> *Kyrie eleison!*

> *Mother of God, Virgin, praised by God, Mary!*
> *Your son, the Lord, chosen mother, Mary!*
> *Secure us with Him, send Him to us.*
> *Lord, have mercy!*

Today's national anthem, called the *Mazurek Dąbrowskiego* ("Dąbrowski's Mazurek," or often mistakenly called "Poland has Not Yet Perished"), was originally called the "Song of the Polish Legions in Italy." These Polish Legions were formed in 1797 in Milan under the command of Jan Henryk Dąbrowski, at a time when Polish soldiers were offering their military services to Napoleon Bonaparte's revolutionary France after the collapse of the Greater Poland Uprising that had taken place three years before. The words of the text were first written down that same year in Reggio nell'Emilia by the preeminent political writer Józef Wybicki. The lyrics were first sung in public on July 16, 1797 during an army parade. The song became very popular among Polish legionaries—one year later nearly all soldiers were singing it—but no one expected that they would become the words of the national anthem.

Around 1831, the leaders of the November Uprising chose Wybicki's lyrics as their official anthem, as large armies of Polish soldiers fighting in Italy against the partitioning powers meant that Poland indeed had "not yet perished." Polish society understood that this servitude to foreign nations would not last forever, and the words gave them hope for a better, independent future. Independence was regained on November 11, 1918. In 1924, the Polish hymn was officially played to honor sovereign Poland in Paris during the Olympic Games. In 1926, the official lyrics were made public by the Polish government and in 1927, the official national anthem was recognized as the *Mazurek Dąbrowskiego*. In 1990, the new, democratic Sejm of Poland unanimously voted it as the national anthem.

The white crowned eagle, white and red flag, and *Mazurek Dąbrowskiego* were used by insurgents as patriotic symbols during the eighteenth- and nineteenth-century uprisings to liberate the partitioned Polish state. During the nineteenth and twentieth centuries these national symbols played an important, if not crucial, role in the process of shaping national awareness, but there was also a religious symbol of paramount importance in the history of Poland—the Black Madonna of Częstochowa.

THE BLACK MADONNA

The origins of this most revered of religious paintings depicting the Virgin Mary and Christ child in Poland are unknown. According to tradition, it was painted by St. Luke on wood that came from the Holy Family's table. Other sources say it was an icon painted on a wooden board brought from Ruthenia by Vladislaus II of Opole (Władysław Opolczyk) at the end of the fourteenth century. The current image was painted over several much older ones, which makes exact dating very difficult, if not impossible. This painting of the Black Madonna, 122 cm x 82 cm in size and dark-tinted in color, is located in a shrine at the monastery of Jasna Góra in the southern city of Częstochowa.

Throughout the centuries, miraculous interventions have been attributed to the Black Madonna. In 1430, a group of Hussites stormed into the church on a plundering rampage, and according to accounts one charged at the painting with his sword and made slashes on the cheek of the Virgin Mary, thus breaking the panel. The painting was renovated in a Krakow workshop, but the scars were left on the Madonna's cheek to remind future generations of this religious profanation. It is also commonly believed that the miraculous painting delivered the monastery of Jasna Góra and all of Poland from the Tatars in the fifteenth century and from the massive Swedish invasion, known as the Deluge (*Potop*) in 1655, when overwhelming

Swedish forces that had overrun the entire country were defeated by a small group of defenders after a prolonged siege of the monastery (see Chapter 9).

In 1656 King John II Casimir Vasa (Jan II Kazimierz Waza) vowed that Mary, the Mother of God, would become the Queen of the Polish Crown, and in 1717 she was indeed crowned Queen of Poland; the ceremony was apparently attended by 200,000 followers. Thus the Black Madonna became the patroness of Poland, the country's most significant religious relic and symbol and the main destination of pilgrimages from Poland and from countries all over the world. John Paul II's second pilgrimage to Poland in June of 1983 was to commemorate the 600th anniversary of the Black Madonna of Częstochowa—the painting of the Black Madonna had also become a symbol of patriotism. The leaders of the Solidarity movement were not afraid to wear small badges with the image of the Black Madonna as a sign of this.

The message of the Pope's visit was unity, implicitly solidarity, although using the very word was illegal at that time. The *Solidarność* sign, created by Jerzy Janiszewski in 1980, was a new take on the national colors of white and red, the Polish flag flowing freely in the wind carried proudly by individuals, united, marching together. This simple sign became a symbol of freedom of the Solidarity movement and was worn as a badge along with that of the religious icon of the Black Madonna.

M.T.

PART II

POLES IN POLAND

CHAPTER 17

THE POLISH MENTALITY

"Like any other nation, it has its idiosyncrasies and nurtures its para-doxes, which are neither more nor less baffling than those of others."
–Adam Zamoyski, *The Polish Way*

There's something about Polish people that you can just never put your finger on. They seem a proud nation, but if you compliment the average Pole and say something like, "Wow! That's great! You really did a wonderful job," they will eye you suspiciously and ask if you're joking, or worse yet, they might even go as far as to accuse you of blatantly lying.

Poles don't like to brag; actually, they never seem to boast about anything—the only exception may be proud grandparents. If they have just bought a new car, you will never know. If their child wins some big sporting competition, they won't tell you that either. So when you do find out, from a third party that is, that a friendly neighbor of yours has won an award for being one of the most accomplished scientists in the country, don't think that neighbor will ever mention that fact to you in person. And if you tell them you just read about their accomplishments in the paper and congratulate them, don't expect to get the lowdown on the whos and whats of everything, because they will be more willing to talk about what they're having for dinner that night than about their personal success story.

If you ask the average Pole to come up with a list of their personal successes and failures, you will get a long and elaborate inventory of failures, whereas the triumphs might have two or three items listed, one item crossed out, and maybe two left by the end. It's difficult for Polish people to talk about themselves in the superlative, particularly when it comes to their own accomplishments. The same goes for Polish humor—most often, it's of the self-deprecating variety. And yet, a current of national pride runs through most Poles' veins, even if it only comes out once they have left Polish borders.

NATIONAL PRIDE

Poles feel national pride, but are sometimes afraid to show it in public. This lack of national self-confidence also manifests itself in Poles' constant comparison of Poland to other countries, which supposedly have better healthcare systems, better roads, more credible governments, more trustworthy politicians, less bureaucracy, better schools . . . The list goes on and on. But when abroad, a Pole will soon start longing for home—for a delicious home-cooked meal, for the annoying Polish voice-over on TV and even the spiteful, middle-aged sales clerk working at the local grocery store. Everything to do with Poland will take on a warm, sentimental tone and will not seem as bad as once thought, and you will probably often hear a Pole remark, "You know, in Poland we do it this way. . . ."

This sense of Polish identity is connected with Poland's historical past, one that has endured foreign invasions, hostile occupation and contemptible Partitions (see Chapter 42). Poland always saw its historic mission as that of the "bulwark of Christianity," an impermeable barrier between Western culture and, usually, non-Christian intrusions from the East. If anything, Poles' attachment to the Roman Catholic tradition (just as to the Polish language) was always stronger than to any ruling political system. And if Poland was in the heart of Europe, then in 1795 the Old Continent lost its most vital organ for over a hundred years. Despite this political dismemberment between Austria, Prussia, and Russia, Polish cultural identity remained intact, and organized uprisings were commonplace in the partitioning powers' territories. From these two main sources of aggravation rose the concept of Poland as the "Christ among nations," a martyred country that had to endure great suffering for itself and in the name of other nations. Then came the atrocities the Nazis and Soviets committed on Polish soil during World War II and, afterward, Poland's fate as a forced Soviet satellite of the Eastern bloc until 1989. But these historical predicaments only impelled Poles to try to find ingenious ways out of hopeless situations, and to regularly do the inconceivable to pull off the virtually impossible against all logical odds.

CHARITY BEGINS *W DOMU*

It is said that Poles can fight for ideals, even if those ideals seem far from being anywhere near realistic. But this belief that the impossible is in fact possible can, and often has, proved to be very successful. Poles possess an almost mythical way of being able to come together when the need arises (or when a common enemy appears on the horizon), of organizing and accomplishing great things. Historically the uprisings and the rise of the Solidarity movement can serve as examples, but more recently whenever a streak of great misfortune comes upon a group of people, Poles band together and help out—such was the case during the floods of 1997 or the Katowice Exhibition Hall roof collapse in 2006. Another nationwide example is the Wielka Orkiestra Świątecznej Pomocy (The Great Orchestra of Christmas Charity), a public benefit organization whose yearly fundraising campaign gathers Poles in Poland and abroad who raise money to provide hospitals and clinics with specialist state-of-the-art medical equipment for children, especially newborns.

Most every Pole will declare that family is most important in their lives, and many Poles manifest this through their respect for their parents, older people and for the deceased, which is especially visible during All Saints' Day on November 1 (*Wszystkich Świętych*), when entire cemeteries emanate a warm, glowing orange from the thousands of lit candles among flower wreaths on carefully polished tombstones.

THE POLISH SENSE OF HUMOR

Perhaps it makes sense for a nation of people who tend not to brag and may be called cynical by some to have a very strange sense of humor, and one that is not always understood, some say hardly ever, by a non-native. It seems the most common, everyday jokes are of the "old woman (*baba*) went to the doctor's and [. . . to be joyfully filled in]" variety, at which point the wise-cracking Pole will put in some kind of noun, e.g. "the old woman (*baba*) went to the doctor's and there she saw another *baba!*" and die of laughter. Umm . . . yeah.

Another example of a typical Polish *kawał* (joke) you might hear at a bar (or forwarded in an e-mail from a Polish uncle) is of the largely self-deprecating kind:

> *A Polish minister went on an official visit to France. One of the objectives of his visit was to have dinner with his French counterpart. Seeing his magnificent villa, with paintings by the great masters on the walls, he asks the Frenchman how he can afford such luxuries on the modest salary of a public official. The Frenchman invites him to the window:*
> *– Do you see the highway there?*
> *– Yes.*
> *– It cost twenty million euro; the company wrote out an invoice for twenty-five and gave me the difference.*
> *Two years later, the French minister travels to Poland to visit his Polish counterpart. When he pulls up at the house of the minister, before his eyes stands the most beautiful palace he has ever seen in his life. He asks immediately:*
> *– I don't understand, two years ago you said that I led a princely life, but compared to you…*
> *The Polish minister invites him to the window:*
> *– Do you see the highway there?*
> *– No.*
> *– Exactly!*

Throughout history, joking about the often-tragic absurdities of everyday life has been a kind of coping mechanism for Poles, particularly during the communist era, when even politicians were not immune (see Chapter 41). While today's political corruption and bureaucratic headaches are nowhere near as bad as they were in those days, much of the humor has remained, and often acts as a mirror held up to Polish society. For abundant examples, one just has to watch a Polish cabaret show (see Chapter 35)—or simply ask any bar patron, particularly an older gentleman, for an example.

Kombinujemy

A Pole will be painfully honest when asked, "How are you?" You will often hear "Awful!" as an answer, or "Couldn't be worse!" If you, in turn, answer that everything's fine then you will raise any Polish person's level of focused attention, and they might even suspect something is seriously wrong with you. But Poles are also sensitive to harm done against those who are poor or less privileged, or to violations of workers' rights, and they are acutely aware of attempts at various forms of exploitation. Perhaps this goes back to the communist times of the Polish People's Republic, the era of the "we" against the "them," when anything the authorities of the ruling regime did was usually considered to be in contradiction with the interests of the "the people." Those times also forced Poles to learn how to get things done—sometimes ingeniously. Some say Polish people never have an elaborate, complex plan, but instead are always ready to go and can easily improvise, modify, change, adapt and use creativity to make something out of nothing, as nothing is ever impossible. Polish sayings seem to be saturated with different ways of saying "It'll be OK": *Jakoś to będzie* (It'll work out somehow), *Coś wymyślimy* (We'll think of something), *Damy radę* (We'll deal with it), and the gloriously untranslatable *Coś wykombinujemy* (We'll think of a way to get it done; we'll suss it out).

Historically multiethnic and multicultural, foreigners see Poles as hungering for knowledge, wanting to know and understand other cultures, and wanting to find out more about the world. It was in Poland that the geographically distant Latin American writers, such as Mario Vargas Llosa, Julio Cortázar, and Gabriel Garcia Marquez, became exceptionally popular and gained a huge readership—and this was during the drab 1960s and 1970s of communist rule.

It is said Poland has constantly been changing its identity since 1989, and that Poles are enthusiastic, hardworking, and patient; that they inspire others; that they are friendly, warm, and kind-hearted; that they are persistent in their spirit of achieving independence and are always on a quest for freedom. Poles do indeed have noble souls.

M.T.

CHAPTER 18

SUPERSTITIONS:
HOLD YOUR THUMBS!

"Science can purify religion from error and superstition. Religion can purify science from idolatry and false absolutes."
–Pope John Paul II

The dichotomy between many Poles' Catholicism and their belief in superstitions tantalizes theologians and sociologists alike. Both most probably stem from Poles' attachment to tradition and folk culture—both of which have intermingled and influenced each other to such an extent that it is now difficult to discern where true religion begins and excessive superstition takes over. What are some of these superstitions? Well, let's see. . . . Polish superstitions can, most generally, be divided into several categories:

First, there are many things or events that bring **bad luck** and, in many cases, these include instructions on how to undo this potential misfortune:

- If you wake up in the morning, whatever you do, do not get out of bed by placing your left foot on the floor first, as getting up on your left foot means the whole day will be one major disaster, and if something is to go wrong, it definitely will. Get out of bed on your right foot. Always. By the way, doesn't that suggest sleeping on the right side of the bed?

- No matter what the circumstances, do not refuse to give a pregnant woman whatever she may want; otherwise, everything in your home will be devoured by mice. Poles rarely see real mice these days anyway, and probably get a chance to see them more often in the countryside than in apartments in the cities, but they still have a hidden fear of not giving a pregnant woman what she wants, as this just might bring bad luck upon them and their household. Strangely enough, pregnant women are considered to be in a "blessed" state and are generally not associated with negative connotations. Unfortunately, some of them seem to take particular advantage of this superstition.

- Speaking of pregnant women, they should definitely not pass under hanging ropes, as this may result in the baby becoming tangled in the umbilical cord.

- Black cats symbolize bad luck. Period. And a black cat crossing the road in front of you is just about as unlucky as it can get. The best thing to do in this situation is to wait for someone else to cross the imaginary line that cat has drawn before crossing it yourself. Doesn't that just sound nice? Or, you might resort to taking three steps back, turning around to your left and spitting over your left shoulder. Polish people are also known to completely change their paths if a black cat has crossed them, even if that means walking a few extra steps or even another hour!

- Generally, it's bad news if you have left the house in the morning and realize that you have to go back because you've forgotten something. Going back home if you haven't really left for good that day, as in for work or school, is just plain bad luck. To undo this most unfavorable of situations, once inside the house, sit down, preferably in a chair, and either count from one to ten, from ten to one, or, as some superstitious Polish people do, raise your feet off the ground for a few seconds. Then you can get up, leave the house and act as if nothing happened.

- Spilling salt, or spilled salt in general, is a total no-no and forebodes an imminent argument. No matter what.

- Friday the thirteenth is unlucky in and of itself. This is the day one should most preferably spend at home, hopefully doing nothing that might potentially bring about failure, disaster, or other potentially dangerous misfortune upon oneself. Some people even refrain from making any important decisions, from buying expensive objects, or going on any kinds of journeys!

- Women should never place their handbags on the floor, as this will cause their money to float away. Bags should always be placed on the backs of chairs or left neatly hanging from the strangest of places in restaurants or in the homes of guests.

- Sitting at the corner of a table, usually due to lack of room or to the large number of guests, is most unlucky for an unmarried woman, as this may just leave her an old maid.

- Do not greet people over a threshold or, in other words, in the doorstep. And whatever you do, do not shake hands over that forsaken doorstep either.

- When it comes to shaking hands, if there are four people standing together and ready to shake hands with one another, they will be careful to make sure that their handshakes do not overlap, as in the shape of a cross.

- You should not give a cross pendant to a baby as a Christening gift. A cross symbolizes a difficult and arduous life, and you would not want the baby to start out this way.

- Also, the very superstitious believe that newborn babies should not be taken outside for a walk until they have been baptized.

- Underwear worn inside out will bring bad luck the whole day, through and through.

- Putting new shoes on the table will bring bad luck.

- Many students believe that if you drop your notebook, you will be graded on that particular subject that day.

- You should not get a haircut before an important exam, and especially not before the *matura* (the final high school exam).

- If a deceased person is not buried and "lies over Sunday," there will definitely be another funeral in the family.

- And finally, perhaps this superstition is most daunting of all: when sharing a *na zdrowie* (cheers!), always look straight into the eyes of the person you are clinking your glass with. If you don't, you risk seven years of bad sex!

There are also plenty of ways to assure you will have **good luck**:

- If you see a chimneysweeper, then... wait—what does a chimneysweeper look like, anyway? Well, if you see one, you will know it. They look like they have just come straight out of a Dickens novel—clothes, soot, and all. It is always a man dressed in a well-fitting black uniform (pants and jacket), most often covered in soot, wearing a traditional, black top hat and carrying a chimney brush attached to a fat, black chain at the end that looks like a big, black fuzz-ball. So, when you see this strange-looking fellow, grab any button you have on you and make a wish. If you then see a bespectacled man (some claim it should be a woman), the wish will come true. When traveling on a bus in Poland you may be witness to seeing all the passengers, especially those looking out the windows, grab hold of their buttons at the same time. Should this happen, without a doubt the bus just passed a chimneysweeper.

- The same goes for if you see a nun. If you do, look around to find a man wearing glasses; if you don't see one, you might just be on a bad luck streak.

- A stork seen in flight or on a nest in spring forebodes good luck; a stork seen standing on the ground is not such good news.

- If your right hand starts to itch, you will soon be greeting somebody; if your left hand starts to itch, you will soon be counting, or receiving, money.

- You might also come across small red ribbons hanging on the inside of baby strollers, or better yet, small red ribbons tied to small, golden pendants with a picture of the Virgin Mary or some saint hanging inside said strollers. The color red supposedly protects babies against all types of evil, spells, or bad luck in general.

- Four-leaf clovers, especially those found in the grass during an afternoon walk, will bring good luck. Horseshoes and small, porcelain elephants with raised trunks will do so also. Yes, the trunk must be raised.

- Students bring all sorts of lucky pens and stuffed animals when taking the *matura* or other exams during the school year or at university. Yes, these are allowed by the examiners! No, cheating is not allowed (though not uncommon).

- The same red underwear should be worn for the *studniówka*, the high school prom held 100 days before high school graduation, and then during the final *matura* exam, during which it should bring good luck.

- If you button up your shirt or jacket the wrong way and someone notices, it will bring good luck.

- And finally, if you want to wish someone luck, rather than saying you'll keep your fingers crossed, say you'll be holding your thumbs (*Trzymam kciuki!*) for them. Legend says this gesture comes from medieval times, when thumbs were essential for holding a sword, so you wanted to keep them protected at all costs.

Then, there are superstitions connected with **weddings** in general:

- The best month in which to get married is one that has the letter "r" in its Polish name: *marzec* (March), *czerwiec* (June), or *sierpień* (August), among others. *Maj* (May) is the absolutely worst possible month to get married, as the saying goes "*w maju ślub—rychło grób*," which basically states, "a wedding in May means quick to the grave."

- Beautiful, sunny weather on the wedding day will guarantee good luck for the newlyweds.

- The bride should be wearing or using something old, something new, something blue, and something borrowed on the day of her wedding, that way she will bring good luck to herself and, hopefully, to her spouse.

- The bride should not be wearing a string of pearls, as pearls symbolize tears.

- The groom cannot, of course, see the bride's wedding dress before the wedding. Why? Because this will, of course, bring bad luck.

- In the church the husband-to-be should never walk in a circle around the bride, as this means he will literally have to run around tending to his wife throughout the marriage.

Finally, there are also many superstitions connected with *Wigilia*, the much-awaited Christmas Eve supper that seems so otherworldly in itself:

- Whoever first enters the house on Christmas Eve is very important. A woman is a bad omen and means large amounts of trouble; thus, it is more preferable that a man be the first to cross the threshold of the house.

- Make sure you always have an extra plate on the table for an unexpected guest; this may either be the spirit of a loved one who has passed away or your next-door neighbor stopping by that evening.

- A single fish scale, especially from the carp that was on your *Wigilia* table, should always be in your wallet. One of those will guarantee loads of money or, at least, that you won't be short of cash. However, carrying around any more means you're too keen to get rich, and bad things will happen.

- At midnight on *Wigilia*, animals can speak with human voices, so you might want to hear what they have to say.

- *Wigilia* should be spent in a warm, family atmosphere because, as the saying goes, "How you spend *Wigilia* is how you'll be spending the rest of the new year."

For more in-depth descriptions, see "Here Come the Holidays" (Chapter 30), "How to Survive a Polish Wedding" (Chapter 22), or "Folk Traditions" (Chapter 31).

M.T.

CHAPTER 19

NAMES: FROM ANIA TO ZENON

Jak Barbara po wodzie, Boże Narodzenie po lodzie.
If it rains on Barbara's name day, there will be snow for Christmas

Na Grzegorza zima idzie do morza.
On Gregory's name day the winter leaves for the sea.
(Polish sayings about name days)

Name days have always been a big deal in Poland. Actually, they were once much more important than birthdays, and only within the last two decades or so have the latter gradually ousted the former among the younger generations of Poles, and especially among little children, who have been won over by birthday parties with colorful balloons, big birthday cakes, fun games and all.

HOLY NAMES

In the past, the list of names to choose from for a newborn child was limited to Christian names and, more precisely, to the names of the patron saints listed in the calendar. Each day of the year was assigned to two main patron saints, so often the child would be named after the saint whose name was celebrated on the day that child was born. If the name of the patron saint was less common, or simply sounded strange even to a Polish person, such as Świętopełk or Rościsława, then the name of another saint close to the birthday was chosen. Some saint's names repeated throughout the year, but the patron saint's

129

name day *after* one's birthday, just to be on the safe side, was usually celebrated. The different regions of Poland also had various preferences for patron saints, so, for example, the Greater Poland region's patron saint, Wojciech, was reflected in the many boys named after him; in Lesser Poland, there were many Stanisławs, and in the area of Białystok a very popular name for boys was Kazimierz—all were names of famous Polish kings. In the noble families of the *szlachta*, historical as well as royal names were commonly popular, with Bolesław, Kazimierz, Władysław, and Zygmunt as the choice for boys' names and Anna, Jadwiga, Elżbieta, or Wanda for girls. Names were also given to pay homage to venerated grandparents and important relatives in a given newborn's family.

In fact, most any other more or less original name not to be found on the pages of the Christian calendar would not be accepted by the priest baptizing the child, so originality was, in a way, out of the question. The baptism also symbolized the ceremonious naming of the newborn child in the presence of its parents and godparents. Into this important religious ceremony were interwoven age-old Slavic religious beliefs and customs connected with the protection of the baby against evil forces. The baptism also symbolized that the child had been given a second pair of guardians, the godparents, who would care for it if the need arose. Often the two witnesses of the parents' wedding ceremony were chosen to be the child's godparents, and in Polish tradition it has always been considered an honor to be asked and entrusted with the care of a godchild.

WHAT'S IN A NAME?

You can pretty much tell when somebody was born by their name; for example, a Zdzisław, Waldemar, Krystyna, or Barbara will probably have been born in the 1950s, and an Agnieszka, Magdalena, Tomasz, or Piotr in the 1970s. Unfortunately, this has led to some major conformism in the choice of names, and it is often the case that in a larger group of thirty-year-old women you will come across six Magdalenas, five Katarzynas, four Joannas, three Annas, two Agnieszkas, and one Małgorzata. The same goes for men, whose names in that age bracket will probably be Marek, Maciej, Tomasz, or Łukasz.

In the last decade or so, priests have become more lenient when it comes to the choice of names, so there has been a visible influx of foreign-sounding (and often non-Christian) names, such as Nikola, Jessica, Brian, Alan, Angelica or Natan, to name a few. These are quite often English names with Polish pronunciation and sometimes mixed Polish-English spelling.

The most common names in the last few years have been Julia, Maja, and Zuzanna for girls and Jakub, Mateusz, or Kacper for boys. Traditional names have also seen a revival, such as Zofia and Maria or Franciszek and Jan. So, the parents' dilemma today seems to be between choosing a popular, modern, traditional, or foreign-sounding name.

Another linguistic curiosity of Polish names are their many diminutive forms, or the variety of ways even one name can be altered to denote that its owner is especially cherished or dear to one's heart. Usually an ending is added to the name, but very often the entire name changes its form altogether. For a woman's name the diminutive will usually end in –sia, so Małgorzata is Gosia, Barbara is Basia, Katarzyna is Kasia and, get this, Joanna is Asia. For men, the ending will usually be –ek, so Tomasz is Tomek, Krzysztof is Krzysiek, and Bartosz is Bartek. But one name can have very many diminutives, so Monika can be Moniczka, Moniusia, Monia, or Monuś, and Waldemar can be Waldek, Waldziu, Walduś, or Waldeczek... the array of choices seems to be never-ending.

Certain name days have become traditional holidays in their own right, though neither necessarily religious nor national. Some of the most commonly celebrated during the year are:

- **St. John's Night** (*Noc świętojańska*) on June 23-24—an age-old folk festival that celebrated the beginning of summer on the shortest night and longest day of the year (summer solstice). Especially known for its bonfires and dances of young, unmarried girls and boys, it is best known for the wreath floating ceremony, when girls prepare hand-woven wreaths, light a candle in them, and let the wreaths float away on the water of a lake or river as a way of foretelling their future.

- **St. Andrew's Eve** (*Andrzejki*) on November 29—in the past young, unmarried women could foretell their future on this magical night, and obviously love and marriage were the main topics of interest. The most important ceremony involved pouring hot wax through a keyhole into a bowl of cold water and then interpreting what its solidified shape represented when its shadow was cast on the wall. These days, *Andrzejki* is still immensely popular among college students, and any bar worth its salt will set up a wax-making contraption for their annual *Andrzejki* party.

- **St. Nicholas Day** (*Mikołajki*) on December 6—this name day commemorates the legendary bishop whose unusual kindness and generosity are manifested in the symbol of Santa Claus. On this day, Polish children are given candy and small presents, supposedly from the patron saint in question himself.

- **St. Barbara's Day** (*Barbórka*) on December 4—the patron saint of miners and those whose death was sudden or unexpected. These day-long *Barbórka* celebrations most often take place in Upper and Lower Silesia among miners and their families, with a ceremonious mass for those who died tragically, further blessings for miners to take on the hardships of labor and dangerous work, a solemn luncheon, and other festivities.

Name days continue to be celebrated ceremoniously, and on this day Polish women receive bouquets of roses and chocolates, men get lots of kisses on the cheek and wishes for success, health and all the best—a true *Sto lat!* They, in turn, bring homemade cakes or doughnuts to work to share with everyone and continue their name day celebration at home with more friends and relatives—eating, drinking, and talking around a richly laden dinner table. Nothing can compare to the typical Polish celebration of one's *imieniny*.

M.T.

CHAPTER 20

POLISH WOMEN: MOTHERS OF THE NATION

"Let the Mother, the Queen, the Handmaid make every Polish woman live like a Mother, be adored like a Queen, sacrifice for the Nation like a Handmaid."
–Cardinal Stefan Wyszyński

Most Polish women who have had contact with foreigners are quite aware of Western perceptions of them; while the keywords "Russian brides" might get more hits on Google than "Polish brides," there's no shortage of the latter, mostly leading to rather questionable websites. But while Polish women are hardly lining up to marry foreign strangers like in poorer regions of Eastern Europe, the stereotype of the "ideal Polish wife" still exists in Western and Polish society: a self-sacrificing woman who puts her children and husband first. While that may be the historical case (and not always, as we'll see), today's Polish women are just as complicated and diverse as their counterparts throughout the world. In essence, there is no such thing as a quintessential "Polish woman" anymore—and yet, many of the conventions of the past are still embedded in modern Polish culture.

Matka Polka

Every Polish woman knows the myth of *"matka polka"* ("the Polish Mother"), "the pinnacle of virtuous self-sacrificing womanhood," as described by gender studies professor Halina Filipowicz. The

(Elzbieta Sekowska / Shutterstock.com)

archetype emerged during the Partitions in the nineteenth century, when Russian and Prussian policies of assimilation and suppression of Polish culture in schools led the Polish home to become the refuge of "Polishness." As the home was the domain of women, they became the guardians of Polishness and took over the role of educating children in Polish language, history, and culture. Polish mothers instilled patriotism in the next generation, a role normally reserved for civil society and the educational system, giving them an unparalleled importance for the survival of the nation. This would continue through modern times, when communist authorities implemented the teaching of a "revised" history in school, leaving children to learn the truth of their nation's past exclusively at home.

While this explains the romantic, patriotic duty Polish women have taken on throughout history, the *matka polka* stereotype also largely emphasizes self-sacrifice—putting their children, husbands, or the nation above themselves. There are countless tales of Polish women giving shelter to insurgents during rebellions, caring for the wounded on the battlefield, sheltering Jews or other persecuted groups during Nazi occupation, or even taking up arms (such as national hero **Emilia Plater**, who fought in the November Uprising). In many cases, the wives of insurgents or intellectuals sentenced to hard labor would follow their husbands to exile in Siberia. In more recent history, whole books have been written (see Further Reading) about the part women—who made up half of the movement's membership—played in Solidarity behind the scenes, leading the struggle when the men had mostly been locked up or otherwise silenced. Nonetheless, when a free Poland emerged, it was the men who received credit and political offices, while the women's sacrifice was viewed as part of their historical martyrdom.

Of course, the *matka polka* stereotype is one that is impossible for any actual Polish (or otherwise) woman to live up to. For one, it associates womanhood strictly with motherhood, thereby excluding any woman who happens to not be a mother. It also places the cause of patriotism above all others, including the fight for women's rights. Finally, there's the inherent paradox of the veneration of the Virgin Mary, which is another feminine ideal celebrated in Polish society throughout history. Mary was a mother while also remaining a virgin—a paradoxical situation. Similarly, throughout history, women's sexuality has been repressed and kept private in Poland, especially in theater and film, when compared to more "risqué" countries like France or Germany.

THE "NEW WOMAN"

Communist rule introduced a different picture of Polish womanhood: the "New Woman." According to doctrine, a good woman was a good socialist, taking care of the home while also putting her loyalty to the Party above all (and even reporting on her husband, if such a situation arose). On paper, women were to take an equal part in the workforce, as seen on propaganda posters portraying tractor-driving mothers and scythe-wielding daughters. And in fact, women's employment did increase steadily following World War II, from 33.1% in 1960 to 46% at the fall of the Iron Curtain. Nonetheless, unemployment levels for women remained higher than for men throughout the communist era, and the transition to a democratic government and a free market economy in the early 1990s did little to better the cause of women at first.

After all, freedom and nationhood were the ideals all Poles, male and female, were fighting for, and issues such as equal pay, workplace gender discrimination, government-subsidized childcare, and reproductive rights were put on the back burner during the political struggles of the first postcommunist decade.

LESS TALK, MORE STATS

So what is it like to actually be a woman in today's Poland? Well, one way to get a good sense is to look at the numbers:

- As of 2011 (the last time these things were properly tallied), women made up 51.6% of the population of Poland.

- As far as employment goes, only 53% of women are gainfully employed, compared to over 60% of men.

- While unemployment in general has hovered near 10% since 2010, it is closer to 18% for women.

- Those women who do work earn 83.6 groszy (that's Polish pennies) for every złoty a man earns in the same profession; the wage discrepancies are the most significant at the highest earning bracket, where women earn just 67% of what men in the same positions earn.

- Meanwhile, women are better educated in general: they earn nearly 60% of college degrees.

- As educated as they are, they are still vastly underrepresented in the top levels of business as well as politics, where women make up just 20% of the Sejm (the lower house of Parliament) and less than 10% of the Senate.

- Part of that might have to do with the fact that women still spend twice as much time on household chores (4 hrs 45 min) as men do (2 hrs 13 min on average).

- Following trends throughout Europe, the median age of marriage has been rising in Poland, and is currently twenty-five for women and twenty-seven for men.

Poland's entrance into the European Union in 2004 led to the *de facto* adoption of EU policies related to the promotion of gender equality. Within EU legislation are directives that stipulate equal pay for equal work and prohibit discrimination on the basis of gender. Nonetheless, it seems that so far, many of these directives have yet to be fully implemented.

POLISH FEMINISM

So what have Polish women been doing to improve their situation? Contrary to popular belief, feminism has existed in Poland since the nineteenth century, though until very recently it has always been overshadowed by the country's problems with its neighbors. Even today it is viewed by many as suspect, either as antitraditional (usually from the Catholic perspective), or a relic of communism, or, worst of all, as a Western import with no place in Polish society. It wasn't really until 2011, when Poland held the rotating presidency of the EU, that women's equality and the problems that are unique to Polish women were being frequently and seriously discussed in the political sphere, thanks mainly to the Third European Congress of Women that also took place that year.

However, modern feminist groups have existed since practically the fall of the Iron Curtain. Their first general focus was reproductive rights, such as trying to stop the passage of anti-abortion legislation in 1993. By 2007, there were over 300 organizations working on all aspects of women's rights, including birth control, domestic violence, and the promotion of women in politics and the workplace. Women's Day (March 8), once celebrated as a communist holiday of all things traditionally female and a reason to give flowers, is now a national day of demonstrations and activism by women's groups.

Today, the issues most important to Polish women are increased access to childcare for young children, so that new mothers can continue to work just like new fathers; a louder voice in politics—a goal that should become closer thanks to the passage of a 2011 law requiring 35% of electoral candidates to be women; and combating workplace discrimination and closing the wage gap. With more women gaining political office in the future, one can hope that these issues will finally be given the attention they have lacked throughout the nation's history.

POLISH WOMEN AND FOREIGNERS

For an amusing introduction to the strange phenomenon that is the prevalence of Polish women dating or marrying foreign men, one just needs to browse Internet forums for English-speakers looking for information on how to please their Polish partners. Forum topics such as "Polish guys, why are your women choosing foreigners?" or "What to expect? My Polish girlfriend wants me to meet her parents" are widespread. The view among many Western men is that Polish women are different from Western women, who are viewed as more independent, assertive, and demanding. Part of this can be explained by the lingering *matka polka* stereotype; part of it is the image of the beautiful Russian bride, which is blindly applied to all women from Central and Eastern Europe. And part of this is rooted in truth, to the extent that feminism is still not as widespread as in Western countries.

But what do the numbers have to say about this? In 2009, nearly 4,000 Polish women married foreign nationals; the majority of these were from the UK or Ireland (549), followed by Germany (327). An interesting side note is that the majority of Polish men who married foreign women chose Ukrainians, Byelorussians, or Russians for brides (645), which points to a curious trend of men originating from countries to the west of their wives. However, this was only a fraction of the total 256,000 or so marriages that were registered that year—which means that despite some reservations on Internet forums, Polish men seem to be doing just fine for themselves.

Today, the idea of the desperate Polish woman jumping at the chance to marry a rich foreigner seems antiquated in Poland. Like women around the world, most Polish women are seeking partners who are supportive and understanding, who see each woman as an individual, and not a stereotype—which, as we can see, has earned its place in the bin of historical curiosities.

A.S.

FURTHER READING

Poles Apart: Women in Modern Polish Culture by Helena Goscilo and Beth Holmgren, ed. Indiana University, 2006.

Polish Women, Solidarity and Feminism by Anna Reading. MacMillan Academic, 1992.

Solidarity's Secret: The Women Who Defeated Communism in Poland by Shana Penn. University of Michigan Press, 2006.

We All Fought for Freedom: Women in Poland's Solidarity Movement by Kristi S. Long. Westview Press, 1996.

CHAPTER 21

POLISH MEN: STEREOTYPES AND REALITY

"Courtesy's not a science too easy, or small.
Not easy, for it is not sufficiently done
With a deftly bent knee, smile at just everyone;
For meseems, such politeness a merchant's is only,
And is not of old Poland, nor yet gentlemanly."
–Adam Mickiewicz, *Pan Tadeusz*

The Polish man, ever since he's but a mere Polish boy, has huge shoes to fill. His childhood is often filled with stories of larger than life national heroes, whether from his parents or schoolteachers. Because Poland regularly found itself at war (see Chapter 9), historically, masculinity was tied to valor on the battlefield. That meant that military virtues like aggression and courage were praised, while cowardice or pacifism were seen as weaknesses. Today, this tradition continues from childhood with toy soldiers and is enforced through such practices as compulsory military service, which was only eliminated a few years ago. In addition, a man is traditionally expected to go to church, finish college, quickly find a job, get married immediately and beget as many children as possible—and above all, to be a provider. At least, that has been the historical case...

THE HISTORICAL POLISH MAN
In Polish literature, particularly that of the Romantics, the ideal Polish man is painted as the archetype of the old fashioned gentleman—the

kind of man who throws his clean coat over a puddle lest a lady soil her boots trying to cross it. In history, the prime example is the Polish officer during the interwar period: he was handsome, brave, intellectual, well placed in society and able to provide for his family. At the same time, he was expected to sacrifice his life for the nation at the drop of a hat. He was also expected to uphold his honor and that of his family, to the point of being prepared to duel should it be threatened.

Obviously, this was a tall order for any man to live up to. On the one hand, throughout Polish history, men have held the power, whether figuratively through politics (women did not get the vote until Polish independence in 1918) or literally, through the use of force in war. Poland has mainly been a patriarchal society—with exceptions under the Partitions, when uprisings and deportations left a general shortage of men—until recently, and it still is in many respects—it's enough to look at the make-up of the Polish Parliament or most company boardrooms to get the gist. On the other hand, the image of the Polish woman is nearly sacred, and women were viewed as the protectors of Polishness. This has led to stereotypes of men and women that neither gender can realistically live up to, though they persist to this day.

POLISH CHIVALRY

Polish men (particularly in the nobility) were also expected to be the embodiment of chivalry—something that has carried on to this day, even in younger generations. It is far more rare to find a man in Poland who does not open the door for a woman or let a woman go first into a room; usually this signifies a foreigner. In the older generations (but not necessarily limited to them), men take women's coats, pull out their chairs, and kiss their hands when introduced. While these customs can be viewed as relics from a different age by some, and even sexist by others, they are largely divorced from any grander meaning than general respect. For most men, this is simply the way they were taught to act around women by their parents, and that is likely how they will raise their sons to act as well, regardless of their personal views on gender equality. In Poland, the staunchest feminist and defender of women's rights will still hold the door open for his female friend.

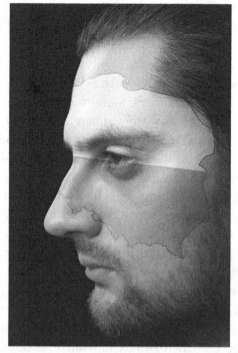

(Shutterstock.com)

Postcommunism and a Crisis in Masculinity

In some ways, the economic crisis that followed the end of communism in Poland in the 90s (see Chapter 12) resulted in a serious crisis of masculinity, and highlighted the need for a new definition of what it means to be a man in contemporary Poland. Traditionally, manhood has been tied to income, and even under communism this led many to take great risks on the black market when there were no other options. Today, men face less unemployment and earn higher wages than women (see Chapter 20 for statistics), but they also have to deal with greater pressure to bring home the *boczek*.

The economic transition of the 1990s hit men the hardest, as the economy shifted from being based on industry to being based on knowledge. The transition particularly affected traditionally male occupations in heavy industry, manufacturing, and construction. In Poland, the definition of masculinity is still largely based on the ability to be a provider, which means that despite rising unemployment during the 90s, men were put under increasing pressure to find good jobs and provide for their families. This became a frequent cause of psychological distress, to the point that over 80% of suicides in the 90s were men.

In Poland, unemployment is highly stigmatized, but mainly for men, as female unemployment is seen as more socially acceptable and even expected for new mothers. Men, meanwhile, face expectations from fellow men as well as many women to be breadwinners, which means that unemployed men feel disempowered or emasculated, and their self-esteem declines the longer they remain unemployed. While this is true in many cultures, it is especially ingrained in Polish society, to the point that being supported by a wife is seen as the ultimate humiliation for most men.

When the economy began to recover at the turn of the century, many men saw this as an opportunity to be breadwinners again, and those who could not find work in Poland migrated to the UK and other EU countries. Many stayed abroad long enough to save for a down payment on a house or apartment in Poland, as being able to provide housing is a large part of a man's traditional duty—something that has become increasingly unrealistic as housing prices have skyrocketed since 2004.

Though attitudes about gender roles in general are slowly transforming in Poland, there are many changes that still need to take place. In addition to a focus on breadwinning, Polish men are expected to not show emotion, not care too much about their appearance and to be able to drink their weight in beer or vodka—which, in addition to leading those men who choose not to drink to be stigmatized, has enabled large-scale alcoholism in the country. Many men also face pressure from their peers to hold sexist and homophobic attitudes and tell or laugh at sexist and homophobic jokes, whether or not they actually share these views, or simply just don't think about them. Which brings us to another difficult topic. . . .

HOMOSEXUALITY IN POLAND

The topic of homosexuality in Poland continues to be a tricky one at best, and in general, it's either something that isn't discussed at all, or its discussion leads to impassioned arguments. There are several well-organized LGBT rights groups in the major Polish cities, and since 2004 there have been marches in support of equal rights—though while colorful in their own way, these differ significantly from the gay pride marches held in the U.S. or Germany. In Poland, they are called "tolerance" or "equality marches" and are quite a different affair, because while pride marches proclaim "We're here, we're queer, get used to it," etc., a tolerance march pleads, "We exist in your country, please stop beating us up the other 364 days of the year."

Though mostly students and other left-leaning young people take part, the marches do draw celebrities and politicians, as well as a blockade of policemen to protect the marchers from the counter-demonstrators, who mostly consist of young men from nationalist parties. The counter-demonstrators hold signs with slogans such as "gayness prohibited" and shout obscenities at the marchers. Many older Poles, used to completely ignoring the issue under communism, see homosexuals and supporters of tolerance events as social deviants, perverts no better than pedophiles, who are corrupting the future of the country. On the other hand, homosexual members of the older generation are also generally against these "displays," which only represent a fraction of homosexuals in Poland—generally younger and from urban areas. However, the marches have gained traction over the years, and every year there's a little less violence and a little more support—but whether these movements lead toward legislative actions remains to be seen.

A.S.

FURTHER READING

Men and Masculinities in Europe by CROME. Whiting & Birch, 2006.

Polack (film) by James Kenney. 2010.

CHAPTER 22

How to Survive a Polish Wedding

Jadą goście weselni!
The wedding guests are coming!
(Polish saying)

The first time you attend a Polish wedding . . . well, let's just say you probably won't understand much of what's going on, but once you've been to three or so it'll be like a piece of (wedding) cake. All Polish weddings will start to look the same after a while, with the exception of the changing pair of gloriously happy newlyweds. Some of them, especially those self-proclaimed contemporary and progressive ones, will want to change this or that during their wedding reception, or do something just a tad different. If their alternative plans actually slide through the planning stage and somehow go unnoticed by either set of parents, then they will definitely be scrupulously analyzed and commented on by the wedding guests—those lovely groups of distant relatives, next of kin, close or estranged family members, friends, and best buddies who make every Polish wedding reception what it is—a truly unforgettable experience.

THE INVITATION
There are two kinds of wedding invitations that can make their way to your mailbox: the *Zawiadomienie* and the *Zaproszenie*. You, the lucky

wedding guest, will only get one of these. The former is the wedding announcement inviting you solely to the wedding ceremony; the latter is the invitation proper, which means the couple will want to have you at their wedding reception as well. Generally either can be sent by mail, but many young couples still prefer to personally give the *Zaproszenie* to the people they have chosen to invite, especially if these are older family members, grandparents, aunts and uncles, godparents or close friends. If you're single, the invitation will say you can come "with a companion," and if you are in a long-term relationship, engaged or married, your partner will also usually be included in the invitation.

Here comes the bride . . .

The ceremony will most often take place in a church on a Saturday, so that the following day can be spent sleeping in after a night of fun and dancing—or continuing the party. Traditionally, the groom and bride-to-be will enter the church together. Most brides no longer wear a white veil to cover their faces; in fact, very few even wear a *white* wedding gown. The colors of today's dresses are ecru, cream, and off-white, as the pure white of yesteryear used to symbolize a bride's virginity and chastity.

As the happy newlyweds step out in front of the church, the guests usually shower them with rice and small coins, which should be picked up by the bride and groom as a symbol of future wealth. Then the guests get in line to give their wishes, hand over a bouquet of flowers to the bride and the wedding card and gift to the groom. After that, most everybody is off to the wedding reception. As the cars leave, some local children, especially boys, will put up blockades by holding a rope across the street, and the cars will have to pay them in small change or candy to pass through.

(Elzbieta Sekowska / Shutterstock.com)

... AND HERE COMES THE FOOD AND DRINK!

The wedding reception will almost always take place either at a restaurant or a small palace or villa specializing in wedding celebrations. The reception will start with the symbolic round loaf of bread and salt given by the parents of the newlyweds as a way of ensuring the couple will always have plenty of food. This will be followed by a glass of champagne for everyone and the newlyweds throwing their empty glasses over their shoulders as a symbol of good luck. Then the wedding guests will commence looking for their places at the tables, and they will not fail to comment on the general seating arrangements. Once that is done, they will start looking around and quietly commenting on the other guests—some of whom they do not know or have not seen in ages.

The wedding menu is probably the one thing that never changes: the *rosół*, or chicken broth soup, then potatoes, pork chops (*schabowe*), beef roulade (*zrazy*), or chicken *de volaille* and some vegetables. If anything else is served the wedding reception will go down in history as having been quite *un*traditional. Of course, this takes the form of what seems like an endless number of courses served throughout the night, accompanied by the usual cold cuts, appetizers, and a variety of sweets for dessert.

THE FIRST DANCE

This is the dance the newlyweds have been practicing for what seems like forever, attending months of dance classes and spending sleepless nights hoping they won't trip. All of the guests will make a circle and observe this special moment. Then others will join in and the proper dance party portion of the evening will begin.

The music itself should most preferably be played live by a band, which will have to be able to play and sing the most popular songs in Polish and English. DJs are generally considered an inferior option. The music should be tailored to the ages and preferences of the wedding guests. It should be played at regular intervals, not too loudly and not too quietly. A good band playing popular music in step to the guests' dancing abilities is sometimes the single most important determinant of the success of the wedding reception.

THE VODKA

Chilled bottles will be standing on the tables along with lots of juice, just waiting to be opened and poured. Drinking is almost always initiated by the alpha males sitting at a given table. It is in no way possible that there will be a shortage of vodka at a traditional Polish wedding. If on the dance floor you hear the band singing, "*A teraz idziemy na jednego, a teraz idziemy wódkę pić!*" and all the guests suddenly stop gyrating and head toward their tables, this can only mean that the "Let's go and have another round of vodka!" alarm has sounded.

THE PARTY CONTINUES

An important part of the wedding reception will be the official ceremony of the newlyweds thanking their parents. After that, usually a brief "thank you" to all of the wedding guests will follow. Most guests will be touched and shed a tear or two during the former and all will be invited to join in a dance during the latter.

Sometime later in the evening, the wedding cake is one of two things that come rolling in on a food trolley. The other is the *płonąca szynka* (literally, the pig on fire)—a big piece of pork, sometimes a whole roasted pig, that rolls in while flambéing. The cake's size and the ham's flames should both make a big impression on the wedding guests.

The *oczepiny* at midnight is a time of games and fun that ends with the bride throwing her wedding bouquet to be caught by one of the unmarried female guests and the groom throwing his bow tie to be caught by one of the unmarried men. The two lucky catchers will then be called the new bride and groom and will have to dance together. Most single guests are never crazy about this part of the wedding reception.

After having consumed extremely large amounts of food, danced like crazy all night, and drunk more alcohol than is usually consumed throughout the entire year, the wedding guests will thank the newlywed couple for the wonderful wedding ceremony and head to bed. Sometimes the guests will also be invited to the *poprawiny* the next day—a type of after-party with more food and drinking.

No matter how scrupulously planned, masterfully designed and refined, every Polish wedding will have some unexpected moments that will be remembered—at least partially, depending on vodka consumption—by all those who attend.

M.T.

CHAPTER 23

F FOR FAMILY

Each family is like a tree
It breaks, it sways, and changes with time
Like in Vivaldi's Four Seasons
Here a pinch of rapture, there a taste of sadness
(fragment of the title song from a famous Polish TV series)

M jak miłość, which translates into "L for Love," is one of Poland's most popular TV series. It portrays the everyday problems, joys, and struggles as well as successes and failures of the archetypical, multi-generational Polish family of the Mostowiaks. On air since 2000, it draws more than nine million viewers per episode.

The revered seniors, Barbara and Lucjan Mostowiak, are the bedrock of the Mostowiak family. Happily married for over forty years, they are the quintessential parents to three daughters and a son, and the ideal grandparents. This elderly married couple's family represents a structure that is still quite important to Polish society, where adult Poles remain in much closer contact with their parents, grandparents are highly respected, and children often move out, if at all, only once they are married. Polish culture tends to foster the concept of three generations living under one roof, and the alternative of a nursing home still carries very negative connotations, with very few seniors placed in such. Family members also tend to support one another, often financially, even when they no longer live together, thus parents help their children out for many years, and later this aid is reciprocated when they themselves grow old. As grandparents, they might also help take care of the grandchildren while the parents are at work, pick the children up from school or help daughters (or daughters-in-law) with their everyday chores around the house.

FAMILY TIES

Despite the fact that one in three marriages end in divorce and more and more people are cohabiting, the value and significance of the family as a mainstay has not weakened. In 2012 the family was regarded as "very important" in life by 92% of respondents, and "rather important" by a near total—99%. This rise in the value of the family is most noticeable among mostly young, educated, and self-employed Poles. The stable family model has, again, gained significance after a reshuffling of the work-life balance among today's younger generations.

Approval of divorce has, in turn, significantly decreased. And it is interesting to note that there is less general consent for divorce mainly among young people and those living in large Polish cities. This perception might be greatly affected by the first generation of young people who have experienced their parents' divorce on a nationwide scale, as well as the trend to marry later than their parents may have.

Though the significance of the family as a concept has not changed, an understanding of what a family *is* has, as more and more Poles consider unmarried couples living together with their children as a family unit. In the recent past this family unit was usually seen as a married couple with two children, known as the "2+2," ideally with a boy and girl, and in that order. Typically both parents would work, either for a corporation or in a family-owned business, go to a shopping mall on Saturdays, to church on Sundays, and spend ideal afternoons on family visits (with cake and coffee) or long walks. That is what one can see on TV in the Mostowiak family. And what about in reality? More often in towns and cities, young people openly choose to live the single life and want to get married much later than their parents did. There are also more single parents who are either divorced or have chosen not to remain with the biological mother or father of their children. This also means more single moms, many of whom openly state that their child does not need to have a father figure. Another phenomenon typical of the newer European Union

(Shutterstock.com)

Member States, such as Poland, is the "Euro-orphan," a child whose parent, or both parents, emigrated in search of work, especially to the UK, Norway, and Germany, and left the child with its grandparents or other members of the family. Many children later move to live with their parents in the new country, but not always. There might be as many as 400,000 such children in Poland today. In the long run, close family ties are weakened in such parent-child relationships, and teachers, psychologists as well as social workers are constantly reminding governmental authorities that large numbers of children, Poland's future generations, are being raised without their parents.

Poles are supposedly highly regarded by other extremely family-oriented nations, such as the Italians, and yes, many Polish kids do continue to live at home well into their late twenties or early thirties, unless they have to move to another city to attend university. But then they usually come back for the weekends to have some of their mother's favorite homemade dinner. And the holidays, such as Christmas or Easter, are almost always spent together with the family.

This perception of the family probably places Polish society somewhere in the middle between relatively individualist cultures, such as that of the United States, and collectivist cultures, such as that of China, although many Poles tend to perceive themselves as quite individualistic. It also seats one-fourth of Poles in front of the TV set every week to watch another episode of their ideal Polish family's (perfectly normal) lives.

M.T.

CHAPTER 24

Going Shopping

Raz poszła więc do fryzjera:
"poproszę o kilo sera."
Tuż obok była apteka:
"poproszę mleka pięć deka."

She went to the barber's once:
"I'll have a kilo of cheese."
Next door was a pharmacy:
"five dekagrams of milk please."
–From a children's poem by Jan Brzechwa about an unusual duck
called "Kaczka Dziwaczka"

Under communism, the life of the typical Polish woman and mother was tough. Not only did she have to commute to and from work every day in a crowded bus or tram, but she also had to do all of the day's shopping in various small stores specializing in a given type of merchandise. Today's working mom (or dad) can simply hop into her car and drive to any of several local supermarkets to buy everything she needs, from cream cheese to a bottle of liquid soap. Many contemporary Polish husbands will say that they too take part in doing the shopping to ease the burden of today's working woman. In the past, however, the list of stores that mostly the women had to visit was extremely long. Most of the specialty stores continue to exist alongside the big, mostly foreign-owned supermarkets, and there are many

Poles who still prefer to shop in these small stores. So, what did the shopping look like when the typical Polish woman did her rounds at the specialty stores?

MAKING THE ROUNDS

The first stop would probably be the *piekarnia*, where one could buy freshly baked goods. Oftentimes the rolls and bread came steaming hot right out of the baker's big oven. Fresh bread would be too hot to be cut into even pieces on the spot, but when cooled many a Polish woman chose this option so that she could quickly prepare a plate of sandwiches for supper. Even today, the smell of freshly baked bread continues to linger around Poland's thousands of bakeries every morning, and this delicious Polish bread is one of the first things Poles abroad mention they miss the most.

The next stop would be the *mięsny*, or the butcher's, where the Polish woman could buy some ham, sausages, or frankfurters, and all kinds of meat for soups and the *obiad*—the main meal of the day. Everything at the meat store was behind a glass counter, so she would show what she wanted and say how much of it she desired in kilos and dekagrams. All of these meat products would be weighed and then wrapped in plastic foil and paper, and the bags soon grew heavy under their weight.

Then the typical Polish woman would visit the *sklep z nabiałem* to buy the dairy products. This specialty store sold milk, eggs, and a whole bunch of dairy products such as sour cream, sweet cream, cottage cheese, and *kefir* (a popular fermented milk product) along with different kinds of yellow cheese, also to be weighed in dekagrams. Sometimes these stores also carried some fruits and vegetables and several other grocery products to widen the assortment of food to choose from.

Next the woman would stop by the *cukiernia*, where she could get a wide array of freshly baked cakes, pies, cookies, and doughnuts. This specialty store also sold freshly baked *drożdżówkas*, sweet buns with filling or without, and usually with a crunchy, sugary topping. Another favorite was a variety of hard and soft candies, with at least a dozen different kinds and flavors to choose from, and all to be bought by the kilo. All of these sweetly tempting delicacies would be

(Jakub Krechowicz / Shutterstock.com)

a necessary component in case a friend or two decided to stop by in the afternoon for a quick, yes glass, of tea or coffee and to gossip for a while. With all these sweets, it's amazing Poles don't spend all of their time at the dentist's.

The *sklep warzywny* would be next on the list. Here the woman could buy fresh vegetables, such as *włoszczyzna* (a bouquet of vegetables) for the soup, dill pickles, and sauerkraut from wooden barrels as well as fruits, especially apples from Poland's many orchards.

If she needed some laundry detergent, toilet paper, or cosmetics, she would have to stop by the *chemiczny*. The *gospodarczy*, in turn, sold everything needed for the kitchen and bathroom, such as pots and pans, cutting boards, dinner sets, utensils, mirrors, and bathroom shelves. If our Polish woman needed the day's paper, a woman's magazine, or bus/tram tickets, she would also have to stop by the *kiosk*, usually a small newsstand on the street with all of the most recent newspapers and magazines clearly displayed. For stationery, envelopes, pens, pencils, and notebooks, she would have to go to the *papierniczy*. A store called *bielizna* would carry mostly women's tights as well as underwear, socks, and pajamas for both sexes. This was a store rarely visited by men, if at all. The *sklep obuwniczy* sold shoes and slippers for the whole family. The *sklep odzieżowy* had clothes for men, women, and children. The *sklep z zabawkami* sold children's toys. The *sklep meblowy* sold furniture, with most stores selling exactly the same furniture from the same factories.

Thus, at the end of the day, and after having run around to all those stores and waited in many a line for her turn, the typical Polish mother would come home literally bending over under the weight of the bags, called *reklamówki*, loaded with the day's shopping to make the *obiad* for her whole family and have an impromptu visit from the next-door neighbor to gossip over tea and a sugar-coated doughnut. The life of the typical Polish woman was rarely the proverbial bed of roses, as even those had to be bought at the *kwiaciarnia*.

ENTER CAPITALISM!

The first nationwide chain of stores selling both grocery and household products was Społem, whose 1960s Sam, Supersam, and Megasam stores, where one could pick merchandise off the shelves as opposed to having to ask the notoriously impatient, constantly irritated, and always tired sales clerk standing behind the counter, were the prototypes of today's local supermarkets. It was probably in stores like these that the infamous photographs of empty shelves with only several bottles of vinegar were taken when the country was experiencing food production shortages during communist times.

Today's Poland claims to have the largest number of shopping malls, usually called *Centra Handlowe* or *Galerie Handlowe*, in Europe, and 730,000 m² more retail space is expected to be ready in 2013, thus leaving such euro-dependent countries as Italy, France, and Portugal far behind. Each shopping mall, in turn, contains at least one supermarket or hypermarket—a huge chain store with just about everything under one roof.

Polish malls carry similar brand names and retail clothing chains to those of any other European mall, such as H&M, Zara, United Colors of Benetton, Marks & Spencer, Esprit, and many others, and more brands are eager to enter the Polish market—Gap, Victoria's Secret, and Toys"R"Us, to name but a few. Many contemporary Polish families spend their weekends at these malls, much to the dismay of the country's religious authorities, but perhaps to the advantage of the Polish woman, who is no longer left alone in her shopping meanders.

M.T.

CHAPTER 25

HOME SWEET POLISH HOME

Komu w domu dobrze, niechaj się po świecie nie włóczy.
Who feels good at home should not wander the world over.
(Polish proverb)

Come and take a virtual tour of the typical Polish home—but remember to take off your shoes when you enter. We begin in the *wiatrołap*, the vestibule—though literally this amusing word means "wind-catcher"—as yet another door will lead you inside to the home's interior proper. The function of this small space, as its Polish name suggests, is to "catch the wind" coming in from the outside—heat in the summer and cold in the winter. It is here that Poles take off their shoes, hang their coats, leave their winter caps, and change into their slippers, which you might even be handed a pair of to put on. Open the door of the *wiatrołap* and you are inside the Polish home. Yes, it has changed over the years since 1989, but some things always seem to stay the same. As you enter the small hall you might notice natural wood paneling, called *boazeria*, on the walls, and ceilings too sometimes. There will be a small picture or two hanging on the wall here and there and perhaps a small cross over some of the doors.

BLOCK LIFE

The typical Polish home in the city is usually in an apartment building, and the older apartments, especially those built until the 1980s, are situated in humongous apartment blocks that are grouped together

Modern apartment buildings, new housing area in Gdynia (Shutterstock.com)

in kilometer-long and wide complexes called *osiedla* (neighborhoods) in the suburbs of Poland's bigger towns and cities. These architectural monstrosities are colloquially called *blokowiska*, a derogatory term for blocks made famous in Polish hip-hop and other pop culture, or *mrówkowce* (anthills), due to the exceptionally large number of apartments squeezed into one such building. Most of these buildings were built using a process called *z dużej płyty*, where large, rectangular sections of prefabricated and prepressed concrete were fitted together and constituted the building's outer layer. Today one in every five Poles lives in such an apartment building, and the tenants come from all walks of life, from university professors to blue-collar workers. This is probably connected with the fact that in the communist past a Polish family, if they were lucky enough, got the keys to their own place after many, many years of waiting—and in that communist reality there were technically no social classes. The comic trials and tribulations of tenants living in such a building are best portrayed in Stanisław Bareja's cult 1983 TV series called *Alternatywy 4*.

If in English we say that an apartment has one, two, or three bedrooms, then in Polish we use the letter M to denote how many rooms the apartment has all together; for example, a *kawalerka* ("bachelor pad") is a one-room apartment with a kitchenette and separate bathroom. An M-2 is a two-room apartment, an M-3—every Polish person's dream during the communist era—has a whopping three rooms. M-4s were rare and considered the *crème de la crème* of urban living standards, and very few Polish families could boast a four-room apartment in the city.

The living room, called the *pokój dzienny*, is where Poles seem to spend most of their day, unless they prefer to sit in the kitchen. Every such *pokój dzienny* will have a *meblościanka* (literally, "wall-furniture-piece")—a single, large wall unit consisting of a closet, bookshelves, cupboards, a desk, and sometimes even a hidden bed all combined in one unit that takes up the entire wall. The shelves used to be full of thick crystal vases, mainly produced in Poland, tea sets, books, and other knick-knacks. During communist times there was a limited selection of furniture and interior decorating products, if any, in Polish stores, and the small amount of space in often cramped apartments forced Poles to make practical purchases, which also meant that most people had exactly the same things in their homes—the functional *meblościanka* being one of these. Interestingly enough, since the early 1960s Poland has been one of the main furniture manufacturers for one of the world's most famous furniture stores, IKEA. The first IKEA store in Poland was to open its doors a whole thirty years later. And most Poles probably do not know that Poland has always been a large exporter of furniture, with countries such as Germany, France, and the UK constituting its main markets today. Furniture design lovers worldwide would probably be surprised to know that since his invention, Michael Thonet's bentwood furniture has been produced for over 125 years in a factory called Fameg in Radomsko, Poland, and that another small factory near Poznań has been the authorized manufacturer of original Arne Jacobsen Egg chairs and other design classics for many years.

Another important furniture element of the living room is the couch, called a *kanapa*, *sofa*, *tapczan*, or *wersalka*—obviously a significant piece of furniture if there are so many names to denote it. The couch served as a general seating place during the day and was opened up to turn into the parents' bed during the night. Another "open-upper" was the *stół rozkładany*, a small dining or coffee table that could "magically" be unfolded to seat at least twenty guests for an important occasion. The table would not have that finished look without a *bieżnik* or *obrus*, a decorative runner or impeccably clean tablecloth, as the table, according to most Polish decorating standards, should always be covered with some kind of decorative fabric.

All Polish windows have window treatments consisting of two elements—the *firanki* and the *zasłony*. The *firanki* are the sheer curtains (almost always white, almost always with a floral motif) that will not allow you to look into a Polish apartment during the day to see what's going on inside. The *zasłony* are the thick, drapelike curtains (almost always red or brownish-gold in color) that are nicely gathered on the sides of the windows, but once the lights go on in the evening the thicker curtains are quickly pulled over the sheer curtains and you will see even less from the outside than before. These two inseparable decorative window elements guarantee some privacy in the closely situated apartment buildings of Poland's urban neighborhoods.

The rest of the rooms consist of small bedrooms, a kitchen and a bathroom, and they also looked very much alike. Wall-to-wall carpeting was rare and rugs, hardwood floors, linoleum, or ceramic tiles were the main choices for flooring. Many siblings had to share a room, and sometimes a smaller *meblościanka* was put into effect there too—often they would place small, colorful stickers on the furniture to cheer up the place. The kitchen, with its tiny table and some stools, would usually be the place where a quick breakfast, *obiad,* or supper could be eaten. And the bathroom always had a bathtub over which clean laundry taken straight out of the washing machine would be hung to dry. Poles do not have drying machines in their homes. Period. But the scariest element to any foreign guest staying in a Polish home is known as the *junkers, bojler,* or *piecyk gazowy*—that small, innocent-looking gas appliance hanging in the kitchen, or more often in the bathroom, whose quiet, little purplish flame would suddenly explode into a massive blaze—until you were certain you would need to call the fire department every time the tap was turned on. One had to be careful to not be burned by the scalding hot water, which sometimes flowed from extremely cold to lukewarm to hot at irregular intervals. It is indeed a scary piece of water heating equipment.

THE (MORE) MODERN POLISH HOME

Today's new apartments and houses are mainly built by private developers and most often sold during the *stan deweloperski*—the stage where the apartment is completely bare and the new homeowners can choose the window sills, floors, tiles, kitchen cabinets, bathroom faucets, built-in closets, and everything else their hearts

(Shutterstock.com)

desire when it comes to furnishing and decorating their homes. A multitude of interior decorating magazines provide the latest news on what is *en mode* and entirely *passé* in the world of interior design in Poland, Europe, and worldwide. Furniture can be bought at the omnipresent IKEA stores or from renowned retailers selling contemporary furniture. Several large chains specialize in furniture that has been designed and manufactured in Poland. Most importantly, Polish families take pride in decorating their homes according to their own esthetic tastes and standards.

And finally, what would a typical Polish home be without the *jamnik*, that long-bodied, short-legged, brownish-tan breed of dogs known as dachshunds in the English-speaking world, which almost every other Polish family used to possess as the final addition to their M-3. In the early morning most everyone would be out to take their beloved pet for a walk, and those typical Polish *osiedla* would come alive again with hundreds of small, elongated dogs and their owners trailing behind. These days, there's even an annual dachshund parade in Krakow to celebrate this ubiquitous breed of canine!

M.T.

CHAPTER 26

POLISH FOOD: FROM *BIGOS* TO *ŻUREK*

A w karcie—okropność!—przyznacie to sami:
Jest zupa jabłkowa i knedle z jabłkami,
Duszone są jabłka, pieczone są jabłka
I z jabłek szarlotka, i placek, i babka!

And on the menu—how awful!—you too will agree:
There's apple soup and dumplings stuffed with apples,
There's stewed apples, baked apples
And apple crumble, cake, and pie!
–Jan Brzechwa, excerpt from the children's poem *Entliczek*
Pentliczek

Polish food? If words like *bigos, barszcz,* and *pierogi* come to mind, then you're on the right track. Polish cuisine is somewhat cosmopolitan in its array of dishes, although these will vary across Poland's geographical regions. These, in turn, played a role in what types of soils crops could be grown on, whether there were forests or natural lakes in the vicinity to serve as sources of game, mushrooms, wild herbs, and fruit, and if farm animals could be raised. Poland's sometimes very turbulent history also had a major influence on what was eaten in the manors of the gentry and among the peasants. Sometimes recipes for various foods came from above and worked their way down to the kitchens of the common people as the food products became more widely available, and many times the "food of the peasants" eventually turned up on the gentry's richly dressed tables. Poland's central position in an ever-changing Europe also resulted in its cuisine being heavily influenced by neighboring nations and by the various peoples and cultures living on Polish lands throughout the centuries, including German, Hungarian, Russian, Ukrainian, Belarusian, Lithuanian, and Jewish influences.

Interestingly, Polish cuisine was also historically influenced by the rulers of Poland, who brought (along with their royal courtiers, furniture, and personal possessions) international chefs to prepare the various dishes these rulers had grown so accustomed to in their native homelands. A contemporary, everyday example is something no average Pole making homemade soup could do without—namely *włoszczyzna* (translated simply as "Italian stuff"), the greens for basic soup stock which consist of a bouquet of carrots, celery stalks, parsley root, and leek that, as culinary history has it, came to Poland along with Queen Bona Sforza, her vegetable seeds, and court chefs in the early sixteenth century (see Chapter 5).

Spices, especially caraway and saffron, were common in gentry kitchens due to Poland's central position *en route* many trade routes. Toruń as a port city in particular was famous for its use of such exotic spices as cloves, nutmeg, ginger, cinnamon, and black pepper to make the spicy, dark-brown dough for *pierniki* (honey-spice cakes). Polish cuisine makes use of large quantities of fresh dill (*koperek*), especially sprinkled over potatoes, marjoram (*majoranek*), allspice (*ziele angielskie*), bay leaves (*liście laurowe*), and parsley (*pietruszka*), mainly on meat, in sauces and soups, as well as caraway seeds (*kminek*), particularly in *bigos*, bread, and some cheeses.

Another important component of Polish cuisine are dairy products, with a variety of white cheeses leading the way. One of these is a Polish specialty called **twaróg**, known as farmer's cheese in English, which is made from soured, thickened milk and sour cream. Poland's Podhale region is also known for its traditional **oscypek** (hard, tangy, smoked sheep's milk cheese usually in the shape of a large, yellowish-brown spindle formed in richly patterned, wooden forms), which was the second regional specialty, after *bryndza* (soft, tangy, ground and grainy *bundz* cheese from fresh sheep's milk) to receive "Protected

Oscypek cheese
(Snowboy / Shutterstock.com)

Designation of Origin" certification in 2007. The best way to enjoy *oscypek* is fresh from an outdoor grill in the winter, with a touch of cranberry sauce. You'll find these at Christmas markets and the bottoms of ski slopes throughout Poland.

It seems that despite its variety of dishes, Polish food can conveniently be divided into general categories of all things meat, cabbage (sauerkraut), mushroom, groats, flour, and potato. Polish soup is a category in itself. *Smacznego!* (That's the Polish equivalent of *bon appétit*).

BRING ON THE MEAT . . .

Brzechwa's poem about the little worm that was living inside an apple with its whole family and felt like eating a steak or, in fact, anything besides apple, actually points to two truths about Polish cuisine—that you can take a product and prepare it in a multitude of ways *and* that many Polish people will only consider a dish complete if it has meat in it. Needless to say, being vegetarian or vegan in Poland, while not impossible, is considerably more difficult than in many other countries.

The most well known meat for *obiad* (dinner), the main meal of the day, is *kotlet schabowy*, a breaded pork cutlet usually served with boiled potatoes sprinkled with fresh dill and traditional Polish salad, such as *buraczki* (specially prepared beetroot). Pork, a contemporary favorite, has actually come a long way in Polish culinary history. A favorite meat of traditional, old Polish recipes, it was ousted in the nineteenth century by the increasingly popular French cuisine and generally more healthy eating habits, when leaner meats such as beef, veal and mutton gained widespread acceptance. World War I and its aftermath changed culinary habits again and pork returned to it place, even reappearing on elegant dinner tables as the main meat dish. Another French favorite is *kotlet de volaille*, a cone-shaped chicken fillet with melted butter, yellow cheese, and ham or mushroom filling. Roasted chicken (*kurczak z rożna*) is a contemporary favorite with Poles who are on the run and have no time to prepare a time-consuming *obiad*. Whole chickens, or cut portions, can be bought directly from vendors selling them in small stalls along the sidewalk. *Potrawka* is a delicate, savory sauce made from chicken fillet pieces. Turkey, though not commonly served today, was once a popular specialty dish and is even mentioned in Sigismund III's royal bills (sixteenth-seventeenth centuries). Red meat, such as beefsteak and roast beef, only became popularized at the end of the nineteenth century thanks to English cuisine. Goose and duck were favorite meats of the Kujawy region in the past. Today, duck is best known for the enigmatically sounding *czernina*, or duck blood soup! *Wątróbka*, or liver from chicken, turkey, goose or duck, is a poultry favorite, especially to make *pasztet*, the Polish version of *pâté*. *Pasztet* became a popular seventeenth-century specialty thanks to the highly renowned French chefs who prepared it. It was usually served warm in the manors of the gentry and on the sumptuous tables of the royalty. Poland is also most famous for its aroma-filled, flavorful hams and various types of sausage (**kiełbasa**), such as the garlicky, grayish-white *biała kiełbasa* served with *żurek* soup or with horseradish for Easter breakfast, *kiełbasa wiejska* (country sausage), *kiełbasa krakowska* (from Krakow), and the thin jerky-like *kabanosy*. Ham sandwiches are often eaten for breakfast (*śniadanie*), brunch (*drugie śniadanie*), and supper (*kolacja*), during which hot sausages are served with spicy horseradish and mustard.

Game is, surprisingly, not common in contemporary Polish cuisine, and 1627 marks the year when the last wild aurochs, having been hunted so heavily, died in the forests near the town of Żyrardów. After that fateful date wild game was no longer to be a commonly found component of Polish recipes. One dish that does retain the remnants of game meat is **bigos**, the most famed of Polish traditional dishes. A rich mix of various types of bite-sized meat (pork, beef, poultry, sometimes game) and sausage chunks, wild mushrooms, and spices left to gently simmer in sauerkraut and less often fresh, shredded cabbage, it is sometimes simply called hunter's stew in English, probably because it was originally eaten during long hunting trips. *Bigos* was served for breakfast, as a dish before soup, and for supper. Supposedly no two Polish families make the same *bigos*, and its variant recipes include *bigos litewski* (Lithuanian *bigos* with apples and fresh, white cabbage), *bigos alzacki* (Alsatian *bigos* with pork knuckle), or simply *bigos* with the addition of tomato sauce, which gives it an orangey color and specific flavor. Repeated cooling and reheating supposedly makes *bigos* taste even better.

. . . AND SOME VEGGIES, IF YOU MUST

The main ingredient of *bigos* is **cabbage**. Grown in Poland since the Middle Ages, white cabbage has always been served in soups and various stuffings, stewed with vegetables, wild mushrooms, and meat. To last longer it was pickled. At first whole cabbage heads were used for the pickling process, but the cabbage lasted longer and tasted better if it was finely shredded before pickling, to which, interestingly, apples were also added in the past. *Kiszona kapusta*, commonly known as sauerkraut, is an important source of vitamin C, especially during the long and cold winter months. It is interesting to note that such a basic Polish food product bears a German name, and that probably the only other people who love and consume pickled (fermented) cabbage in such large quantities are eaters of the traditional Korean favorite—*kimchi*. Cabbage seems to be one of the most universally applied vegetables in Polish dishes. Eaten raw only in certain salad recipes, it comes in many forms in Polish dishes, with *gołąbki* (wrapped cabbage leaves usually with a ground meat and rice filling) topping the list. Sauerkraut, in turn, can be eaten cold in salads (*surówki*) or fried hot with pork cracklings, or stewed with mushrooms, the most popular of which is as a *pierogi* filling, as the main ingredient of *kapuśniak* and *kwaśnica* (traditional soups), or in *łazanki* (a dish with homemade macaroni, often served on Christmas Eve).

Another Polish favorite are dill **pickles**—small cucumbers that have been cured in brine. Brine consists of salt water, dill, especially the parachute-shaped frond, garlic, horseradish root, mustard seed and other spices, which differentiates this pickling process from marinating pickles (*ogórki konserwowe*), which is done mainly with the use of vinegar and sugar. Cucumbers have been used in Poland since the early Middle Ages. Besides being pickled or marinated, they are most commonly served raw in a salad called *mizeria* with sour cream, fresh dill, and a drop of lemon juice. Polish cuisine, partially due to Lithuanian culinary influence in the past, is famous for its art of pickling food in general—from wild mushrooms, beets and red cabbage to apples and even rye bread.

Polish forests and fields have always been abundant with **mushrooms**, which grow in the wild from mid-April to the end of November, but can most easily be found from July to October. Whole Polish families or groups of friends go mushroom gathering, and when traveling through Poland you will see people selling baskets of freshly picked mushrooms along the roads. There are many poisonous mushrooms that look very similar to the edible varieties, which is why it's important to always go mushroom picking with an expert—just about any elderly Polish grandmother will do. About thirty species have officially been classified as edible and can be commercially sold in Poland. The Polish language differentiates between the word *pieczarka,* which means the common, white mushrooms (*Agaricus bisporus)* that are grown commercially, and *grzyb*—which denotes any general wild type of mushroom. Also, because they are so important in Polish cuisine, various species of mushrooms have their own common names, such as *rydze, maślaki, podgrzybki, koźlarze, kanie,* and *boczniaki,* to name a few. *Kurki (Cantharellus)*, small, yellowish flat-shaped mushrooms, were so commonly found in Polish forests that they were considered to be of no culinary value and are not to be found in very old Polish cookbooks. Today they are most commonly served stewed in a heavy sweet cream sauce or fried with scrambled eggs. Another very popular variety in Polish cuisine, *borowiki (Boletus),* was rarely consumed until the eighteenth century, only to make its way onto the Polish table via French cuisine. Mushrooms can be marinated, fried, cooked, baked, served in mushroom soup (*zupa pieczarkowa*), especially on Christmas Eve and, of course, stewed with cabbage or sauerkraut for a variety of dishes. Strings of dried, wild mushrooms (*grzyby suszone*) were and still are a Polish cook's most valuable culinary commodity.

Another Polish culinary classic is **kasza**, or groats. *Kasza* is the hulled grains of a large variety of cereals, which, along with flour, was a staple foodstuff in Poland for hundreds of years, only to be ousted by the widespread potato in the eighteenth century. It can be cooked to be loose (*na sypko*) or as a more unified mass (*na gęsto*). Some of the more popular varieties are *kasza gryczana* (buckwheat goats), *kasza jaglana* (millet groats), *kasza jęczmienna* (barley groats), and *kasza manna* (semolina). Groats were served equally eagerly in rural homes as well as in dishes of the nobility and royalty—supposedly the sixteenth-century queen of Poland, Anna Jagiellon, liked *kasza krakowska* (groats from Krakow) so much that she had it sent to her court in Warsaw. *Kasza* is often served with savory meat and mushroom sauces and as a *pierogi* filling. The popular Polish *krupnik* is a thick soup made with barley groats, meat, potatoes, and vegetables. Another specialty is *kaszanka* or *kiszka*, a sausage made from buckwheat groats with pig blood and ground pig offal, and usually served fried with onion (it's better than it sounds, really). A regional dish, especially from the Podlasie region, is *bliny*—thick pancakes most commonly made from buckwheat flour, which gives them their characteristic brownish color.

THE MIGHTY *PIEROGI*

The generic English word "dumpling," used to denote a filled or unfilled dough ball, does not do justice to what can be made from dough that consists of sifted flour, water, salt, and sometimes eggs. The most famous Polish dumplings are **pierogi**. Making the dough demands a lot of rolling—the dough has to be soft, thin, and moldable—cutting out round shapes, adding just the right amount of filling, tightly sealing the edges and cooking in lots of boiling water until the *pierogi* float up to the surface. The Podlasie and Lubelszczyzna regions are most famous for their wide variety of *pierogi* fillings, which are generally divided into two categories: savory and sweet. The most well known savory fillings are *mięsne* (ground, cooked meat), *ruskie* (the "Russian" kind, with cooked potatoes, farmer's cheese and onion), and *z kapustą i grzybami* (with sauerkraut and mushrooms). Sweet fillings include *z serem* (farmer's cheese), *z owocami* (with fruit such as sweet cherries, sour cherries, plums, or blueberries), or *z makiem* (ground poppy seed filling with raisins and honey). *Uszka* are small, ear-shaped, mushroom-filled *pierogi* served with Christmas Eve beetroot *barszcz* or mushroom soup. Another variant, *kołduny litewskie*, are the Lithuanian type of very small *pierogi* with beef filling,

(Shutterstock.com)

although originally these were small lamb-filled dumplings. The great Polish poet Adam Mickiewicz is said to have had a great admiration for these small dumplings.

Another type of dumplings made from flour are *kluski*, which are basically a variety of homemade noodles. Their various names suggest exactly how they are made or their telltale features. For example, *szare kluski* (gray noodles) come from the Greater Poland region—the raw, grated potatoes added to the dough give them their characteristic dark gray color. The dough is placed in boiling water, and they are served with fried onion and bacon bits as well as with fried sauerkraut. *Kluski kładzione* (laid noodles) are made of dough put in boiling water off the tip of a spoon. *Kluski lane* are egg-batter noodles that are poured directly into *rosół* or other types of soup. *Zacierki* are egg-dough noodles that are either grated or have tiny, oval shapes that are also served with soup. *Pierogi (kluski) leniwe* are called "lazy *pierogi*" because they come with no filling, thus are far less time-consuming to make. Farmer's cheese is added and they are cut into rhombus-shaped, flattened pieces—often served with butter-fried breadcrumbs or with sour cream and sprinkled with sugar. *Łazanki* are flat homemade noodles served with either cabbage or poppy seed.

The third type of dough used to make Polish dumplings is made from flour and, most often, minced cooked potatoes. These are, for example, *kopytka*, colloquially known as "little hooves"—dumplings made from cooked potato and flour dough, cut into bite-size pieces from a long piece of dough and served with melted butter, with meat or with butter-fried breadcrumbs. *Kluski ziemniaczane*, also known as *kluski śląskie* (Silesian noodles, although they're not actually noodles), have cooked potatoes added to the flour dough, are molded into round, flat balls with a pinched hole in the middle and served with pork cracklings, butter, savory roasted meat or mushroom sauce. *Knedle* are round and made from flour dough with cooked potatoes and have a filling— again either savory (ground meat, mushroom, or farmer's cheese) or sweet—with fruit (apples, plums, strawberries, apricots, peaches, or sour cherries). *Pyzy ziemniaczane* are made from dough consisting of mixed raw and cooked potatoes with flour and are molded into big, round balls, which can also come with a ground-meat filling.

Dinner time!

Potatoes, so popular in the dumpling recipes and in Polish cuisine in general, first appeared in Poland along with German settlers during the reign of Augustus the Strong at the beginning of the eighteenth century. Even a century later potatoes were still less popular than cabbage or carrots—and it took another hundred years for them to oust groats—but by the beginning of the twentieth century over fifty ways to prepare potatoes were to be found in contemporary cookbooks. Most Poles, young and old, love *młode ziemniaki* in the springtime— these are boiled, walnut-sized young potatoes in thin jackets served with melted butter and fresh dill. Potatoes are generally always a part of the *obiad*, along with meat and a Polish-style salad. They appear in most soups, are used for salads and fillings, served with *słonina* (pork cracklings), baked with sausage pieces and cabbage and popular as French fries with fish on Fridays, when many Poles prefer to fast. *Placki ziemniaczane* are another potato favorite—made from raw, grated potatoes and mixed with flour, eggs, and sometimes finely chopped onion, these fried, hash brown–like pancakes are served either savory, with a sprinkling of salt, sour cream, goulash or mushroom sauce, or sweet—sprinkled with sugar.

The main meal of the day, *obiad*, actually consists of two courses—
soup as the first course and then the main meal, *drugie danie*—although
today many Poles have just one or the other. Polish cuisine seems to
appreciate soup, with its *włoszczyzna* and meat portions, more than any
other cuisine in the world. A classic and truly Polish soup is *rosół*, which
Mickiewicz even mentions at the beginning of his Romantic epic poem,
Pan Tadeusz. The Polish version of this classic soup is a clear chicken
bouillon served with noodles and fresh parsley. Another famous Polish soup is the enigmatic *flaki*—hearty tripe morsels cooked in spicy,
seasoned bouillon; some people actually prefer not to know what is in
flaki and just enjoy its zesty taste. *Żurek* is a tangy Polish specialty that
is made from soured ryemeal (*zakwas*). Thickened with sour cream, it
is most often served with hard-boiled egg wedges, sausage slices, or
both, and sometimes with a side dish of cooked potatoes. *Kwaśnica*, a
specialty of the Podhale region, is a sauerkraut soup with potatoes but
no added vegetables, which is similar to *kapuśniak*, its added-vegetable
counterpart in the other regions of Poland. Another soup mentioned
above, *krupnik*, literally means made from groats, as *krupa* is an old
word denoting *kasza*, its main ingredient.

In the fifteenth century, cabbage, beets, carrots, cauliflower, tur-
nip, and peas were eaten as vegetables, but vegetable soups as such
only became popular in the eighteenth century thanks to French cuisine. In the Middle Ages, thick, hearty soups called *bryje* were made
with groats, legumes, lardy bacon, vegetables, and meat, but the significance of Queen Bona's introduction of *włoszczyzna* lay in the fact
that vegetables were an uncommon food to be consumed by courtiers
and the upper classes, who considered greens food for farm animals
and vegetables "fit only for peasants!" Nowadays, Polish cuisine
has a wide variety of vegetable soups, such as *ogórkowa* (dill pickle),
pomidorowa (tomato), and *kalafiorowa* (cauliflower), just to name a few.
Soups can also be served chilled in the summer, with the originally
Lithuanian *chłodnik* being the most popular Polish version. This soup
is made from beetroot and sour cream, fresh dill and grated cucumber.

Probably the most classic and well-known soup is **barszcz**
(borscht). Its tart flavor comes from a basic component—beet-sour
(*zakwas buraczany*), which is the juice of beets that have been covered
with garlic and some bread crust and left to ferment in sweetened

water. Beets were first mentioned in fifteenth-century Polish documents. Called *ćwikła* at that time, they were intensively grown in Poland in the eighteenth century, when *barszcz*, salads, sauces, and meat dishes with beets began to appear. *Ćwikła* is a zesty relish made from cooked, creamed beets with horseradish and sometimes finely grated apple. It was first mentioned as a recipe over 400 years ago by Mikołaj Rej, one of Poland's best-known early Renaissance poets.

Fish have always been popular in the traditional dishes of Polish cuisine. The ways of preparing fish date back to the Middle Ages, when there was a lot of compulsory fasting going on (even up to 200 days out of the year). Fish came from breeding ponds or Poland's thousands of lakes, especially in the regions of Kujawy, Warmia, and Masuria. The Baltic Sea was a natural source of many species of fish, with the **herring** (*śledź*), served in a multitude of ways, becoming a favorite, particularly as a vodka chaser (see Chapter 28). Fish can be marinated, cooked in broths, served cold, jellied, baked, fried, and grilled. Queen Bona and her master Italian chefs brought along many recipes for oysters and mussels, but because these were not readily available, difficult to transport, and thus expensive, shellfish in general never made its way into traditional Polish cuisine, although a rich array of seafood recipes can be found in the oldest Polish cookbooks.

So, what did the little apple worm have to eat instead of steak? Apple and cinnamon pierogi, sauerkraut with grated apples, *szarlotka* (apple pie), stewed apples, *bigos* with apples, baked apples, apple mousse, apple jam, *ćwikła* with finely grated apples, apple compote, and baked duck with apple stuffing.

M.T.

FURTHER READING

Authentic Polish Cooking: 150 Mouthwatering Recipes, from Old-Country Staples to Exquisite Modern Cuisine by Marianna Dworak. Skyhorse Publishing, 2012.

Old Polish Traditions in the Kitchen and at the Table by Maria Lemnis and Henryk Vitry. Hippocrene Books, 1996.

CHAPTER 27

(Famous) Polish Hospitality

Gość w dom, Bóg w dom.
A guest in the house, God in the house.
(Polish proverb)

Polish hospitality is famous the world over. It is a hospitality that is honest and down to earth, and manifests itself in a unique kind of selfless sympathy toward guests, tourists and foreigners alike. The old Polish proverbial saying that hosting a guest is like having God over implies that both should be treated with the utmost respect and cordiality—thus Poles' authentic care for guests in their homes.

This legendary Polish hospitality probably goes back to the age-old beliefs and traditions concerning social norms in the Polish countryside. The most important social unit was that of the family; several families constituted the closest neighborhood, neighborhoods were part of a village, and surrounding villages comprised a particular, local area.

Like a good neighbor

A neighbor was thus treated as someone close, a person whose personal joys and sorrows one could not be oblivious to. If the neighbors had a problem or hardship, everyone in the local neighborhood tried to help out. This sense of community developed over hundreds of years and brought with it a set of social norms and customs concerning neighborly relations. The most notable of these was the sense of respect one showed toward one's neighbors, which was reflected through courtesy, assistance in case of need, and hospitality.

Neighbors, even those from distant villages, would always greet each other in passing and courteously stop to exchange a few words. The topics of their small talk were health, work on the farm, the success or failure of a certain undertaking, or updates concerning relatives and other people from the local area—the usual. Neighbors would also help one another out in everyday tasks which one person or family would not have been able to do alone: they would help in the building of a house or the digging of a well, and in emergency situations such as putting out a fire, helping care for someone who had fallen ill, or during other maladies. Neighbors also willingly came to the rescue during the merciless labor of harvesting—the farmer who received this neighborly aid was obliged to provide something to eat and drink to everyone working out in the field. It was a selfless form of joint work for a common cause.

After a day in the field or doing the household chores the neighbors would meet in their homes to talk, exchange advice or simply gossip, and paying visits to one's neighbors was an amiable pastime. Upon their arrival the guests, dressed in their best attire, greeted the host and hostess solemnly with carefully chosen wording—the host was usually complimented for being the steadfast head of the family and the hostess for how well she took care of and kept order in the home. Impoliteness or lack of courtesy in these cases was indubitably seen as bad manners. Even today most Polish children are taught to say *Dzień dobry* (Good day) when entering a room full of adults and *Do widzenia* (Goodbye) when leaving it.

TABLES OVERFLOWING WITH FOOD (AND DRINK)
During communist times cafeterias or restaurants were few and far between, so it was naturally far more preferable to invite guests to one's own home. The table had to be laden with a large number of hams and cold cuts, sandwiches and warm dishes, and sometimes it would literally be bending over from the weight of the food. Time was then spent on eating, talking, drinking and, yes, singing *Sto lat* together into the wee hours of the night. *Sto lat* literally means "100 years," in the context of "may you live to be a hundred years old!" It

is sung (loudly and festively) on birthdays, name days, when taking a drink, on the night bus home at four in the morning, or whenever a similarly good occasion arises.

Polish hospitality is known for one's being able to drop in for a visit without notice (*bez zapowiedzi*) and knowing that your host will be genuinely happy to see you, will gladly invite you in, and naturally ask *Czego się napijesz?* (What would you like to drink?). This unexpected visit can last up to a few hours, with drinking, eating, and gossiping about family and friends, or other neighbors for that matter, taking up most of that time. Yet older generations of Poles tend to complain that the constantly busy and career-oriented younger Poles are no longer as willing to invite unexpected guests in.

Poles are said to be friendly, hospitable, and generous when they have guests in their homes for a longer stay. They might even take time off work to show them around, spend time together, or take them along to visit other friends and family members if the guests are from out of town. Every new household visit will come complete with an array of cakes, cookies, cold cuts, sandwiches, lunches, dinners, drinks, suppers, and an insurmountable amount of tea and coffee in between meals.

Some foreigners say they have felt dined and wined to death by Poles. This is because a guest that is hosted in a respectable Polish home cannot go hungry—so you will continuously be asked if you would like something to eat or drink. If it is time for breakfast, lunch, or supper you will be seated with the rest of the host's family and will have to eat along with them. Polish hosts, and especially hostesses, see no other possibility than to make sure that the guest is doing a large portion of the eating. No one at the dinner table will take your "No, thank you" for an answer. If you say you just ate you will hear, "No problem, you can eat some more," and if a Polish person finds out you're "on a diet," they will take it as absolute nonsense when it comes to receiving seconds.

Drinking is governed by rules of its own. The bottle of vodka (or increasingly, wine) on the table can miss no one. So if your hosts feel that you have not been keeping up with the drinking, you will have to drink an extra round (the so-called *karniak*, or penalty drink) to make up for the rounds you supposedly missed; whether you did so purposefully or totally unknowingly will be a point of no discussion. There can be no empty bottle standing idly on the table, and it will always be replaced by a new, full bottle of vodka to be poured.

Poles will treat you first before they help themselves to something—be it a homemade cake, a piece of chocolate, or a cigarette. If there is visibly not enough, they will skip their portion and give it to you. If invited to your *parapetówka* (housewarming party) every guest will come with something (usually practical) they have bought for your new home. If you have a baby they will bring a box of diapers, baby clothes, or toys as presents. If you have small children they will bring a chocolate bar or a small present for the kids when visiting. And for a party you're throwing they will come with bags of potato chips, food, and an extra bottle of wine.

If a Polish person considers you their good friend, they will openly show it, will always invite you over, bring presents, and usually try to never say anything negative about you. Your birthday, name day, and all types of important anniversaries will be scrupulously noted down in calendars, and you will receive long, elaborate, poemlike text messages with birthday wishes, name day wishes, or wishes for the holidays. These important dates will be remembered forever.

M.T.

CHAPTER 28

DRINKING IN POLAND: *NA ZDROWIE!*

Wypijmy za to!	*Na zdrowie!*	*Do dna!*
Let's drink to it!	*Cheers!*	*Bottoms up!*

(Popular Polish toasts)

There seem to be so many stereotypes about Poles and their drinking habits that no words said here will be able to abolish them. Thus, let us take a look at some questions commonly asked by non-Poles and see if certain preconceived notions regarding drinking in Poland can be clarified.

DO POLES DRINK A LOT OF VODKA?

Not really. In fact, Poles' consumption of alcohol is actually below the European Union average. According to a study published by the World Health Organization in 2011, the European average of alcohol consumed was 10.85 liters per person, and the figure for an average Pole was less than that—10.6 liters. In comparison, the average Czech citizen drank 15 liters, the French 12.3, the German 11.87, and 10.82 liters were consumed per person in Great Britain. These statistics thus show that Poles are far behind their European neighbors when it comes to heavy drinking.

ARE POLES NATURALLY RESISTANT TO VODKA?

Vodka is a potent alcoholic beverage that contains about 40% alcohol. It is very often drunk neat, chilled and at one gulp, sometimes with a glass of juice on the side to help get it down (*popitka* in Polish). Vodka drinking glasses range from 25-100 ml, so one such shot is one gulp. But no respectable Pole will pour himself (or herself) a shot of vodka and down it himself (or herself) in the company of others. And the general rule is that once a vodka bottle is on the table, no one leaves before it is empty. Even the visit of an unexpected guest is a good excuse to bring out a bottle of chilled vodka that was waiting for that "special occasion." And when it comes to alcohol consumption, Poles are always looking for these occasions to have a round together, be it a birthday, a promotion at work, or a day that ends with y. There is also one more secret to consuming those many shots of vodka—the *zakąska*, or bite-sized snack, such as a piece of herring in oil or a pickle, will help one's stomach in the intervals between toasts of *Na zdrowie!* Nevertheless, foreigners claim that there is no use in trying to outdrink a Pole, and drinking vodka can especially be a true challenge for amateurs.

WHY IS THE STEREOTYPICAL POLISH MAN A HEAVY DRINKER?

Half of all the alcohol drunk in Poland is consumed by under ten percent of all its drinkers, although research studies in the mid-1990s showed that it was men with a poor or basic education, mostly unskilled physical workers and farmers, who drank the most. The majority of Poles do not drink often, especially if there is no special occasion to do so, and thus rarely get drunk. Poland's Central Statistical Office has also noticed a visible decline in the sales of premium spirits, of which 3.7 liters account for that 10.6-liter average, so consumption of spirits, namely vodka, has actually been declining over the last few decades in Poland.

WHAT OTHER TYPES OF VODKA ARE THERE?

The most commonly known vodka is unflavored and clear—or *czysta*. But vodka also comes flavored and in a variety of colors, and can range anywhere from very sweet to extra dry. For example, Żołądkowa Gorzka, or "Bitter vodka for the stomach," quite a nice name, is called such due to its supposed medicinal properties. This is a vodka flavored with herbs and spices that has the color of golden amber. It has a unique aroma and a slightly sweet taste, and not bitter as the name suggests. Another vodka is Krupnik, a sweet vodka made from mead and herbs. In winter it is served with hot water or tea, lemon, and spices. Poland's

Carnival party c. 1960 in Łódź (Elzbieta Sekowska / Shutterstock.com)

most popular overseas vodka exports are Wyborowa and Luksusowa, both also commonly consumed in Poland. Other deluxe brands such as Chopin, Sobieski, and Belvedere are considered to be true "export brands" and as such are not drunk often in Poland.

IS THERE A POLISH VODKA WITH A BLADE OF GRASS IN IT?

Yes, and it's called Żubrówka. Each bottle contains a long blade of bison grass, which comes from no other place but the primeval Białowieża Forest in northeastern Poland, home to the famous *żubr*—from which it proudly takes its name (see Chapter 2). Obviously, those *żubry* (European bison) love to munch on that bison grass. The vodka also has a light yellow tint to it, a delicate fragrance of mown grass, and a subtle, floral taste. It is most commonly combined with chilled apple juice, and you can typically tell where a person is from by whether they call this mixed drink a *tatanka* or a *szarlotka*. However, if you buy a bottle of Żubrówka from a *Polski sklep* in Chicago, don't be surprised if that blade of grass is missing. Like absinthe, the vodka was banned by the U.S. FDA until 2011, when a grass-less version was finally approved.

WHAT IS *BIMBER*?

In communist times some Poles made their own alcohol, commonly called *bimber* or *gorzała*, in the four walls of their homes. It usually had a 90% alcohol content and ranged in taste from sweet to cognaclike.

This was obviously an activity that was entirely illegal, but quite a few engaged in it and actually saw the procedure as a type of hobby. Stories have been heard of huge vessels unexpectedly exploding under the pressure of the fermenting alcohol and the owners frantically trying to clean up the mess before the neighbors downstairs smelled it, or worse yet, saw the liquid trickling down their ceilings and walls.

DO POLES ONLY DRINK VODKA?

No, they also consume large amounts of beer—the 6.1 liters of that 10.6 alcohol total in 2011. Beer has seen visible growth in liters consumed over the last several years. Poland's brewery tradition goes back to medieval times, and today Poland is said to have some of the best pilsner-type lager beers in the world. Some of the most common brands of beer include Lech, Tyskie, Żywiec, Okocim, and Warka. Increasingly popular are regional or local breweries making their own branded beer, usually unfiltered or unpasteurized and dark or cloudy, such as the brewery in Czarnków and other beer brands, like Fortuna, Amber, or Ciechan. Some popular bars and restaurants also sell their own brewed beer.

Another traditional type of alcoholic beverage is mead (*miód pitny*), which is brewed from honey and contains 13-20% alcohol. Sometimes very sweet, the drink comes in different strengths depending on the proportion of honey to water used, such as *półtorak*.

A national specialty is also the homemade or store-bought *nalewka*, an aged, infused liquor made from fruits, herbs, and spices with a 40-45% alcohol content. Just about every Pole has an aunt or uncle known for their *nalewki*, especially around the holidays.

AND WHAT ABOUT WINE?

Only 0.4 liters of that 10.6-liter total were drunk in the form of wine in 2011, although the general tendency is to consume alcohol with a lower alcohol content level, so wine consumption is steadily on the rise. Wine is mostly imported from western, central, and southeast Europe as well as from both Americas. Good wines are served in literally every restaurant, bar and café, especially with the large number of French and Italian restaurants that have opened up within the last few decades. Poland also produces some of its own quality wines in various regions of the country, and most larger towns and cities have stores specializing in the tasting and sales of wine. A popular beverage in the wintertime is *grzaniec* (mulled wine), which is red wine heated with a slice of orange and spices, such as nutmeg, cinnamon, and cloves.

IS HOT TEA SERVED IN GLASSES WITHOUT HANDLES?

That was usually the case in communist times, when hot tea, and coffee too, was served in a clear glass and there was no way to grasp the thing. Sometimes the glass would be put in a metal holder with a handle, but not always and not everywhere. Generally, Poles love to drink tea with and in between meals, but today tea is rather served in a cup or mug.

DO POLES DRINK COFFEE WITH THE GROUNDS FLOATING IN IT?

In communist times, coffee tended to be a rare commodity—it was also one of the most popular products to be handed over as a bribe when a Pole wanted to get something done. *Kawa parzona* was a spoonful or two of coffee grounds in a, you guessed it, glass, with boiling hot water poured over them. And yes, the coffee grounds floated around in the glass and would often get stuck between the teeth. Today Poles enjoy all types of coffee served in a variety of ways, such as Viennese coffee, espresso, caffe latte, latte macchiato, or cappuccino. The latter have become popular with the pervasive coffee culture that has made itself at home in Poland, with coffee shop chains such as Coffeeheaven, Costa, or Starbucks.

AND FINALLY, IS IT OK TO DRINK TAP WATER IN POLAND?

Generally, drinking water with a meal did not make it into Polish tradition, as tea and compote have always been more common. Tap water, especially in the larger cities, used to be of very poor quality and drunk only after it had been filtered and boiled. Today, with many state-of-the-art water treatment facilities, water can usually be drunk from the tap. Poles also consume large amounts of bottled water, either carbonated (*gazowana*) or noncarbonated (*niegazowana*), which mostly comes from Poland's famous mineral water springs. Unfortunately, if you ask for water at a restaurant it will always be bottled and you will have to pay for it.

M.T.

CHAPTER 29

BACK TO SCHOOL

| - Kto ty jesteś? | - Who are you? |
| - Polak mały. | - A little Pole. |

| - Jaki znak twój? | - What's your sign? |
| - Orzeł biały. | - The white eagle. |

| - Gdzie ty mieszkasz? | -Where do you live? |
| - Między swymi. | - Among my own. |

| - W jakim kraju? | - In what country? |
| - W polskiej ziemi. | - On Polish land. |

| - Czym ta ziemia? | - What is that land? |
| - Mą ojczyzną. | - My homeland. |

| - Czym zdobyta? | - How acquired? |
| - Krwią i blizną. | - By blood and scar. |

- A w co wierzysz?   *- And what do you believe in?*
- W Polskę wierzę!   *- In Poland I believe!*

- Czym ty dla niej?   *- What are you to it?*
- Wdzięczne dziecię.   *- A grateful child.*

- Coś jej winien?   *- What do you owe it?*
- Oddać życie.   *- To give my life.*

- Czy ją kochasz?   *- Do you love it?*
- Kocham szczerze.   *- I do sincerely.*

—Władysław Bełza, a famous children's poem written in 1900 in the form of a Q&A, known as "Katechizm polskiego dziecka" ("The Polish Child's Catechism"), often taught in schools.

Imagine you're back in school. You wake up early in the morning. You hesitantly get ready, quickly eat breakfast and make yourself a sandwich with ham or cheese to take to school. You put the sandwich into your backpack with all the books and notebooks you will need that day and head for the bus. No, not the school bus. The bus, as in public transportation. Most school buses are only available to the kids who live in the countryside or in very small towns and villages, where there is no other source of transportation to get them to and from school—well, besides maybe walking a couple of miles down a road with no sidewalk and trucks and cars perilously zooming by. The bus stop is usually close by, but if you live in one of the larger cities you might take the tram (an electric-powered streetcar that looks somewhat like a small train) or the subway instead, or you might have to take the tram and the bus, and not necessarily in that order, to get to your school.

You wait at the stop, but for some reason the bus doesn't come. It doesn't come for a long time, so a whole bunch of other people start gathering there and you have no idea how all those people, including you, are going to get on that one bus once it does appear. The bus finally arrives, a whole fifteen minutes late, and you push your way in with all the other people. The doors of the bus can barely close with everyone pressing on one another, and you imagine what a canned sardine feels like. As you try to get some room to breathe you start thinking about today's classes. And thinking about that makes you worry more than the stuffy bus you're on with all the other people trying to get somewhere. You are happy to get off at your stop and walk to the school building.

The sign above the main entrance proudly reads: VII Liceum Ogólnokształcące im. Dąbrówki, which basically means you're attending a Polish public high school named after Dąbrówka, the Polish princess. It also means you've been part of the Polish educational system for at least half your life, as compulsory education begins at age five or six (depending on birth month) at *przedszkole* (kindergarten), or grade 0 as it's also known. You spent the carefree days of first through sixth grade at a *szkoła podstawowa* (primary school), after which you took an exam—your first of many to come—to determine which *gimnazjum*, or middle school, you would attend. Three years later and it was time for another exam, one approached with even more stress and anxiety, as it would determine which *liceum*, or high school, you would spend the next three years (or four, for a *technikum* or vocational high school) of your life. But that's all in the past. Right now, you still have a full day of classes to get through.

As you enter, the *woźna*, if it's a woman, or *woźny*, if it's a man, the equivalent of a janitor, makes sure that you head straight for the *szatnia*—the coatroom. You bring along your clean tennis shoes to change into, as walking around in the same dirty shoes you just had on a minute ago will get you in trouble with that *woźna*. You leave your coat and shoes and head for the classroom. Your classmates are waiting next to the locked classroom door, so you get a chance to talk and gossip a little before your *wychowawca*, or homeroom teacher, comes to unlock it. The *wychowawca* will be your homeroom teacher throughout your entire stay at the school. The same goes for the other people in your class. You will be seeing the same faces of your homeroom classmates in every single class, every single day of every single year you are at the school.

Your homeroom teacher will start the day off by talking about some parent-teacher meetings and reminding you that you will be getting your first semester report cards soon (everyone makes a loud noise of disapproval at this point) and then will tell you to pull out your books. Your homeroom teacher might also be your mathematics, physics, or chemistry teacher. There will usually be a blackboard in front of the class and he or she will write today's date and the subject of today's lesson on the board in clear, legible handwriting. Then, he or she will sit down and open up the *dziennik*, the class register with everyone's names, grades, and subjects written down. Attendance will be taken, and then the teacher will say in a solemn tone: "Today's subject is…" and will drone on for the next forty-five minutes or so while everyone makes notes of what he or she says. The bell will then ring and you will be happy to have a whole five or ten minutes to eat your sandwich. Your homeroom teacher will take the *dziennik* and hurry to the Teacher's Room, the place where all teachers meet during the breaks and recesses. Then the bell will ring again and this time the history teacher will enter the classroom with the same *dziennik* in his or her hand. The *dziennik* will travel from teacher to teacher like that all day, and sometimes, if your class is very lucky, you will be able to look into it and see the grades, or any other strange marks your teachers might be making next to your names. "Lucky" meaning the teacher has left the room and everybody flings themselves at the *dziennik* or lucky in the sense that you bribe the priest (or nun) with donuts during religion class to get a glimpse at it.

Your history teacher will go through the same routine, plus or minus some formalities, and will then sit down. A silence will befall the classroom as she carefully examines the same list of names in the *dziennik*. She will call out a name, either randomly or according to some secret logic of hers that is still unbeknownst to you, and the person whose name is called out will stand up on unsure feet. This is the beginning of *odpytywanie* or *odpytka* for short, a phenomenon some believe exists only in Polish schools—the most dreaded of all things that can happen during class, the ultimate source of sleepless nights and the root of all things most unpleasant—the wonderful Q&A session one can only experience with one's teacher, in front of the classroom, and always reaching inhumane levels of stress. What is this

Q&A session you may ask? Well, your history teacher, in this case, will start by asking you what you remember from last week's lesson. Let's say the subject was the aftermath of the French Revolution, Napoleon Bonaparte's rise to power and his direct influence on Poland's foreign policy. You will be asked about important dates, places, treaties signed, battles, important politicians, and whatever else comes to your teacher's mind. You will have to answer in full sentences, give details, provide analyses and throw around dates and figures like the history teacher herself. If she is only satisfied with your answers to her questions, you might be lucky enough to get a 3 (the equivalent of an American "C"); if she liked your answers (and probably likes you too), you just might get a 4 (a "B"), and if you show some stroke of historical genius you might even get a 5 (an "A"). She will ceremonially write the grade down next to your name in the *dziennik*, you will sit down feeling satisfied, relieved, and intellectually drained (happy to know that the chances of being picked again are zero for the next couple of weeks or so), and the whole class will sit in silence as the teacher chooses her next victim. When this Q&A nightmare is over, she too will write down or dictate today's subject and will talk for the rest of the lesson about dates, facts, and figures. Everyone will listen attentively and take notes, usually in their notebooks with "Historia" and their names written on the front cover. The notes will usually be long stretches of information, run-on sentences with dates underlined twice. You will then study your notes for the rest of the week and probably the night before your next history class, as the Q&A session will start all over again the next time you have history, the only difference being that the questions will pertain to today's lesson.

The next class might then be chemistry, so you will leave that classroom and go to another one, the chemistry teacher waiting for you with, of course, nothing other than the *dziennik*. The chemistry teacher will call on some people and ask them to write out the complicated chemical formulas from last week's lesson on the board, and if someone doesn't remember or know how, the chemistry teacher might give that person a 2 (an "F" or failing grade). Sometimes the teacher will explain the reactions again and will tell you all as a class to learn them by heart this time (or else!). Or the teacher might tell the whole class to pull out a piece of paper (a pop quiz) and will dictate some questions and formulas to write out. Another chance to earn a grade—though not necessarily a good one.

The next class might be physics, but your homeroom teacher will come in and tell you that the physics teacher called in sick. You will all happily rejoice, knowing you have a whole 45 minutes to yourselves and one Q&A session less to worry about today. You will probably spend that time talking, laughing, eating and preparing (which means reviewing last week's material) for the class following physics. Then you'll have your lunch break, and will probably go to the lunchroom, walk around the school halls to see your friends from other classes or go outside for some fresh air. Your Polish teacher will enter the classroom an hour later and will ask if everyone has read the *lektura* (a book considered mandatory reading) she assigned. Most everyone will answer "Yes," even though some may not have read it, and you will spend the rest of the lesson discussing "What the author had in mind..." when writing the book or poem you were supposed to read. You will take notes during this classroom discussion, as everything said by the teacher in the classroom might be used in the form of questions during another Q&A session. A potential, lingering Q&A session is always there in the back of your head, and you never know what question you will be asked.

The last lesson of the day might be a foreign language, such as English, French, or German—most Polish schoolchildren learn at least one, and usually two, beginning in primary school—or a physical education class. If you happened to attend a specialized high school, such as a music or art school, you will have additional classes in those subjects, as well as after-school activities such as playing in a student orchestra.

You will then head back to the *szatnia*, change your shoes once again, and be happy to go back home, usually commuting in the same conditions as you arrived, but with one day of school behind you, enriched with a whole new dose of knowledge and an array of *przepytkas* and quizzes awaiting you the next day. You have just spent a typical day at a Polish school—and a fairly carefree one at that, considering you still have a few years of this to go before the dreaded *matura*, the Polish equivalent of the SATs and A-levels rolled into one, which will determine your chances of getting into the university of your choice.

Overall, most Poles regard education as incredibly important, and educators have earned a respected place in Polish society, albeit rarely with the salaries to match. Polish students have also done well for themselves on the world stage, coming in twelfth place in reading (well ahead of the U.S. and UK), nineteenth in math, and thirteenth in science in the 2009 OECD world education rankings, despite education budgets of less than half of similar performers such as Norway or Germany. If they successfully pass the *matura* exam, many students will go on to attend Polish universities or private colleges, where they can earn a *licencjat* degree (the equivalanet of a U.S. bachelor's) after three years, an *inżynier* (engineer) degree after three-five years, or, the most common choice, a *magister* (master's) after five years. The really ambitious and academically minded students will study for another three to four years to obtain the title of *doktor*.

M.T.

CHAPTER 30

HERE COME THE HOLIDAYS

Święta, święta i po świętach...
Holidays, holidays, and the holidays are over...
(a Polish saying about the holidays)

As a rule, Poland has a multitude of holidays honoring various saints, historical events, and other excuses to take a day off work, which many visitors only learn about when they suddenly find all the shops closed. Nonetheless, the main holidays are the same as in most Western countries, and are inevitably tied to Poland's Catholic tradition.

Some of the finest Polish holiday customs go back to age-old rural festivities connected with the natural cycle—changing seasons of the year, vegetation cycles connected with farming and harvesting, the rhythm of human life, love and fertility and, finally, remembering the souls of those who have passed away. Most contemporary Poles happily take part in observing the traditional rites and customs of the holidays without being aware of their origins or what they initially symbolized. The most important religious holiday in the liturgical calendar is Easter (*Wielkanoc*), although it is Christmas (*Boże Narodzenie*) that brings smiles to the faces of both adults and children in Poland. Celebrated over several days, it comprises the long-awaited Christmas Eve (*Wigilia*), or the day of presents, the joyous Christmas Day, and the solemn December 26 to commemorate St. Stephen, the first Christian martyr (*św. Szczepana męczennika*).

THE THREE DAYS OF CHRISTMAS

The Polish word *Wigilia* comes from the Latin term *vigiliare*, which means, "to watch, to stand the night guard," as Christmas Eve is a day of fasting and should be spent on silent prayer and vigil while awaiting the birth of the Christ child—though most Poles, especially children, mainly await the exchange of presents that night brings. It is considered, and rightly so, to be the most beautiful holiday of the year, a time of peace and harmony in a joyous home atmosphere with no grievances, quarrels or fighting among family members—"jaka Wigilia, taki cały rok"—as the Polish saying goes, which means the atmosphere in which this exceptional evening is spent portends the rest of the new year to come. But the Wigilia is also a time of eager anticipation, of high spirits and exciting running about preparing long-awaited dishes and Christmas decorations. According to custom, everything in the house must be cleaned, cooked, and ready before the first star appears in the sky for the ceremonious evening meal. Embedded in a long past of vestigial beliefs and traditions, the Wigilia is rich in symbolic customs and rituals during a night that has always been considered full of mystery, magic, and mysticism.

Originally, that is after the adoption of Christianity in Europe, Christmas was introduced to counterweight the pagan solstice celebrations that took place during that time of the winter, when the days were shortest and coldest and people most needed a reason to celebrate. Christmas marks the beginning of the solar year and the yearly vegetation cycle in farming, with its own set of rites in the folk tradition. Christmas Eve fell on the night of the winter solstice, the longest night of the year when the rays of the rising sun had long been awaited, as the sun symbolized victory over darkness and chaos. This had been a day of worship of the birth of the sun and the light in ancient Rome and was thus adopted as the birthday of Jesus Christ. The pagan Slavic tribes had celebrated the winter solstice both as a harvest festival and a day of remembering the souls of those who had passed away, thus many of the pre-Christian as well as Christian customs, rich in their symbols, have blended and survived, albeit in altered form, until today.

(blackman / Shutterstock.com)

BREAKING BREAD

The most important religious symbol of the long-awaited Wigilia is the *opłatek*, a paper-thin wafer made from flour and water with religious reliefs on it. Usually the oldest and most revered member of the household commences the act of the breaking and sharing of the wafer with the rest of the family members around the richly decorated table. This sharing of the wafer symbolizes reconciliation, forgiveness of any past faults and grievances, and involves wishing others lots of health, happiness, peace, joy, and success in the year to come. The custom goes back to the old Christian rite of sharing bread as a sign of brotherhood and belonging to the Christian community. The wafer was introduced in the Middle Ages as a substitute for bread; it was also added to food that was prepared for the farm animals during this magical night as it was believed they could speak in human voices that one day of the year.

Hay has a very important symbolic meaning—it is placed on the table and covered with a pristine white tablecloth. This reminds the family members gathered around the table that Jesus was born in a humble stable and placed on hay in a manger. Sheaves of hay are placed in the corners of the room to guarantee abundance in the year to come, and evergreen branches are hung from the ceiling—these were traditionally decorated with apples, nuts, and colorful wafer cutouts. The Christmas tree, which only became popular in the nineteenth century, symbolizes vitality and the rebirth of life.

Grain, spread out under the tablecloth along with the hay, is also a symbol of prosperity and abundance for the following year. It is seen as a life-giving force symbolizing immortality and wealth. The nuts symbolized mystery, money, and fertility, and the apples were symbols of love and health. Hung on the Christmas tree, they were to provide the family members with strength and long lives.

When setting the Christmas Eve table, Poles made sure to leave an empty place setting for deceased loved ones whose spirits may feel like returning that mystical evening, guided to their family homes by a lit candle. Today this symbolic extra seat is reserved for an unexpected guest, or perhaps to invite someone who would otherwise be spending this holiday time alone.

The Wigilia supper should consist of an even number of meatless dishes, but most preferably twelve, symbolizing Jesus' twelve disciples. Cabbage, one of the main ingredients of Wigilia dishes, such as sauerkraut with mushrooms or in pierogi, was the source of a life-giving force thanks to which nature awakened to a new life, scared evil away, and brought health and abundance to all the members of the household. Yellow peas were added to Wigilia dishes because they protected the household members against disease and guaranteed a good harvest. Honey, a main ingredient of the *kutia* dish in the Podlasie region, guaranteed abundance and happiness, the favors of supernatural forces, and a long life. Poppy seeds, such as in the staple Wigilia dish of homemade noodles and poppy seeds of the Kujawy region, symbolized fertility and offspring, and were eaten in hopes that material goods would soon multiply.

An important part of the Christmas celebrations after the satiating Wigilia supper is the singing of Christmas carols, and some say the Polish ones are some of the world's most beautiful and melodic—the pompous "Bóg się rodzi" (God is born), the lullabylike "Lulajże

Jezuniu" (Lullabye for Jesus), or the solemn "Wśród nocnej ciszy" (In the quiet night), just to name a few. These Christmas carols, *kolędy* in Polish, were also sung by carolers *(kolędnicy)*, usually a group of boys and young men from the local area who dressed up in various strange-looking costumes representing animals and symbolic figures, walked from household to household with a richly decorated carolers' star *(gwiazda kolędnicza)*, staged merry performances, gave their good wishes to the household and received small holiday gifts of food or money in return. The star symbolized the Star of Bethlehem guiding the Three Wise Men to the place where Jesus had been born—it was an age-old symbol of upcoming important events, a sign of happiness and hope that people would be able to get together for the holidays.

These carolers also often carried a *szopka*—originally woodcarved nativity scenes of the Holy Family and the Christ child in the manger. Since the mid-nineteenth century the most famous and intricately ornamented nativity scenes have been the Christmas Cribs from Krakow *(szopki krakowskie)*—finely detailed and colorful versions of Krakow's historic churches and buildings with all of their miniature architectural elements, proudly displayed by the Krakow stone masons who make them for the traditional yearly competition that takes place in the Krakow Market Square in early December.

Christmas Day is celebrated by attending mass (if you missed the Midnight Mass, called the *Pasterka*), and as a ceremonious day of eating meat dishes, such as *bigos*, candy, chocolate and cakes, including the poppy seed-filled *makowiec*, and just simply relaxing and spending time at home together with the family. According to tradition, only the closest relatives may pay a visit, as Christmas Day is reserved for immediate family members. The next day, December 26, commemorates the stoning death of St. Stephen, Christianity's first martyr. It is also a day of more Christmas feasting and visiting family and friends, and like the British and Canadians who have Boxing Day, Poles enjoy this extra day off work as well.

M.T.

CHAPTER 31

FOLK TRADITIONS

Czerwone korale, czerwone niczym wino
Korale z polnej jarzębiny
i łzy dziewczyny i wielkie łzy

Red coral beads, red like wine
Beads made from wild rowan
and a girl's tears and big tears
(Chorus of a contemporary folk song by the band Brathanki)

Cepelia is a nationwide chain of stores that promotes and sells Polish folk art, handicraft products, and pottery as well as embroidered and woven fabric. But their most recognizable product has always been the small, proudly standing lifelike dolls, usually coupled in pairs and finely dressed in their traditional folk costumes representing an ethnically distinct region of Poland. These folk costumes were generally worn only on special occasions in the countryside, during important ceremonies and religious holidays. The choice of materials and fabric to make them reflected a given region's general wealth. These were usually linen, wool, flannel, felt, and, less often, satin, velvet, and tulle. The costumes also varied in their number of layers and colors, which were different for men and women, their choice of headdress, embroidery, lace, ribbons, beads, accessories, and overall ornamentation. These richly decorated and painstakingly created pieces, usually constituting blouses, skirts, and bodices for the women and shirts,

Lowicz dances performed in Warsawon on May 30, 2010, to mark the 200th anniversary of Chopin's birth.

(Stanislaw Tokarski / Shutterstock.com)

pants, and coats for the men, were very different from the everyday attire that was worn to work or in the home. But unique folk costumes are just a part of Poland's rich folk heritage, along with regional music and unique folk customs (see Chapters 16, 22, 30, & 32), distinctive types of architecture and local legends (Chapter 3) as well as regional cuisine (Chapter 26).

TRADITIONAL AREAS OF POLAND

The traditionally distinct region of **Kashubia** in north-central Poland either takes its name from the long overcoats (*sukmany*) that had to be tucked up and under during work or from its marshy areas near the Baltic Sea. This is a land of beautiful lakes and forests as well as fields and meadows. It is well known for its jewelry and ornamental products made from amber—a natural product of the sea. The traditional folk costumes are mostly white and dark blue for both men and women, with characteristic Kashubian embroidery (*haft kaszubski*) on the women's aprons. These are symmetrically embroidered delicate blue, yellow and red flowers with small, green leaves on a white background. Another important element is Kashubian music, with folk songs full of wordplay sung in the regional Kashubian dialect that enumerate and describe everyday objects, which are drawn as hieroglyphic pictures on a stave, called *Kaszubskie nuty*, and cover children's themes, the sea, holidays, the beauty of the region, and the toils of everyday work.

The **Kujawy** region, centrally located between Greater Poland and Mazovia, is known for its many rivers, lakes, forests, and fertile soil. Crop cultivation, especially wheat, initially brought wealth to the region's inhabitants. Folk costumes were mainly red and blue in color. The women wore at least three layers of skirts (convenient for those cold winters), and it was the custom for married women to always wear a headdress to cover their hair. Red coral beads were an essential component of a woman's jewelry, and were often part of the bride's dowry.

The **Biskupizna** region in Greater Poland takes its name from the fact that the land had once belonged to the bishops of Poznań (*biskupi*). Fertile lands and a bustling trade route brought prosperity to its inhabitants, which is clearly visible in the choice of fabrics and number of layers in their traditional costumes. A characteristic element of the men's folk attire was a waist-length red or amaranth buttoned jacket. This is also the only region to use a bagpipe (*dudy* or *kozioł*), which was always played during weddings. Every dance commenced with individual or group singing, but without instrumental music.

The **Podlasie** region in the central-eastern part of Poland is mostly covered by wild forests, marshes, and rivers. It is an area rich in folk crafts, such as blacksmithing, weaving, and pottery. The folk costumes were mainly white and black, with yellow, red, and green ribbons sewn onto the women's skirts and aprons. Colorful, hollow and easily breakable glass beads (*dętki*) were an important part of the women's accessories.

The **Kurpie** region in Mazovia and Podlasie was isolated by two great forests (*Puszcza Zielona* and *Puszcza Biała)* and inhabited by the ethnically distinct Kurpie people. The region was rich in game, thus hunting was an important element of everyday livelihood. Meat, leather skins, wood, amber, and honey were also important commodity products. Beekeeping, originally in the hollows of tree trunks and later in hives, is an age-old tradition (*bartnictwo*). The Kurpie area has its own distinct dialect, woodworking methods, and ornamental jewelry made from amber, which, as opposed to Baltic amber, is mined from underground deposits. Amber necklaces and a tall, black velvet headdress are also important elements of the women's traditional costume, whose colors, like the men's, are predominantly red, white, black, and green. The region is also known for its tall, richly decorated Easter palms.

In the heart of Poland is the region of **Łowicz**. With its dense forests it was a favorite hunting ground, especially for Mazovian dukes and later Polish kings. The inhabitants of this area were quite affluent, which was reflected in their rich and colorful traditional costumes. The women's costumes had bodices with richly embroidered flowers in red, yellow, and green on a black background, and aprons in colorful stripes. Łowicz is also known for its lively dances, such as the polka, and music, especially ballads, pastoral songs, and lullabies. These were performed during traditional, pompous weddings. The region's most recognizable folk products are its colorful cutouts made from paper (*wycinanki łowickie*). Cut by hand with great precision, and most often using large sheep shearing scissors, these portray complex, geometric patterns of folk motifs, usually symmetrical flowers and farm animals.

The Olza River cuts through the **Cieszyn** region that lies near the Czech border, with Cieszyn being one of the oldest towns of Silesia. The region's fertile soils brought its inhabitants wealth, and this was especially visible in the women's traditional costumes, in which the skirt's edges were embroidered with thin silver or gold thread. The dress was so costly that it was usually passed down from mother to daughter. The colors of the folk costumes were mainly white for women and blue and white for men. The region is also known for its filigree—delicate ornamental work using thin, threadlike wires of gold, silver, or other precious metals to make jewelry or belts.

Ziemia Lubuska is centrally located on the Oder River, with its many marshy areas, in western Poland and partly in Germany. The women wore at least three skirts, scarves as headdresses, and white tulle or lace to wrap around their necks. The area's tumultuous history strongly influenced its architecture, with a mix of medieval and Renaissance buildings as well as stylistically eclectic castles.

Ziemia Krakowska, as the name suggests, covers the historical region surrounding Krakow. The folk costumes, black, red, and white in color, and especially the men's overcoat and red four-cornered cap, inspired the official uniform of Poland's nineteenth-century freedom-fighting insurgents. The women wore black velvet bodices that were richly embroidered and decorated in flower motifs, two layers of flowery skirts, and white aprons with red coral necklaces as jewelry. The men's caps were decorated with peacock feathers and either red ribbons or small, artificial flower bouquets, while their pants were vertically striped.

The region is known for its magnificent Christmas nativity scenes (*szopki krakowskie*) and for the symbol of the *lajkonik*, a bearded horseman warrior dressed in Tatar attire who rides a wooden hobbyhorse through Krakow during the Lajkonik festival every June. The jolly horseman begins his journey at the Norbertine Convent near the edge of the city and winds his way to the Market Square, taking "ransom" money along the way, and, as some locals claim, swigs of alcohol offered by business owners as he passes, so by the time he reaches the square he's quite cheerful indeed. The region is also well known for its *krakowiak*, a lively dance that inspired Fryderyk Chopin as well as many other composers and musicians.

For the traditional folk customs and costumes of Poland's **highlanders** (*górale*), see the following chapter.

Interestingly enough, it seems modern-day Poles are not that interested in or attached to folk customs, yet folk-dancing groups, such as the Mazowsze Polish Song and Dance Ensemble, continue to travel around the world to present various traditional Polish folk dances and songs, furniture companies are introducing folk motifs into contemporary design and furniture, and folk-inspired art, such as the paper cutout motifs, adorn modern ladies' bags, clothing, and jewelry.

M.T.

FURTHER READING

Polish Customs, Traditions and Folklore by Sophie Hodorowicz Knab. Hippocrene Books, 1996.

CHAPTER 32

THE HIGHLANDER LIFE

Góralu, czy ci nie żal
Góralu, wracaj do hal!

Highlander, have you no remorse
Highlander, go back to your pastures!
(Popular folk song)

Polish highlanders (*górale*) have always been surrounded by a mysterious, perhaps even mythic, aura. Maybe this is due to the fact that they live so far south, high up somewhere in the mountains among their close-knit family and social structures, that they can easily tell if a person is from another region; they speak their own distinct dialect (*gwara góralska*), pronounce many words differently and use some vocabulary that is unknown to those people "from the lowlands," such as the word *cepr* to denote anyone who comes from another region—especially a tourist. As always, what is unknown or difficult to understand tends to become romanticized, which seems to be the case with the image of the Polish highlander.

Most Poles associate Polish highlanders with those from the Tatra Mountains, and more specifically from Zakopane, the most famous and oft visited summer and winter vacation resort nestled at their foot. These are the highlanders from the Podhale region, but they are not the only ones—other groups of highlanders live in the Beskid Mountains and in the Pieniny Mountains. These distinct groups include highlanders from around the towns of Żywiec, Orawa, or Spisz—although these neighboring groups have also influenced one another's traditional customs throughout the course of Polish history.

High(lander) fashion

The choice of clothing of the Polish highlanders was dictated by what was readily available and by their tendency to work outside in harsh weather conditions. Linen, sheepskin, and leather were the main materials used to make the clothes, which also had to be comfortable, as they would be worn for many hours at a time. The land was not very fertile, but in certain areas grain crops were harvested and pigs and cows were raised. Most often the highlander men were shepherds who had to traverse long distances away from home, so their pants had a narrow fit and were easy to walk in. The highlander men in the Beskid Mountains, in turn, also worked in nearby forests and quarries, so they wore a *kożuszek* all year round—a sleeveless sheepskin vest that protected them from the cold in the winter and from the heat in the summer. A *kożuch* was a sheepskin coat with long sleeves that was worn in the cold of winter. The men also wore felt waterproof hats to protect them from the sun and rain. Their pants were made from white cloth and had few if any decorative elements. Another typical overcoat thrown over the shoulders was a knee-length *gunia*, which was made from cloth and was turned inside out when it rained. The *gunia* was sewn in such a way as to allow the man to move freely while working and to be able to cover himself when asleep. *Gunias* were very practical and weatherproof, and served as outerwear for many years. They were also decorated with colorful strings, called *lemki*, the colors of which originally allowed one to tell which village the highlander was from.

A typical overcoat of the highlander women from the Beskid Mountains was a *łoktusza*, which was made from a large sheet of canvas that nearly covered the woman's entire body. Unmarried women had to keep their heads uncovered all year long, wearing neither caps nor scarves, even in those changing mountain weather conditions. They always wore one braid, which they decorated with two ribbons, either pink or red in color. One ribbon was woven into the braid and the other was tied at its end. Scarves and caps were only worn by either married or pregnant women, or both for that matter. *Kierpce* are the traditional pointed-toe shoes, worn by both men and women, which were made from one piece of tan-colored decorated leather.

The Beskid highlander women, and especially those from the town of Koniaków, have always been famous for their crocheted lace called *koniakowskie koronki*. These elaborate crochet patterns resemble stars, rosettes, or fans. The lace, mainly white or cream in color and round or oval in shape, is often made into doilies or tablecloths, like those for church altars. It has been presented to European royalty and popes, and is even said to have been on President Kennedy's dinner table. The younger generation of women lace-makers in Koniaków recently came up with the idea, albeit controversial, of making colorful crocheted lace thong underwear to supply the ever-growing demand for something traditional and practical, yet with an unusual modern twist. An exhibition of this famous crocheted lace can be found at a museum dedicated entirely to this traditional folk art—the *Muzeum Koronki* in Koniaków.

The climate of the Podhale region did not allow its inhabitants to farm the land, thus they made their livelihood out of raising sheep. One main product they produced was *oscypek*—a hard, smoked cheese traditionally made in the mountains by highlander men called *bacowie* (see Chapter 26). The *baca* was responsible for looking after the sheep and for the production of this and other types of cheese, which was done with the help of assisting shepherds, called *juhasy*, whom he oversaw. It was he who had to make sure there was always a fire going in their shepherds' hut on the mountainside, called the *bacówka*. The *baca* was hired by the group of landowners (*gazdy*) that owned the sheep he helped tend to; he was very much revered by the local community and was also usually one of the wealthier farmers, as his personal assets served as collateral for the owners' sheep.

The traditional folk costume of these highlander men from the Podhale region was a white shirt with a brass clasp under the neck and fitted white-cloth pants with decorative flower motifs on the thighs. The pants had bottom slits on the sides so that they could be easily tucked into the shoes. Over this they donned a medium-length overcoat made from thick white cloth with decorative floral motifs on the shoulders, a wide leather belt that had pockets for money, tobacco and a pipe, and always wore a black felt hat with a row of small snail shells sewn onto a thin red leather strap. Unmarried men also added bird feathers onto the straps of their hats. A characteristic accessory was a *ciupaga*—a richly decorated, tapered wooden cane with a small hatchet at one end that was originally used to cut wood or as a weapon, and later served as a decorative part of the folk costume on holidays. It was also the main fighting weapon to be used by the legendary Janosik, the famed but noble robber of the Carpathian mountains who, like Robin Hood, took from the rich and gave to the poor. It now commonly serves as a choreography element during the men's folk dances, and ersatz *ciupagas* are sold as popular tourist souvenirs from Zakopane.

The folk costume of Podhale women was a white, mid-sleeved blouse with a wide collar, both of which had a lace design. The skirts were usually red with floral motifs, and the black bodices were tightly fitted, laced up with a red ribbon and had beaded embroidery designs of flowers, such as lilies, edelweiss, or chrysanthemums. The costume was topped off with red coral beads around the neck, white socks, and *kierpce* on the feet.

ZAKOPANE STYLE

The rich folk tradition of Zakopane has also become famous for its architectural design, known as the Zakopane Style (*styl zakopiański*). Its history goes back to the second half of the nineteenth century, when Zakopane was already a famous health resort and where its more affluent tourists had started building their vacation homes in the alpine architectural style that was so very *en mode* at that time. **Stanisław Witkiewicz**, whose son was the famous Polish painter Witkacy (see chapters 35 & 37), was himself a renowned painter and architect who had become mesmerized by the local folk architecture. He was asked by a friend, Zygmunt Natowski, an avid collector of folk art from the Podhale region, to design his summer home. Instead of going for the prevalent alpine style, Witkiewicz suggested incorporating folk elements of the surrounding architecture that he so commonly saw on the cottages of the local highlanders. This vacation villa, called Koliba, was the first of many buildings to be designed in this innovative architectural style in 1893. It was similar to a traditional Zakopane highlander cottage in its layout, yet with an enlarged interior and stories added on. Built from wooden beams sitting on a high foundation laid out in chipped stone slabs, the construction also had a steep, sloped roof—a practical as well as decorative element that prevented snow from piling up and causing cave-ins. The roof was decorated with vertically mounted wooden decorative elements in the shape of flowers or crosses, and the door and window frames were adorned with wooden suns made from thin laths nailed in place around a radius. This new style was also implemented in furniture, musical instruments, and

Highlander from Transcarpathia in national dress, circa 1928
(IgorGolovniov / Shutterstock.com)

even porcelain. Today a good example of the *styl zakopiański* is the Church of the Holy Heart of Jesus in Zakopane.

Over time, many highlander men have had to, reluctantly, leave the mountainside in search of work, and they usually sent for their families once they had settled in another region of the country or abroad. Many would never return to the Polish mountains of their youth, thus the words of the folk song above that speaks of the Polish highlander's longing to return to his place on earth.

M.T.

Further Reading

Tatra Highlander Folk Culture in Poland and America by Thaddeus V. Gromada. Tatra Eagle Press, 2012.

CHAPTER 33

POLES ON VACATION

Lato, lato, lato czeka,
Razem z latem czeka rzeka
Razem z rzeką czeka las
A tam ciągle nie ma nas.

Summer, summer, summer's waiting
Along with summer the river's waiting
With the river the forest's waiting
And still we are not there.
–Ludwik Jerzy Kern, fragment of a song from
the film *Szatan z Siódmej Klasy*

Vacationing used to be easy. The kids would be sent to the *kolonie* (organized summer camps for children) and the parents would go either to the Baltic seaside or the Polish mountains; that is, those living along the northern seacoast would usually go to the mountainous south, while those from that region would travel north. Many families would also opt to vacation together with their kids at the *wczasowe ośrodki zakładowe* (employer vacation resorts). Such vacations used to be grossly financed by employers, and were informally known as *wczasy pod gruszą* ("holidays under the pear tree"). Going abroad was simply very costly, especially with the differences in the value of the Polish złoty against any foreign currency, and notoriously time-consuming when one started the whole process of trying to obtain all the necessary formal documents, such as permits, visas, and passports, which were required in order to leave the country—not to mention the fact that many Poles were simply banned from foreign travel for political reasons. In 1966, only every thirtieth Pole declared having been abroad at least once in his or her lifetime, and in many cases this had been a "forced" stay abroad connected with the war or a postwar exodus. In 1990, only one-half of Poles declared having been abroad, despite the fact that for nearly twenty years traveling to other socialist countries had become more widely available.

No more borders

All that started to change in the early 1990s, when Poland's borders were no longer as impenetrable and allowed for more traveling opportunities between countries. Poland's accession to the European Union in 2004 (see Chapter 49) opened up the borders even more, but it was the country's accession to the Schengen zone at the end of 2007 that finally gave Poles the freedom to travel without major border controls. One could cross into Slovakia on a hiking trip through the forest or enter German territory by crossing a meadow, and "shopping" trips or looking for work across the border became more commonplace. A daylong car trip could take one to the ritzy French Riviera or to Italy's idyllic Tuscany. Or one could board a charter flight and swim in the warm, tropical waters of Thailand. It seems the only limit was, ultimately, the family budget.

Poles choose to go on foreign holidays for two main reasons. First, the value of the Polish złoty has remained relatively high in comparison with other currencies, so more and more Poles can afford to vacation abroad. Second, Polish hotels and package holidays are, generally, not cheap, and Poles' expectations regarding accommodation standards are quite demanding. Thus, many have noticed that a vacation at the Polish seaside is sometimes even more costly than a package holiday trip to Egypt. Another factor is the weather in Poland, when one can spend the whole summer waiting for a few hot days in a row, or when the water in the Baltic Sea is still freezing cold in the middle of July. Mediterranean Europe, in turn, almost always guarantees splendid, hot weather. Polish travel agencies have noticed that Polish vacationers are seeking more luxury packages and that the choice of their vacation stay largely depends on the agency's offer. In this respect, Poles do not differ much from the vacationers of other countries in terms of making destination decisions according to personal preferences.

Yearly trends and statistics vary, but popular vacation destinations in Europe have always been Italy, Greece, Spain, France, Croatia, Turkey, and Bulgaria. Egypt has always been a hit with Poles—the numbers show between 250,000 to one million Poles traveling there on a yearly basis! Many are also choosing to visit Tunisia, Morocco, or the Canary Islands. Other non-European countries that have seen a growing number of vacationers from Poland are China, Hong Kong, India, and Australia. There has also been growing interest in trips to more exotic parts of the world, such as safari trips to Kenya and the palest yellow beaches of the Dominican Republic, Mexico, and Cuba. Many travel agencies also comment that the Unites States would be a true vacation gold mine if only the requirement for mandatory visas for Poles was abolished.

In 2012, 34% of Poles declared that they had not crossed the Polish border, and a large part of those said they would probably not do so in the future. The reason for this was not always a low budget. Some stated that their job would not allow them to leave their family-run farm, small store, or workshop; others referred to their own poor health or that of a family member, their not knowing how to speak a foreign language, or simply the general reluctance to travel at all, particularly to any "foreign" place.

Therefore, some 10% of Poles choose to spend their vacation time in Poland. There are plenty of quality hotels, motels, guesthouses, and campsites to accommodate visitors. Numerous castles and palaces have also been wonderfully renovated and invite guests year-round.

A POLISH VACATION

So, what can one do while on vacation in Poland? Well, there certainly is much to choose from, as there are:

- Historic man-made sites, such as the oldest medieval brick bridge in Grudziądz, dating from the first half of the thirteenth century, which has been renovated and is in operation today, or the European Route of Brick Gothic, connected with the history of Hanseatic League cities and their Brick Gothic architecture.

- Man-made and natural sites listed on UNESCO's World Heritage List, such as the pioneer, seventeenth-century, timber-framed evangelical Churches of Peace in the towns of Jawor and Świdnica, which were built in less than one year.

- Historic cities and towns with their Old Town Squares (*Stary Rynek*), such as the largest European one in Krakow, for starters. Every respectable medieval *rynek*, besides having such must-haves as a town hall, trading stalls, and a water well, also had a nice little pillory (*pręgierz*) to expose offenders to public scorn and ridicule. Today, Poznań's restored *pręgierz* is a well-known meeting place for, ironically, first dates or groups of fun-loving teenagers.

- Hundreds, actually thousands, of various museums, the most modern, high-tech ones such as the Copernicus Science Center (*Centrum Kopernika*) or the Warsaw Rising Museum, or perhaps Poland's only museum documenting railroad rescue work (*Muzeum Ratownictwa Kolejowego*) in Poznań; the smallest museum, located in Łowicz, with its registered office in a nineteenth-century trunk, has an exhibition of over 2,000 buttons... yes, buttons.

- Ethnographic museums and open air parks (*skanseny*) with entire traditional villages, cottages, barns and buildings, tools and farm equipment, or folk arts and crafts.

- Century-old wooden churches, the oldest of which was built from wood dating back to the year 1373 (St. Nicholas' Church in the Greater Poland region).

- Historic (yet still functional) wind and watermills, such as the brick, eighteenth-century watermill in the Silesian village of Brzeźnica. It was here that the Romantic-era Silesian-German poet, Joseph von Eichendorff, was inspired to write poems about his unrequited love for the miller's daughter.

- Baltic Sea beaches and seaside resorts, such as Poland's longest beach in Gdańsk (20 km) or the historically fashionable

Sopot, boasting Europe's longest wooden pier (*molo*) that is over half a kilometer long.

- Agro-tourist attractions (*agroturystyka*), which means relaxing in the countryside in adapted cottages, with no cell phone coverage or Internet, where you can see real farm animals, take a walk in the nearby woods or pastures, swim in a nearby lake or river, pick wild mushrooms or berries, observe the birds or storks, read a good book or sit around a bonfire and eat grilled Polish sausages; there are around 6,000 such farms in Poland.

- Haunted castles; for example, the ghost of the *Czarna Dama* in Janowiec near Kazimierz Dolny is a ghouly treat; other supposedly haunted castles are in Niedzica, Kórnik, and Grodno.

- Palaces and manor houses with their surrounding gardens and permanent exhibitions of period art, furniture, and interiors. The largest collection of original residential furnishings is housed in a large palace in Pszczyna, located in Silesia.

- Sailing or windsurfing in the Baltic Sea (especially off of Hel, Poland's longest peninsula) or on the great lakes of the Masuria region (whose sailing capital is the town of Mikołajki).

- Historic forts and their ruins, such as those in Kożuchów in the Lubuskie Voivodeship, where the longest and most well-preserved fortification walls of medieval Poland and Europe can be visited; or as the saying in Danish supposedly went— "You're not safe if you're not protected by Szczecin's walls," which testifies to the impenetrable fortifications of the towns spotting the Pomeranian coast.

- Hundreds of caves, such as the magnificent Jaskinia Niedźwiedzia in the Sudetes or Raj in the Świętokrzyskie Mountains, supposedly not for the faint-hearted.

- Hiking trails in the mountains, in the Bieszczady, Beskidy, Sudetes or Świętokrzyskie, or in the Alp-like Tatras for the more experienced.

- Skiing, and not only at Kasprowy Wierch or Gubałówka in Zakopane.

Sopot: the longest wooden pier in Europe, built 1827. (Nightman1965 / Shutterstock.com)

- Rock climbing in the picturesque Jura Krakowsko-Częstochowska, around Krakow or Zawiercie.

- Odd local festivities, such as the World Gold Panning Competition in Złotoryja, whose first inhabitants were German gold miners in the early thirteenth century; fairs or medieval festivals, such as the Viking Festival on Poland's largest island, Wolin, which was a Viking homestead in the ninth century, before the Polish tribes settled there; or festivals with knights presenting horse tournaments or famous Polish battles, such as annual re-enactments of the great medieval Battle of Grunwald that took place in 1410.

- Music festivals, such as Wrocław's international Wratislavia Cantans festival of choir music; pop music concerts, such as the OFF Festival in Katowice; jazz, such as Warsaw's Jazz Jamboree; or country music, such as the Mrągowo Country Picnic music festival.

- River rafting, such as taking a picturesque tour in the Pieniny Mountains down the Dunajec River.

- Underwater diving around ship wreckages off the Baltic seacoast, in the deep Masurian lakes, or the flooded quarries of Upper and Lower Silesia.

- Relaxing at the *sanatoriums*, now state-of-the-art spas to rejuvenate the body and soul, with those in Krynica-Zdrój, Ciechocinek, or Ustka just to name a few, or in the former Bochnia Salt Mine, which currently houses the largest, underground, man-made space with a sports field, restaurant, disco, and hotel for 250 guests.

Poles and foreigners visiting Poland are becoming increasingly aware of the fact that there is much to do and see within this country's borders, making vacationing in Poland a much more popular trend in recent years.

M.T.

Part III

Poles in the Limelight

CHAPTER 34

WRITERS & POETS:
BEYOND MIŁOSZ & MICKIEWICZ

"Polish literature is one: wherever a beautiful poem in the language of Norwid arises, it belongs in its reach."
–Julian Przyboś, poet

Polish literature has traditionally possessed many aspects of Western literature, more so than other Slavic literatures, despite linguistic similarities. Due to its specific history, Poland was historically cosmopolitan, a place where many cultures and languages existed (and influenced each other) simultaneously, especially when it was divided between Vienna, St. Petersburg, and Berlin.

And yet, aside from a few names such as Miłosz or Conrad (both émigrés), Polish literature is little known in the non-Polish-speaking world, particularly when compared to its neighbors Russia and Germany. Most English-speaking high school students will tackle Dostoevsky, Tolstoy, or Goethe, but will never hear of Adam Mickiewicz or Henryk Sienkiewicz. Part of this may have to do with the historical, religious, or patriotic focus of most Polish literature; part may have to do with language, as Latin was the main language of publication until well into the Renaissance, leaving reading and writing as pursuits of the nobility. Nonetheless, the Polish language has a rich literary tradition, starting in earnest in the Romantic period and continuing to this day.

THE ROMANTICS

When the nation of Poland ceased to exist during the Partitions (see Chapter 42), the job of maintaining Polish identity and traditions fell to Polish artists within Poland and abroad, particularly writers and poets. The written word was used not only for propaganda or nostalgic purposes, but also as a way of keeping the Polish spirit alive through the active use of its language. This gave rise to Polish Romanticism, a period marked by an idealization of folklore and the countryside, emotionalism, and, above all, nationalist ideals and independence.

Nowhere is this better personified than in **Adam Mickiewicz**, the most famous Polish poet and author of the national epic *Pan Tadeusz*, which tells the tale of two noble families living under Russian rule in 1811. Like many Polish writers during the Partitions, Mickiewicz spent much of his life outside of Poland, and *Pan Tadeusz* was published in Paris, safe from the Russian censors. The opening lines (known by every schoolchild in Poland) refer to the historic lands of the old Polish-Lithuanian commonwealth:

> Lithuania! My homeland! Thou art like fine health.
> How much thou should be appreciated, will only know
> One who has lost thee. Thy beauty today, in all its splendor
> I behold and portray, for I long after thee.[*]

Other notable Romanic writers include Cyprian Norwid, Józef Ignacy Kraszewski, Aleksander Fredro, and **Juliusz Słowacki** and **Zygmunt Krasiński**, who together with Mickiewicz are known as the three bards of Polish literature.

Polish writers were also very much tied to the political and military realities of the times. For example, a poet named Apollo Korzeniowski, the father of Józef Konrad (better known as Joseph Conrad), was one of the instigators of the January Uprising of 1863. This was also the case with Mickiewicz, who died in Constantinople while attempting to organize Polish troops to fight against the Russians in the Crimean War.

---

[*] Translation by Marta Turek

The movement that immediately followed Romanticism, called Positivism, was largely a backlash against the Romantics and a call for reason, pragmatism, and skepticism. It came as a reaction to the failed 1863 Uprising and its consequences, one of which was the banning of the Polish language in schools and government institutions—making the very act of writing in Polish a form of protest. Those writers publishing within former Polish territories also had to elude the censors.

Positivist writers were more critical of Polish history, ascribing blame to the failings of the Polish nobility, rather than portraying the country as a victim of its aggressive neighbors as the Romantics had. The straightforwardness of the novel was better suited to Positivism than the flowery poetry of Romantic writers. Within the Positivist movement, notable names include Aleksander Świętochowski, Stefan Żeromski, Piotr Chmielowski, and Eliza Orzeszkowa—though the best known among them was **Bolesław Prus**, a novelist and humorist with a scientific background. Reading his works, such as his masterpiece novel *The Doll*, is a great way to gleam a picture of everyday life in late nineteenth century Warsaw.

Another considerable figure of the era was **Henryk Sienkiewicz**, who was initially known as a journalist and for his travels across the United States in the 1870s, even helping establish a Polish colony in California. However, his most famous novels broke away from the Positivist tradition and were historical, set in the seventeenth-century Polish-Lithuanian Commonwealth. Known collectively as *The Trilogy*, they consisted of *With Fire and Sword*, *The Deluge*, and *Fire in the Steppe*. The novels were initially serialized in newspapers, and reached a popularity akin to Tolkien or today's J.K. Rowling, fan mail and all. *The Trilogy*, together with his later novel *Quo Vadis?*, have all been made into films and won Sienkiewicz a Nobel Prize in 1905. However, Sienkiewicz's works are decidedly more fiction than history, where bad guys and good guys are easily recognizable and war is presented as a romantic, noble pursuit rather than the bloodbath it really was.

INTO THE TWENTIETH CENTURY

At the turn of the century, Polish literature once again returned to romantic ideas with a modernist movement called *Młoda Polska*

(Young Poland). Though the movement was derived primarily from France, it was unmistakably Polish in this incarnation, very much looking back to the Polish Romantic writers who had been such an influence in the past.

Once Poland regained its independence following World War I, it also regained its chance for an independent national literature. Avant-garde and absurdist literature resurged, now that writers no longer had to focus on nationalist themes and the fight for independence was over. Though the period spanned just twenty years, there are far too many noteworthy works and authors to name, and English-language readers will find plenty of them available in translation, including Witold Gombrowicz, Maria Dąbrowska, Bolesław Leśmian, Bruno Schulz, Aleksander Wat, and Jarosław Iwaszkiewicz.

LITERATURE UNDER OCCUPATION (AGAIN)

Under the Nazis, official publishing in Polish was not allowed, but clandestine publishing thrived, and Poles printed and published everything from new to Romantic literature, and even staged poetry readings and theatrical performances. Underground journals rose from about thirty in circulation in 1940 to about 600 in 1945.

World War II also once again divided Polish literature between an émigré faction (see Chapter 48) and a domestic faction, each with its own representatives and movements, though in the end both must be taken into account as comprising Polish literature as a whole during the era. Naturally, the period experienced a revival of Romanticism, reflecting back to the last time Poland had ceased to exist; however, this literature also harbored a strong self-criticism and even ridicule of the interwar Polish society the writers felt had allowed World War II to happen. The war also brought a temporary end to experimental and avant-garde poetry and theater, which had begun to develop in the 1930s, and which would not be revived until 1956.

The most powerful works of the immediate postwar period were not fiction or poetry but stories and narratives barely disguised as fiction. An excellent example is **Tadeusz Borowski's**

This Way for the Gas, Ladies and Gentlemen, a poignant, realistic and often tragically humorous account of the author's experience at Auschwitz.

With the imposition of Stalinism and the declaration that Socialist Realism would be the only acceptable art form in 1949, a large number of writers who had begun publishing immediately after the war went silent, and the writing produced officially in that era was of definite inferior quality. Under communism, the government had complete control over almost all legal publishing, including subsidizing writers, all channels of distribution, and controlling all revenues of publishing houses and appointment to important posts.

After the thaw of 1956 and relaxing of censorship, increased freedom for writers as well as a revival of vangardism hit Polish letters, and writers found themselves much freer to experiment than in previous years. Echoing the periods of the Partitions, literature gained a guiding and vital role, and writers gained a respected position in Polish society. Significant writers of that period include Wisława Szymborska, Zbigniew Herbert, Tadeusz Różewicz, science fiction great Stanisław Lem, Sławomir Mrożek, and Ryszard Kapuściński, whose travel narratives are now known around the world. One of the best-known writers under communism, **Czesław Miłosz**, spent most of his life abroad, yet made a significant impact on Polish writing. His *History of Polish Literature* is also the definitive English-language text on the subject.

1968 brought a new generation of writers to the forefront who incorporated the moral and linguistic experiments of the 1956 generation while finding their own voice, one often protesting against totalitarianism and the censor. The generation of 1968 was obsessed with language, and strongly believed that those who had control over language had control over the people; they developed this view from a lifetime of witnessing the manipulation of language by the authorities, and strove to bring meaning back into words. These writers were bolder in their style and embraced rebellion, often publishing under pseudonyms and in journals based abroad that would then be smuggled into Poland. Together with artists and other creative intellectuals, writers in the 1970s became adept at delivering messages of protest right under the censors' noses, while audiences were always hungry for more. This preoccupation with the censor also brought literature written underground in Poland closer to literature written abroad, while distancing it from the literature appearing in the official publishing houses at the time.

The 1970s also saw the rise in popularity of Catholic writers. The Catholic Press became an alternative for those writers banned by official publications for their criticisms of the system. However, the writers declaring themselves Catholic and publishing in official Catholic publications rather than underground or in émigré journals were often limited by both the censor and by the doctrines of the Church. On the other side of the coin, writers who considered themselves socialist or at least leftist, though they did not agree with the Party as it ran Poland, were numerous as well. An apt example would be **Adam Michnik**, who still believed a Polish form of socialism was possible despite the failures of 1956.

In 1980, with the temporary victory of Solidarity, censorship practically ceased to exist and writers experienced not only freedom in what they wrote, but an influx of previously forbidden literature, both from clandestine publishers at home and Polish publishers abroad, so that for the first time all Polish literature could be discussed as one body. However, the freedom writers faced during the early years of Solidarity was crushed brutally when martial law was imposed. Many continued publishing in the thriving émigré publications, which would then be smuggled into the country for Polish readers. Consequently, the underground presses during this time did amazingly well. One of the most memorable (and banned) writers from the final years of communism is **Tadeusz Konwicki**, whose excellent novel *A Minor Apocalypse* is a biting satirical parody of the communist system akin to *Brave New World*.

POSTCOMMUNISM

It could be argued that communism, a force writers seemed to be constantly struggling against, was better for literature in Poland than the democracy that these writers had fought so long to gain. The 1989 to early 1990s transition from socialism to the free market and democracy shocked Polish society (see Chapter 11), but among the heaviest hit were practitioners of the arts, including writers. In particular, the hardest new reality to face for writers was their fall from esteemed upholders of morality to a feeling of relative obscurity and apathy outside the creative intelligentsia.

Under martial law, shocking numbers of people risked their careers or lives to publish and distribute clandestine journals and books, and many more risked their freedom just to possess such materials. After 1989, when once-forbidden books and periodicals were freely available to purchase, the majority of society seemed to have better things to worry about now instead of something as trivial as literature.

Free market capitalism had indeed hit the Polish economy, and like in most Western societies, what sold was no longer dictated by what was actually good, but by what was popular, which amounted to lowbrow literature and mass translations of mostly American best sellers. Since the immediate transition, the situation of Polish publishing has changed somewhat. Some of the most influential names publishing today include **Andrzej Stasiuk**, known as the Polish Kerouac, Olga Tokarczuk, Grazyna Miller, Paweł Huelle, Jerzy Pilch, Stefan Chwin, and young popular talent Dorota Masłowska.

However, even if Polish society is reading again, the role of the Polish writer remains drastically different today from that of previous centuries. Many writers can only be loosely tied together as postmodernist and lack an overarching style such as Romanticism. The challenge for Polish writers today is to establish a new, nonpolitically motivated yet culturally significant role in society, so that Polish literature may continue to exist at the same high standard developed over hundreds of years.

A.S.

FURTHER READING

Ashes and Diamonds by Jerzy Andrzejewski. Northwestern University Press, 1997.

The Collected Poems: 1956-1998 by Zbigniew Herbert. Ecco, 2008.

The Doll by Bolesław Prus. New York Review Books Classics, 2011.

The Elephant by Sławomir Mrożek. Grove Press, 1985.

Ferdydurke by Witold Gombrowicz. Yale University Press, 2000.

The History of Polish Literature by Czesław Miłosz. University of California Press, 1983.

Pan Tadeusz by Adam Mickiewicz. 1834.

Poems New and Collected by Wisława Szymborska. Mariner Books, 2000.

Primeval and Other Times by Olga Tokarczuk. Twisted Spoon Press, 2011.

Quo Vadis: A Narrative of the Time of Nero by Henryk Sienkiewicz. 1896.

Solaris by Stanisław Lem. Harvest Books, 1987.

The Street of Crocodiles by Bruno Schulz. Penguin Classics, 1992.

Tales of Galicia by Andrzej Stasiuk. Twisted Spoon Press, 2003.

CHAPTER 35

THEATER (& CABARET) OF THE ABSURD

"Whether you want it or not,
your genes have a political past,
your skin a political tone.
your eyes a political color.
...you walk with political steps
on political ground."
–Wisława Szymborska

Like Polish literature, which it is strongly tied to, Polish theater and especially cabaret have a long tradition of being anti-establishment (which usually meant anti-occupying forces) and wavering between the patriotic and the absurd. While theater in Poland is still a fairly popular pastime, most performances are of plays written in the Romantic or interwar period or under communism. The Polish cabaret, however, has changed significantly since its heyday at the beginning of the twentieth century, and has taken on a very modern form—though keeping the cultural references and political satire that made the original legendary. What might be called sketch comedy or variety shows on British or American TVs are generally classified as cabaret in Poland, with the genre taking the place of stand-up comedy—and enjoying the same popularity. Historically and today, cabaret reflects Polish society and allows Poles to laugh at themselves and the situation of their country—something they are quite fond of doing.

ROMANTIC THEATER

If one were to name just a handful of the most influential figures in Polish theater, **Aleksander Fredro** and **Juliusz Słowacki** would certainly top the list. Both men wrote at the height of the Romantic period and produced some of the most notable plays (as well as poetry) in the Polish canon. Słowacki, in fact, is dubbed the father of Polish drama, while Fredro's works, such as the comedy *Zemsta* (*The Revenge*), have been translated into several languages and performed around the world.

A contemporary of the bard Adam Mickiewicz, Słowacki was not too fond of his more popular rival, and even considered challenging him to a duel. Both men were part of the émigré community in 1830s France, though Słowacki was later forced to move to Switzerland and then Italy before returning to Paris. While he never gained popularity and his works were not performed on stage during his lifetime, he became a posthumous inspiration to the Young Poland movement in Krakow, where today the city's most prestigious theater is named in his honor.

ZIELONY BALONIK

If you mention a green balloon to a Pole of the older generation, particularly a Cracovian, you might just get a knowing wink. That's because the **Green Balloon** (Zielony Balonik) cabaret was a Polish institution from 1905 until 1915 among its cultural elite. Thanks to its long cultural tradition and the lenient laws of the Austro-Hungarian rulers, Krakow became the last bastion of Polish culture within former Polish lands before the nation regained its independence, and its artistic and literary scenes flourished. The Green Balloon was a natural result of these circumstances, and the cabaret tended to focus on political satire by some of the edgiest writers of its days (such as the legendary **Tadeusz Boy-Żeleński**)—often accompanied by art exhibitions and general debauchery. It eventually ran out of steam, however, as censorship increased while the original cabaret troupe ran out of fresh material.

Today, visitors to Krakow can still visit the Jama Michalika café, which looks like it has hardly changed in the past century. The green Art Nouveau style café still displays many souvenirs of the early twentieth century on its walls.

CRICOT AND ITS REINCARNATIONS

In the 1930s, the Cricot Theater largely inherited the Green Balloon's tradition. Begun in Krakow by a group of artists and avant-garde writers led by Józef Jarema and his sister Maria, it moved to Warsaw in 1938, and lasted until World War II broke out. It was innovative for its involvement of the audience and improvisational elements.

Cricot rose from the dead in 1955 in the form of Cricot II, begun by visionary Krakow artist and playwright **Tadeusz Kantor**, together with Maria Jarema (her brother would never return to Poland after the war). Some of the first productions put on by the theater group were written by **Stanisław Ignacy Witkiewicz (Witkacy)**. In addition to being a superb painter and writer, Witkacy wrote nearly two dozen plays, some of which have been staged in New York and other cities in the U.S. as well as the Edinburgh Festival, such as *The Madman and the Nun* and *The Water Hen*.

As for Kantor, he often added his own artistic elements to Witkacy's work as well as designing elaborate sets. He introduced several innovations into Polish theater, including using mannequins in place of actors and extending the stage so the audience could feel closer to the action. He would also direct and sometimes act in his own plays, such as *Dead Class*, in which he played teacher to a "classroom" of mannequins. Once communism fell, Kantor's works began appearing in the U.S., though Kantor himself died in 1990.

Today, Kantor's vision is being revived once more, in the form of Cricoteka, a museum dedicated to Tadeusz Kantor along with a new theater in his name that is being built in Krakow's Podgórze district.

TWENTY-FIRST CENTURY CABARET

While the U.S. has *Saturday Night Live* and the UK had *Monty Python*, Poland's preferred form of comedic entertainment is the modern, televised cabaret. One of the most legendary Polish cabarets was called *Potem* (After), which established the benchmark for quality abstract comedy and was the Polish equivalent of *Monty Python*. Today, some of cabaret's bigger names include **Maciej Stuhr**, who is the son of renowned actor Jerzy Stuhr and the creator of the *Po Żarcie* (Post Grub/Joke) cabaret. It was one of the acts that regularly performed at Krakow's Rotunda club, which would then launch TVP Channel 2's *Cabaret Scene* program in 2004, jump-starting the careers of many current comedy stars. Because modern cabarets focus on very Polish themes like politicians and institutions and are full of references to Polish pop culture, they are nearly impossible to translate to a foreign audience—not to mention the frequent use of wordplay and double entendres that simply cannot be translated. This explains why they are seldom exported outside Poland; however, within the country they are one of the most popular forms of entertainment for young and old alike.

International Festival of Street Theatre. Anakolut–Krakow Dance Theatre. July 11, 2010, Krakow.
(Milavanava Anastasiya / Shutterstock.com)

A.S.

FURTHER READING

A History of Polish Theater, 1939-1989: Spheres of Captivity and Freedom by Kazimierz Braun. Greenwood Press, 1996.

Insatiability by Stanislaw Ignacy Witkiewicz. Northwestern University Press, 1996.

A Journey Through Other Spaces: Essays and Manifestos, 1944-1990 by Tadeusz Kantor. University of California Press, 1993.

Tadeusz Kantor by Noel Witts. Routledge, 2010.

The Wedding by Stanislaw Wyspiański. Oberon Books, 1999.

CHAPTER 36

Capturing Reality on Film

"The dialogues are very bad, sir. In fact, there is no action.
Nothing happens."
(A quote about Polish films from Marek Piwowski's 1970 film *Rejs*)

In a telling and symbolic scene in **Krzysztof Kieślowski**'s film *Amator* (*Camera Buff*, 1979), the main character, an amateur filmmaker who has been observing and filming others, decides to turn the camera and focus it on himself. This can be understood as his realizing the importance of his own story, his own reality, as opposed to the stories of those he had chosen to film, some of which, by the way, have gotten him in trouble with his employers, local authorities, and even his closest family—but in a wider context it can be understood as Polish cinematography in general, whose most powerful films have been those which mainly focused on Polish reality, past or present, realistic or absurd. The films this amateur filmmaker makes, just as all post-WWII, state-funded Polish films made until the early 1990s, were subject to censorship by institutional authorities. And, ironically, many contemporary Poles say such good movies are never to be seen again. Any list of Polish films and Polish directors would be too short and superficial, thus only some of the many films that have made an impact in Poland are described below.

Communist-era cinema
Polish cinematography quickly rose from the ashes of World War II and turned to themes dealing with the people and everyday problems

of the last days wrought by the war. The first feature film after WWII was **Leonard Buczkowski**'s *Zakazane Piosenki* (*Forbidden Songs*, 1947), whose main "heroes" were actually Polish patriotic songs, full of catchy tunes and witty, sometimes hilarious lyrics which, sung about everyday life under German Nazi occupation, had helped Poles survive through those days with subtle patriotic defiance.

Andrzej Wajda's *Kanał* (*Canal*, 1957) was a vivid picture of the tragic heroism and ultimately futile attempt of a small group of Warsaw Uprising insurgents making a retreat from the Nazis through an underground labyrinth of reeking sewers in order to join the last fighting Home Army (AK) soldiers in Warsaw's downtown area. We observe strong, determined men and women trying to survive in a world that is falling apart, and it slowly becomes inevitable that their personal worlds are also doomed. Wajda succeeded in making a poignant commentary concerning the patriotically charged but ultimately failed Warsaw Uprising of 1944, one which cost hundreds of thousands of Polish lives, especially those of Warsaw's many civilians, and concerned the recent past he had been witness to. Another important film by Wajda was *Popiół i Diament* (*Ashes and Diamonds*, 1958), whose main "hero" is an AK soldier at the eve of the end of the war who must decide between trying to return to a "normal" life or remain faithful to the political and social ideals of the comrades he had fought alongside and lost in the Warsaw Uprising. The film is a reflection of the Polish nation's destiny as it dealt, more universally, with the internal conflict that took place in the hearts of the young generations to come—of men and women trying to adapt to the surrounding socio-political reality in Poland.

The 1970s brought about films depicting the total absurdity of everyday life in communist Poland. The most famous symbolically multi-layered film is **Marek Piwowski**'s *Rejs* (*A Trip Down the River*, 1970). His insightful commentary concerning Polish society is filled with absurd humor, hilarious dialogs, and situations among a group of people of various ranks and positions gathered on a cruise ship—like a picture of early 1970s Poland in a surrealistic, distorted nutshell.

The year 1976 marked the beginning of the "cinema of moral anxiety" (*kino moralnego niepokoju*), when several Polish directors demanded the right to openly speak about, make, and show films

concerning Poland's socio-political issues without being censored—
to present an individual's moral condition when he or she was con-
fronted with situations where an ethical choice had to be made, about
the hardships of everyday life under external, usually corrupt, author-
itarian pressure, and about staying true to one's ideals. No matter
what the decision, it seemed the individual always lost to the system.
An important first was Wajda's *Człowiek z Marmuru* (*Man of Marble*,
1977)—a political and historical study that reveals many aspects of
life in the 1950s and 1970s—with absolute governmental control over
everything that was filmed, publicly stated, and broadcast. Wajda
continued the story in *Człowiek z Żelaza* (*Man of Iron*, 1981), which
showed the momentous, historic changes taking place among the
shipyard workers in 1980 Gdańsk, with original footage of protests
against the government and the beginnings of free labor unions and
the Solidarity movement. Some of the other films representing this
new wave were *Przypadek* (*Blind Chance*, 1981, Krzysztof Kieślowski),
Kontrakt (*The Contract*, 1980, Krzysztof Zanussi), and *Kobieta Samotna*
(*A Lonely Woman*, 1981, Agnieszka Holland). This trend in Polish cinema ended with the introduction of martial law in 1981.

The 1980s are also known for the comedy films and TV series
made by **Stanisław Bareja**, most of which have gained cult status in
Poland. These films expose everyday human weaknesses that result
not only from mere human nature but, most decisively, from the comically distorted context in which the heroes and heroines have come
to live in. The many interdependencies between average people that
were hidden under several layers of meaning subtly criticized communism, which was shown as a socially complex plethora of totally
ridiculous rules, and only those who had mastered them and were
able to bend them in their own favor could achieve any sort of plau-
sible success. Bareja's most famous comedy of communist absurdities
is *Miś* (*Bear*, 1980), which shows many short scenes from Polish milk
bars, offices, and shops and reveals the starkly hilarious side of everyday existence in the 1980s.

An entirely different comedy from 1984 is the futuristic science
fiction *Seksmisja* (*Sexmission*, **Juliusz Machulski**). The action starts out
in 1991 and shoots forward to the year 2044, but again, everything is
set in a futuristic Poland. Two male scientists wake up from a planned

three-year hibernation experiment only to realize that actually fifty years have passed. Then they find out that a worldwide nuclear bomb has killed all men, that they are the only two living specimens carrying male genes, and that the planet has become a matriarchy ruled entirely by women. Made when communism was still going strong in Poland, this well-received, extremely funny comedy has been analyzed as a satirical commentary on Polish society, the effects of a totalitarian regime and the dangers of blind fanaticism, but it is the straightforward humor and witty dialogs in this Polish futuristic world which have gained *Seksmisja* cult status.

POLISH REALITY ONCE AGAIN

At the end of the 1980s Poland became flooded with millions of privately imported VCRs, one of which most every Polish family wanted to have at home in addition to a color TV set. This "video cassette culture" led to the opening up of large numbers of local video rentals, the consumption of B- and C-class movies, and the popularization of the Western way of life as seen in those movies. The onset of the 1990s, marked most significantly by the fall of communism, meant an end to censorship and the state's monopoly on distribution. The most significant movies made during those times commented on the newly budding, free market reality in Poland—with all its vices and virtues.

Psy (*Dogs*, 1992, **Władysław Pasikowski**) was one of the first movies to deal with Poland's at times rough transformation from communism to democracy among the ranks of the Security Service police, whose main job had been to penetrate and control all areas of Polish social and political life to ensure that communist principles were being maintained. The former Security Service officer, Franz Maurer, is lethally brutal but continues to abide by certain principles—his character introduced a new version of the Polish hero of the 1990s.

Other films that tried to reflect the changes taking place in an adapting society were *Młode Wilki* (*Young Wolves*, 1995, Jarosław Żamojda), about high school friends wanting to make quick and easy money by working for gangster-type bosses in a newly democratic Poland, and the joke-filled comedy *Kiler* (1997, Juliusz Machulski), which showed a comically simplified vision of the Polish gangster underworld. A turning point in this thematic matter was Krzysztof Krauze's *Dług*

(*Debt*, 1999)—considered one of the most important films of the time and inspired by a true story of two entrepreneurial businessmen from Warsaw, the film presented how they unwillingly became involved in the brutal mechanisms of a gangster-type acquaintance who was constantly raising their supposed financial debt.

Finally, *Dzień Świra* (*Day of the Wacko*, 2002, **Marek Koterski**) is a bittersweet yet genuinely funny comedy presenting the agony of the everyday life of a Polish language teacher, Adam (Adaś) Miauczyn-ski. We are witnesses to the main character's emotional inner dialogs and spitefully funny comments to what is happening around him. Adaś represents a disillusioned individual caught up in the superfi-cial consumerist society of the late 1990s, whose patriotic ideals end up meaning nothing. This painfully bitter yet quite accurate descrip-tion of Polish reality was all the more disheartening since Adam knew that life for him could have been different if he had adapted, that is conformed to, society's new rules. The lesson to be learned is that life in Poland had simply never been easy.

M.T.

FURTHER READING

The Red and the White: The Cinema of People's Poland by Paul Coates. Wallflower Press, 2004.

Wajda on Film: A Master's Notes by Andrzej Wajda. Acrobat Books, 1992.

CHAPTER 37

POLISH ARTISTS: FRAMED BY HISTORY

"Art is not afraid of propaganda—art is afraid of mediocrity."
–Jerzy Nowosielski

Try as it might, like literature, Polish art could not escape from Polish history. Each of its movements began as a reaction to the country's political situation, or as a reaction to that earlier reaction, and no individual Polish artist was truly immune from his or her surroundings. While many Polish artists studied and were influenced by parallel artistic movements in Western Europe, particularly France and Italy, Polish art is distinctly its own entity, with its own distinguished, troubled, and often larger than life personalities.

JAN MATEJKO AND ROMANTICISM
Some of the best-known Polish art and artists were products of the Enlightenment and the Romantic Movement that followed. Much of the art produced in the last years of independent Poland was under the patronage of King Stanisław August Poniatowski, who introduced a new system of art education that brought Polish art closer to European trends. Particularly popular were Italian and French Classicism, and later Viennese and English portraiture.

Though Romantic tendencies had been in the air since the final partition of 1795, the Romantic era of Polish art officially began in 1822, with the publication of Adam Mickiewicz's *Poetry* (see Chapter

Stańczyk, by Jan Matejko, on postage stamp, circa 1968
(Boris15 / Shutterstock.com)

34), and lasted until the failure of the January Uprising in 1863. While the period featured a variety of styles and themes, its overarching attribute was a patriotic and pro-independence stance. Themes were ideological in nature and portrayed in a realistic style, following trends in the art of Western Europe of that time, particularly French Romanticism. Created in an era when Poland did not exist (see Chapter 42), Romantic art took it upon itself to uphold Polish patriotism, often throwing in patriotic allusions in Biblical or classical scenes. Historical events, portraits and natural landscapes were ever-present, though the public of the time demanded accurate historical depictions. Nonetheless, compared to later realism, the Romantic artists portrayed historic events in a highly idealized way.

Polish Romantic art had a tendency toward the epic—both literally, in the vast scale of some paintings, as well in its subject matter, which often depicted heroic battle scenes and the most magnificent and tragic moments of Polish history. The best example of this trend is the work of **Jan Matejko**. Just as one cannot mention Romantic literature without mentioning Mickiewicz, the most significant figure in Romantic art was decidedly Matejko. He is best known for his historical battle scenes, such as *Kościuszko at Racławice*, where each of the dozens of soldiers depicted wear exaggerated expressions and are shown in dramatic poses. In Matejko's works and those of others of the era, even the animals are rendered with expressions of sorrow for the Polish tragedy.

After 1863, Polish art began to step away from Romantic depictions of history and began to favor truth and objectivity over the ideal. Contemporary issues became more important than historical ones, and the common man became the principal subject matter. As Polish art moved toward Realism and Naturalism, everyday scenes depicting the gentry as well as the peasant classes became popular. From the 1870s, Impressionism and Symbolism took hold in Poland, with a partial adaptation of French Impressionism, though the styles were decidedly Polish. The works of Jacek Malczewski and Józef Chełmoński are very representative of Polish art of this era.

STANISŁAW WYSPIAŃSKI

By the turn of the twentieth century, Polish art had almost succeeded in shedding its Romantic tendencies, and the transformation was completed by the *Młoda Polska* (Young Poland) movement. Like their literary contemporaries (see Chapter 34), the artists valued the autonomy of art above all—art that was not in the service of any causes, but existed for its own sake. Because of this, the art of that era, particularly at the beginning, was often humorous and bordered on the absurd, though it was also stylistically quite diverse, with some similarities to Impressionism.

One of the most influential and representative artists of the turn of the twentieth century is **Stanisław Wyspiański**, who was also an accomplished dramatist, stage designer, poet, and writer. A pupil of Matejko, Wyspiański departed from Romanticism and represented a tendency toward Art Nouveau and modernism, particularly in his striking portraits, which are some of the most splendid in Polish portraiture as a whole. He is also known for his dramatic works in stained glass, such as the windows he originally designed for the Wawel Cathedral in Krakow—which were deemed too shocking by Church authorities for the actual cathedral and never installed there. Today, you can see them in Krakow's Wyspiański Pavilion in the heart of the city.

Other significant artists working alongside Wyspiański include Józef Mehoffer, who also produced stunning stained glass works; Leon Wyczółkowski, Józef Pankiewicz, Olga Boznańska, Wojciech Weiss, Jacek Malczewski, and many others whose works hang in museums all over Poland and throughout the world.

WITKACY

One of the most interesting figures in Polish art of any era was **Stanisław Ignacy Witkiewicz**, or **Witkacy** as he was known to his friends. Witkacy studied under Józef Mehoffer in Krakow, and is associated with a movement called Formism, which valued form over content. In addition to painting, he was an accomplished poet and playwright. However, one of Witkacy's most memorable accomplishments is a series of paintings he did from 1924, when he founded "The S.I. Witkiewicz Portrait Painting Firm" in jest, in which he would take commissions to paint people's portraits and then sign them with his name and a list of the narcotics he was on while painting. His favorite was peyote, though he was also quite fond of cocaine, opium, morphine, hashish, or just plain caffeine. He took his own life when he learned of the Soviet invasion of Poland on September 17, 1939.

Speaking of interesting artists, a contemporary and friend of Witkacy whose work is highly representative of the Polish interwar period was **Zofia Stryjeńska**. Her style was mostly Art Deco, though her biography is just as colorful as her paintings. She studied at a Polish fine art school for women, but her dream was to enroll at the Academy of Fine Arts in Munich, which did not admit women. So she took her brother's name, applied and was accepted (a feat in itself as the competition was quite tough), and disguised herself as a man while at the academy. She produced the bulk of her work between the two wars, was forced to emigrate with the imposition of communism, and spent the rest of her life in relative obscurity in Geneva.

In that same period, one of the few Polish artists to gain worldwide fame was another woman, **Tamara de Lempicka**, though she spent the bulk of her life abroad (see Chapter 48).

COMMUNIST ERA

Though Witkacy died in relative obscurity, his works, both in the theater and in art, were popularized by another artist and theater director, **Tadeusz Kantor**. Today Kantor is known more for his theater work (see Chapter 35), but as an artist he was at the forefront of the Polish avant-garde of the communist era.

Under communism, the official doctrine regarding art was socialist realism. One Polish artist who embraced this style early on but managed to make it his own was **Andrzej Wróblewski**, who rejected such conventions as Cubism or Surrealism and instead pushed for a clear, photographic style of art, the kind that could hang in factory halls and be embraced by the common man. Though he died in an accident at age twenty-nine, Wróblewski was a prolific artist and managed to produce over 150 paintings and hundreds of drawings, many of which can be found in Polish museums. Later communist era art was dictated by the *Wprost* (direct) group from Krakow, who admired Wróblewski but opposed the totalitarian system and its indirectness.

THE POLISH POSTER

In addition to painting and sculpture, since the 1950s Polish graphic artists have especially been known for their poster art. In fact, the **Polish School of Posters** is an entire genre in itself, with many adherents throughout the world. Posters have been used in Poland for artistic and advertising purposes since the turn of the century, but under communism they were also often used to mock propaganda and in protest. An iconic example would be the "High Noon" Solidarity poster designed by **Tomasz Sarnecki** in 1989 for the first semi-free elections, or the Solidarity logo itself, designed by **Jerzy Janiszewski**.

A.S.

FURTHER READING

Contemporary Polish Posters in Full Color by Joseph Czestochowski. Dover Publications, 1979.

Jan Matejko by Juliusz Starzynski. Arkady Publishers, 1979.

Out Looking In: Early Modern Polish Art, 1890-1918 by Jan Cavanaugh. University of California Press, 2000.

Tamara De Lempicka by Laura Claridge. Bloomsbury Paperbacks, 2001.

CHAPTER 38

Composers & Music: More than Chopin

"Sometimes I can only groan, and suffer, and pour out my despair at the piano!"
–Fryderyk Chopin on Russia's domination of Poland

The musical tradition in Poland can be traced back to the Middle Ages, when, like art, it was usually connected with religious tradition. Later, the golden age of Polish music took place during the Renaissance, where musical education flourished in Krakow in particular. In modern times, Polish music is largely associated with the Romantics, and Chopin in particular. However, Polish music continued to evolve after Chopin, and is littered with fascinating and talented individuals.

Maria Szymanowska
Before Chopin was even born, **Maria Szymanowska** was one of Europe's first celebrated virtuoso pianists, touring throughout Europe and Russia, often performing for royalty, while also composing pieces for piano, chamber, and voice. She's also recorded as one of the first (if not the first) virtuoso pianists who played from memory. In Weimar, she famously performed for Goethe, who called her "the charming Almighty of Sound." Though she wrote over 100 pieces for piano, they are little known to this day, with the exception of her short

Fryderyk Chopin (mrHanson / Shutterstock.com)

etudes, dances, mazurkas, and nocturnes. Her work is very much considered a prelude to Chopin and the Romantics. Ironically (or perhaps not), one of her daughters, Celina, ended up marrying Romantic poet Adam Mickiewicz.

FRYDERYK CHOPIN

It's no stretch to say that **Fryderyk Chopin** is Poland's best-known composer, as well as one of the greatest Romantic composers the world has seen. Born in Żelazowa Wola near Warsaw to a Polonized French father and Polish mother, he was surrounded by both music and Polish language and culture from an early age thanks to his parents. His older sister began teaching him the piano as a child, and by age seven he was performing concerts for the public and publishing Polonaises. By age eleven, he was performing for the Russian Tsar.

Chopin spent his teenage years in Warsaw, though he would travel to the countryside in the summers, where he absorbed folk culture and melodies that he would later use as inspiration. He studied at the Warsaw Conservatory, after which he made his debut in Vienna in 1829. This opened the door for him to tour Europe, and in 1830 he set out on what was to be his first longer trip from home. However, historical events made it his final trip, and the last time he would step foot on Polish soil.

A month later, the November Uprising broke out, and as Chopin heard news of its failure he was overcome with grief for his homeland, as well as the realization that he may not be able to return. He arrived in Paris the following year, where his first performances and publications were met with wide acclaim. Chopin soon became a star of both the Polish expatriate scene in Paris, centered around the Hôtel Lambert (see Chapter 46), as well as with the Parisian artistic and musical elite of that time, often performing in well-known salons. It was there that he began his ten-year relationship with French writer George Sand after an unsuccessful engagement to a Polish noblewoman. However, throughout his life his health had always been poor, and his condition worsened over the years to the point where he could scarcely travel, only spending longer time abroad in London and Scotland in 1848.

Chopin would go on to compose and publish hundreds of mazurkas, etudes, nocturnes, waltzes, polonaises, piano sonatas, and other works, mostly for solo piano, though he seldom performed concerts due to his poor health. In 1849, his illness taking a turn for the worse, he asked his sister to come to Paris one last time. Chopin died at the age of just thirty-nine, likely of a type of tuberculosis, though the exact cause is still debated today. Though Chopin would never return to his homeland, in correspondence, attitude, and spirit he remained thoroughly a Pole until his death.

CONTEMPORARY COMPOSERS

While Chopin placed Polish composers on the world map, several of his followers continued the tradition. In the world of opera, **Stanisław Moniuszko** is credited with inventing the Polish national style. He is best known for *The Haunted Manor*, a comedic opera with nationalistic overtones (like most works written during the Partitions), with a Romantic musical style. Needless to say, it was banned by the Russian authorities.

Ignacy Jan Paderewski followed closely in the footsteps of Chopin, also choosing the piano as his main instrument, and pioneered the Polish neoromantic style. In addition to his immense talents as a composer and pianist, Paderewski was known as a statesman, talented orator, a patriot and intellectual, and was fluent in seven languages—which came in handy when performing over a thousand concerts all over the world. But unlike many composers who gained fame only after their deaths, Paderewski was a turn of the century pop star, particularly in the U.S. His performances would regularly sell out, and famously one night in New York City he managed to compete with himself, when both a performance of his opera and his own recital (in Carnegie Hall, no less) sold out. To top it all off, he also served as the Polish prime minister and minister of foreign affairs for one year after the country regained its independence—though after that brief stint in politics, it's no surprise that he returned to musical performance and composition soon thereafter.

In addition to Paderewski, another Polish composer stands out at the turn of the twentieth century: **Karol Szymanowski**. Szymanowski best represents the Young Poland style also seen in Polish literature and art at that time (see Chapters 34 & 37). Like Paderewski, he traveled extensively throughout Europe and the U.S. during his career, and also took a break to pursue another passion. His, however, was literature, and he wrote a novel that was unfortunately lost when Warsaw burned in 1939.

In 1933, two great Polish composers were born: **Krzysztof Penderecki** and **Henryk Mikołaj Górecki**. Penderecki is best known for his symphonies and orchestral pieces, most notably *Threnody to the Victims of Hiroshima* and *St. Luke Passion,* as well as his opera, *The Devils of Loudun*—not to mention his pieces that have appeared in film soundtracks, including in *The Exorcist, The Shining,* and several David Lynch movies. Górecki, on the other hand, did not gain fame abroad until his Symphony No. 3 (*Symphony of Sorrowful Songs*) became a best seller around the world—about a decade after it was well known in Poland. At home, he was always at the forefront of the Polish avant-garde.

Two other contemporary Polish composers are best known for their work in film music. **Wojciech Kilar** has written scores for hundreds of films, including those of Krzysztof Kieślowski, Krzysztof Zanussi, Andrzej Wajda, and Roman Polanski, though perhaps his most famous is the soundtrack to Francis Ford Coppola's *Dracula*. **Zbigniew Preisner** has also composed scores for Krzysztof Kieślowski, as well as working in television and composing several well-received orchestral works.

ALL THAT JAZZ

During the interwar period, Poland was swinging to Gershwin and the likes with the rest of the world, in addition to local Polish and Jewish acts. However, the introduction of communism suppressed anything that did not fit into the socialist realist mold, including jazz, swing, and any music that involved a fair bit of hip shaking. This means that between 1945 and the thaw of 1956, marching bands and non-patriotic classical composers had the approval of the authorities, while jazz, the music of the enemy, had to go underground. Nonetheless, it flourished in the private homes and hidden salons of the heppest cats of every town, and in the late 1940s the group **Melomani** emerged to become the center of the underground jazz scene—and managed to do it with almost no exposure to Western jazz music.

From the mid-50s, jazz as a genre was once again officially allowed and began to be broadcast on the radio and jazz ensembles formed en masse, along with the first jazz festivals (some of which survive to this day). Jazz became extremely popular not just for its own sake, but because it was one of the only expressions of the "decadent West" that was allowed. As the access to jazz increased, so did the talents, and the stars of Poland's jazz era of the 60s and 70s were born, most notably pianist **Krzysztof Komeda**—who was also an eminent composer, writing the scores of Polanski's *Rosemary's Baby* and several others—trumpeter **Tomasz Stanko**, whose Stanko Quintet reached legendary status in Europe in the early 70s, and violinist **Zbigniew Seifert**, who was originally part of Stanko's quintet before becoming one of the greatest European jazz violinists until his tragic death at age thirty-two. Many Polish jazz musicians would make their mark on American jazz as well in the 70s and 80s, including **Michał Urbaniak**, who released his groundbreaking album *Fusion* in the U.S., as well as **Adam Makowicz**, who now lives in Toronto.

THE MUSIC BIZ TODAY

In many cases, some of the historical jazz clubs of the 50s and 60s exist as rock venues today, where mostly international acts perform, such as Warsaw's Stodoła and Krakow's Alchemia—though some of the biggest and oldest European jazz festivals do still take place in Poland. As a whole, today's Polish music scene and musicians are as diverse as in most European countries, and there's no one such entity called "Polish music," but rather Polish representatives of just about every genre, from classical to rock to hip hop. Some of the best (or at least most popular) acts can be seen annually at the **Open'er Festival** in Gdynia or the **Jarocin Festival**, which began as Poland's answer to Woodstock in the 1970s and continues to showcase Polish and foreign rock and punk talents.

A.S.

FURTHER READING

Beats of Freedom (film) by Leszek Gnoinski and Wojciech Slota, 2010.

Chopin: Prince of the Romantics by Adam Zamoyski. HarperCollins Publishers, 2011.

Chopin's Letters by Frederic Chopin and E. L. Voynich. Dover Publications, 1988.

Polish Music Since Szymanowski by Adrian Thomas. Cambridge University Press, 2008.

A Polish Renaissance by Bernard Jacobson. Phaidon Press, 1996.

A Romantic Century in Polish Music by Maja Trochimczyk. Moonrise Press, 2010.

Szymanowski on Music by Karol Szymanowski. Toccata Press, 2010.

CHAPTER 39

SCIENTISTS: POLONIUM & MORE

"A scientist in his laboratory is not a mere technician: he is also a child confronting natural phenomena that impress him as though they were fairy tales."
–Marie Skłodowska-Curie

Throughout history, Poles have made enormous contributions to science—though unfortunately they remain largely unknown as Poles outside of Poland. How many non-Poles know Nicolaus Copernicus as Mikołaj Kopernik? Or that Marie Curie was born Maria Skłodowska in Warsaw? Or in recent history, that it was thanks to the efforts of Polish codebreakers that the Enigma machine was cracked, which was one of the main contributions to the Allied victory of World War II? Or that one of the oldest universities in the world, and the second oldest university in Central Europe, is Krakow's Jagiellonian University? Often, these stories have remained hidden because Polish scientists and academics had to work in less than ideal conditions during occupations or were forced into exile, continuing a tradition of scholarly exchange between Poland and the rest of Europe that began in the fourteenth century and continues to this day.

COPERNICUS OR KOPERNIK?
Nicolaus Copernicus is perhaps one of the best-known astronomers in history. Born Mikołaj Kopernik in Toruń, which was at that time a town within the Kingdom of Poland, to Polish-German parents, Copernicus spoke Polish, German, and Latin fluently, though he would end up publishing his works in Latin, the language of

academia in those days, and thus he is known by his Latinized name today.

Copernicus studied at the University of Krakow (now the Jagiellonian University), where he received the foundations of the mathematical and astronomical knowledge of the day, as well as a grounding in philosophy and the humanities. He would then go on to study law in Bologna and medicine in Padua. Copernicus traveled between Italy and Poland several times before settling in Warmia, northeastern Poland, where as a clergyman he would serve as the economic administrator for his bishop, lead Polish troops while defending Warmia from the Teutonic Knights, and occasionally treat patients as a medical doctor, all while making regular astronomical observations and working on his revolutionary heliocentric theory.

He would go on to make numerous astronomical observations and discover the variability of earth's orbital eccentricity, create a reformed calendar, and of course, publish his most important discovery in *De revolutionibus orbium coelestium* (*On the Revolutions of the Heavenly Spheres*), which turned scientific thought upside down and discredited the previous geocentric model that had been relied on for millennia.

MARIE SKŁODOWSKA-CURIE

Born Maria Skłodowska in Warsaw, **Marie Skłodowska-Curie** is responsible for a staggering number of firsts: she was the first person to ever receive two Nobel prizes (in physics and chemistry), the first person to describe the phenomenon of radioactivity, the first woman to earn a PhD in a scientific field in Europe as well as the first woman to win a Nobel Prize in physics. She discovered two elements, was the first female professor at the University of Paris, and has served as a role model for countless women in the sciences.

Skłodowska-Curie began her education in a somewhat unconventional way. Unable to enroll in a normal university in Russian-occupied Poland because she was a woman, she attended the clandestine Flying University in Warsaw—so called because it had a habit of moving from place to place (usually private residences) in order to evade the authorities. After a few years of studying, working, and training in a chemical laboratory run by her cousin, Marie had saved enough money to join her sister in Paris, where the latter was studying

Marie Skłodowska-Curie. (fmua / Shutterstock.com)

medicine. She enrolled at the University of Paris and studied physics, chemistry, and mathematics while barely eking out a living to support herself. She met Pierre Curie, an instructor and physicist, soon after graduation, when he provided her with a laboratory. As they began to work together they grew closer; he proposed marriage and, unable to receive an academic position in Poland because she was a woman, Marie decided to take up his offer, stay in Paris, and pursue a PhD.

Together with Pierre, she would go on to discover the radioactive elements radium and polonium (named in honor of her homeland), develop the concept of radioactivity, and receive a Nobel Prize in physics together with Henri Becquerel in 1903. After her husband's death in 1906, Marie took his chair at the university and would go on to create and head the Radium Institute and isolate the element radium, for which she received a second Nobel Prize, this time in chemistry, in 1911. Marie had two daughters with Pierre, one of whom, Irène Joliot-Curie, also received a Nobel Prize in chemistry. She died at the age of sixty-six from cancer due to her long-time exposure to radiation.

Jan Szczepanik

Dubbed the "Polish Edison" (though with a rather enviable mustache), **Jan Szczepanik** was an inventor who contributed greatly to the science of filmmaking, photography, and television. Some of his several hundred patents include the silk ballistic vest, the telectroscope (the subject of a short story by Mark Twain), sound recording and playback equipment, a colorimeter, and an electric rifle—which doesn't include his unpatented work on helicopter and submarine concepts.

Kazimierz Funk

Another Polish scientist working in emigration was **Kazimierz Funk**, a biochemist credited with the discovery of vitamins. Born in Warsaw, Funk studied in Switzerland and would go on to live and work Paris, Berlin, and London before immigrating to the United States in 1915, though he would return to work in Warsaw and Paris until the outbreak of war, when he moved to the U.S. for good. Funk studied the nutritional components of such diseases as scurvy and rickets, and determined that they were caused by a deficiency of a substance he called "vitamines"—later renamed vitamins. He would also go on to make important contributions in the fields of hormones, cancer, diabetes, and ulcers.

Stefan Bryła

Among Polish engineers, **Stefan Bryła** is probably the best known. Born in Krakow, Bryła graduated from the Lviv University of Technology, where he then worked as a professor, followed by the Warsaw University of Technology. His most significant contribution was the design of the first welded road bridge in the world, which spanned the Słudwia River. He was also a pioneer in high-rise building methods, designing the still standing (after postwar renovations) Prudential building in Warsaw. In 1943, he was arrested by the Nazis for his clandestine teaching activities, and executed together with his family.

Leopold Infeld

A prominent Polish scientist also of Jewish descent was **Leopold Infeld**, a contemporary of Albert Einstein. Born in Krakow when it was still a part of the Austro-Hungarian Empire, Infeld studied physics at the Jagiellonian University as well as the University of Berlin, where he met Einstein. He then worked with Einstein at Princeton University before the outbreak of World War II, where they wrote *The Evolution of Physics* together, and then immigrated to Canada. After the war, Infeld became a peace activist and staunchly opposed the use of nuclear weapons, for which he was criticized and labeled a communist, particularly when he returned to Poland in 1950. Nonetheless, he felt that his contributions were needed more in postwar Poland, and he would teach physics to a new generation of scholars at the University of Warsaw until his death.

MARIAN REJEWSKI

Many people have heard of the role of Bletchley Park during World War II, and many more of Alan Turing, but the name **Marian Rejewski** is still quite obscure, even in Poland. However, the former would not have succeeded if it were not for the latter. Rejewski, a mathematician and cryptologist, was the first person to crack the infamous Enigma machine used by the Germans. Rejewski was recruited by the Polish Cipher Bureau while still in college in 1929. In 1932, he began work on the Enigma I, a state of the art (at that time) German cipher machine. In the course of breaking the cipher, Rejewski pioneered several mathematical codebreaking methods, including one that was described as "the theorem that won World War II." With the war imminent, the Polish Cipher Bureau informed the French and British about their discoveries in July 1939, and the latter would base the Ultra project at Bletchley Park on the work of Rejewski and his colleagues **Jerzy Różycki** and **Henryk Zygalski**. When war broke out, Rejewski fled to France and then Britain to continue helping with the codebreaking efforts. His contributions remained unknown for decades until documentations about the Ultra program began to be declassified.

RECENT CONTRIBUTIONS

Though we already know of the great contributions Polish pilots made to British aviation in World War II (see Chapter 9), **Władysław Fiszdon** was an aerodynamist, aviator, and mathematician who made scientific contributions as well. Working at the Lublin Aircraft Plant at the outbreak of war, he fled to France when the plant was bombed early on. When France was invaded, Fiszdon fled once again, this time to Britain, where he would work to modernize and improve the airplanes used by the Royal Air Force during the war. After the war, he returned to Poland to rejoin his wife and son, who had been forced to stay behind, and continued to direct research for the Aviation Institute in Warsaw.

Marian Kryszewski made significant contributions to the field of polymer science. Perhaps his most important contribution to Polish science was the co-founding of the Center of Molecular and Macromolecular Studies of the Polish Academy of Sciences in 1972, which resulted in pioneering research into electric conductivity and photoconduction.

Finally, Polish astronomer **Aleksander Wolszczan,** another graduate of the Nicolaus Copernicus University, discovered the first extrasolar planets in 1992 together with American astronomer Dale Frail. Wolszczan is currently a professor at Pennsylvania State University.

A.S.

FURTHER READING

The Book Nobody Read: Chasing the Revolutions of Nicolaus Copernicus by Owen Gingerich. Walker & Company, 2004.

Enigma: The Battle for the Code by Hugh Sebag-Montefiore. Wiley, 2004.

Marie Curie and Her Daughters: The Private Lives of Science's First Family by Shelley Emling. Palgrave Macmillan, 2012.

Marie Curie: A Life by Susan Quinn. Simon & Schuster, 1995.

CHAPTER 40

SPORTS & ATHLETES: "POLSKA GOOOOOOOOOL!"

"Human life is like a giant sports game,
in which we are both participants and spectators."
–Antoni Gołubiew, historian and writer

If you were to take the graffiti scrawled on suburban Polish buildings seriously, you would think that club football (soccer for you Americans) is the most important—nay, the only—sport that matters in Poland. While some Poles do take their football very seriously, to the point where local rivalries and hooliganism are serious public issues, most are content to cheer for the national team every few years, or for the Polish-born stars playing on the German national team (also a mixed point of pride and contention). Many are just happy to cheer for whatever sport a Polish team is playing, as long as it's on the TV of the local pub.

In addition to spectating on sports, Poles are a rather active bunch themselves, especially in the summer months. In the parks, you will see plenty of adults as well as children running, biking, rollerblading (yes, some are still stuck in the 80s), shooting hoops, kicking around a ball, playing tennis or badminton, or perhaps a friendly game of chess following a walk if they're in their golden years. Swimming is also extremely popular, though most public pools are indoor ones, as the weather does not permit outdoor swimming for most of the year. Schoolchildren participate in mandatory physical education classes throughout their primary and secondary school years, in addition to playing their favorite sport on an after school team. Come winter, Polish, Slovakian, and increasingly Alpine ski resorts swarm with Poles zooming down on skis or snowboards.

While football is the most popular sport in Poland by a long shot, with hundreds of professional and semi-professional teams (the association football league is known as the *Ekstraklasa*), there are plenty of other sports that tend to gain popularity when Poles do well in them. Throughout recent history there have been several phenomenal athletes who not only broke records in international arenas, but also made their whole nation excited over their sport, including some obscure ones like handball or ski jumping. Sports fans or not, most Poles know at least some of the following names by heart.

A TALE OF TWO SPRINTERS

Two women were born in 1946 that would change the face of Polish track and field, though one's story unfortunately ends in tragedy. Irena Szewińska and Ewa Kłobukowska were both phenomenal Polish sprinters during the golden age of Polish track and field. Together, they ran the 4x100m relay during the 1964 Olympic Games in Tokyo and won gold for their nation. However, after that historic event their paths would take very different turns.

Irena Szewińska was born Irena Kirszenstein in what was then called Leningrad, USSR, to Jewish Polish parents who soon after returned to Poland, where she grew up. At eighteen, she competed in her first Olympic Games where, in addition to the afore-mentioned relay gold, she swept up a silver each for the 200m and long jump. Szewińska would go on to have one of the most illustrious track and field careers ever, winning a total of seven medals (three gold) as well as ten European Championship medals (five gold) between 1964 and '78. To this day, she is the only athlete, male or female, who has held world records in the 100, 200, and 400m events. Oh, and to top it all off, she is the only runner in history so far to win medals in four consecutive Olympics—during which time she also managed to give birth to a son!

The story of **Ewa Kłobukowska** begins in a similar fashion. Born the same year in Warsaw, after winning gold in the 1964 relay (and bronze in the 100m) she set a world record for the 100m the following year. In the '66 European Championships, she took two golds for the relay and 100m and a silver in the 200m. However, it was in 1967 that her career would take a downturn, when she was slated to compete in the European Cup in Kiev. That year, the IOC had implemented mandatory gender testing, and Kłobukowska would fail—falsely, it turned out years later. Further studies would determine she had an inactive chromosome that resulted in a false positive, but by that time her career was already ruined when she was barred from all future competitions. Her disqualification was a real shock to her Polish fans, particularly because it came from Poland's "allies"—the USSR and GDR—whose runners Kłobukowska had beaten numerous times. Kłobukowska was stripped of her medals and the matter was hushed in the typical communist fashion. It wasn't until 1992 that officials admitted she was wrongly disqualified—though to this day she has not received an official apology.

A POLITICAL KNOCKOUT

To lighten the mood a bit, next we have a tale of boxing and politics, two subjects that usually do not mix (unless you count the verbal matches held regularly between Poland's two main parties). Another veteran of the Tokyo Olympics, **Jerzy Kulej** won a gold medal each in '64 and '68 in the light welterweight boxing division—the only Polish boxer to ever do so. After stepping out of the ring, Kulej took to the podium, first joining the Communist Party until it collapsed in 1990. In 1993, he initially ran for Parliament unsuccessfully as a member of the Polish Beer-Lovers' Party (yes, that's right—see Chapter 41 for more). He was finally elected in 2001 as a member of the Democratic Left Alliance. In addition to politics, Kulej had a short-lived career in film and as a sportscaster—hardly a lightweight.

THE YEAR ENGLAND WOULD RATHER FORGET

If you're a hardcore football fan, you may recall the qualifying campaign for the 1974 World Cup with either pride or sorrow, depending on whether you root for Poland or England. The fateful day was October 17, 1973; the place was Wembley Stadium in London. The teams were England—who had won the Cup in '66—and Poland—completely unknown on the world stage. The stakes were nothing less than the privilege to play in the 1974 World Cup. And the score ended up being 1–1, something no one expected, even though the

English team had already lost 2–0 to Poland in a previous qualifier. In the end, England was eliminated, and Poland had secured its second appearance in football's most important tournament.

England should not have felt too bad, though—in the actual tournament Poland would take third place, beating Argentina, Italy, Brazil, and Sweden before finally succumbing to West Germany (the eventual champions) in a heartbreaking 1–0. Of course, while Poland had a phenomenal squad that year, it was striker **Grzegorz Lato** that can take much credit for how far Poland made it. He scored seven goals in the tournament and won the Golden Boot to boot. Lato was also on the squad when they again placed third in the 1982 World Cup, tying with eventual champions Italy and beating France and Belgium but losing to the Italians the second time around in the semi-finals.

Unfortunately, things went downhill for the Polish National Team after that. 1986 was the last World Cup Poland would play until 2002, in which the only team they managed to beat was the U.S. The next hope for the white and reds came in 2008, when they qualified for the European Championships. Unfortunately, Poland's tradition of losing to Germany in the most painful way possible continued—this time the only goals scored against the Polish side were by Polish-born German star **Lukas Podolski**, who obviously seemed conflicted about his victory when he donned a Polish jersey after the match.

In 2012 Poland co-hosted the European Championships with Ukraine. While the tournament as a whole was a success, neither host made it out of the group stage, with Poland suffering a particularly upsetting defeat to the Czech Republic after showing potential in earlier matches.

MAKING TENNIS POPULAR

Another star from the golden age of Polish sports is **Wojciech Fibak**, whose weapon of choice was the racquet. In 1978, he won the Australian Open doubles, and he reached a no. 3 world ranking the following year, though the height of his career was undoubtedly 1980. That year he would reach the quarterfinals at the French and U.S. Open and at Wimbledon. Perhaps what was most interesting about Fibak, however, was his effect on tennis in Poland. Before Fibak, tennis as a sport was not very popular; after Fibak, every child in Poland begged for a tennis racquet as a communion or Christmas gift. It is mostly thanks to his legacy that Poland has tennis stars on the world stage today. Fibak would even go on to use some of his winnings to establish the Polish Tennis Club, as well as acquiring one of the largest collections of Polish art outside of Poland.

THE MUSTACHE FLIES

For a country without any real Alpine-class ski mountains, Poland sure has had a soft spot for ski jumping since **Adam Małysz** came on the scene in 1995. The ski jumper was known as much for his style as for his facial hair, earning the nickname "the flying mustache" early on. Though he had several impressive initial wins, he really exploded on the world stage at the 2002 Salt Lake City Olympics, where he took a silver and a bronze home for Poland. In 2010 he would repeat the feat, this time with two silvers. However, it was the World Ski Championships where he would really shine, taking home four golds, a silver and a bronze between 2001 and 2011, the year he retired. Winning three World Cups in a row was a first, and it gained him numerous fans in Poland and brought ski jumping to new heights of popularity in the country.

RECENT ATHLETES TO KNOW

If you ask a Pole today which Polish athletes they admire, you're likely to hear at least one of the following names: champion heavyweight boxer **Tomasz Adamek**, Robert Kubica, Justyna Kowalczyk, Agnieszka Radwańska, and most recently, Jerzy Janowicz. The latter two are a legacy of Fibak's impact on Polish tennis. While the U.S. has the Williams sisters, Poles are equally proud of **Agnieszka Radwańska** and her younger sister, **Urszula**, both native Cracovians. **Robert Kubica**, on the other hand, is a rising star in Formula One racing, while **Justyna Kowalczyk** is a cross-country skier and the only one in history to win at the Olympic Games, World Championships, World Cup, and Tour de Ski.

A.S.

FURTHER READING

Behind the Curtain: Travels in Eastern European Football by Jonathan Wilson. Orion, 2006.

CHAPTER 41

PROTESTORS, REBELS, AND RABBLE-ROUSERS

"How can you take a police officer seriously when he asks you: 'Why did you participate in an illegal meeting of dwarfs?'"
–Waldemar "Major" Fydrych

As long as there have been reasons to protest, Poles have risen to the occasion in spectacular fashion. Even in the English colonies of the seventeenth century, it was Poles who held the first ever strike in the New World. More recently, protestors and rebels have found interesting, unique, hilarious, and sometimes downright absurd ways to showcase the issues important to them, and the rebellious tradition proudly continues to this day.

THE FIGHTING MOUSTACHE

When speaking of Polish protesters, rebels, and rabble-rousers, it's impossible not to mention the most famous one of them all, Nobel Laureate and former president **Lech Wałęsa**. While you can read the background of the events of 1980 in Chapter 10, the story of the electrician-turned-revolutionary hero is quite interesting in itself. It begins in 1970, the year Wałęsa first marked himself as a troublemaker when he helped organize illegal strikes in the Lenin Shipyard in Gdańsk, where he had worked since 1967. As the economic situation worsened, he continued to campaign for worker's rights, which led to his

Lech Wałęsa speaks at a press conference on November 30, 1989 in London. (David Fowler / Shutterstock.com)

firing in 1976, and his continued surveillance by the secret police and regular arrests. However, he only ramped up his activism and when the right moment finally came in August 1980, he would lead the most important strike in Polish history. On August 14, ex-employee Wałęsa hopped the fence and joined the disgruntled workers of the Lenin Shipyards. For two weeks they would draw up demands, help organize similar strikes and continue their activism while receiving food and supplies from sympathetic friends and strangers through the shipyard's fence.

The strikes spread throughout Poland despite the authorities' attempts to keep all news quiet. On August 31, Wałęsa and the other strikers finally got their way: the strikers and the communist authorities signed the Gdańsk Agreement, which not only allowed future strikes but legalized the formation of an independent trade union. And so Solidarity was born, with Wałęsa at the helm as its chairman. As news of Solidarity's success leaked west, this also thrust Wałęsa into the international spotlight, where he would find himself again in 1983 when he was awarded the Nobel Peace Prize after spending eleven months in jail under martial law.

Wałęsa would bide his time and continue working underground throughout the 80s, until his next chance came in 1989, when the government agreed to enter into the Round Table Negotiations. Once again at the lead, Wałęsa fought for the relegalization of Solidarity and the chance for its participation in national elections. The rest, of course, is history, and on December 9, 1990, Wałęsa was elected the first noncommunist president of Poland in fifty years (despite his motto of "I don't want to, but I must"). He would serve from 1990-1995, a time of incredibly rapid social and economic transition (see Chapter 11).

MEET THE MAJOR

One of the most effective anticommunist campaigns in the entire Soviet Bloc had a simple strategy: make 'em laugh. This is exactly what **Waldemar "Major" Fydrych** and his cohorts did in the 1980s, and the results were not only hilarious, but quite effective as well. The Major created and led the Orange Alternative (Pomarańczowa Alternatywa), a student group whose goal was to showcase the absurdity of the communist regime. They began by painting little orange dwarves in the spots where authorities had painted over antigovernment slogans throughout the city. They expanded their activities to all kinds of happenings and pranks that seemed absurd and harmless at face value, which meant that by arresting Orange Alternative members, the authorities just made themselves look rather silly. Examples include members handing out toilet paper and sanitary pads on the street—a harmless gesture in most places, but in 1987 Poland it was a clear protest against the lack of consumer goods—or hanging posters with the slogan "Citizen, help the militia, beat yourself up." Their antics allowed ordinary citizens to laugh at situations they would normally fear.

As for Fydrych's nickname, the story is just as good: when reporting for his compulsory military service, which Fydrych was none too keen to do, he pretended the opposite, showing up dressed like a major and barking orders. Fydrych was declared mentally unsound and rejected for service, but the nickname stuck.

WHO DOESN'T LIKE BEER?

Though Polish politics of the 1990s were interesting at best and chaotic at worst, there's one political party that really took the cake—or the keg, as the case may be. In 1990, a comedian and satirist by the name of Janusz Rewiński was tired of the rampant drinking of vodka, a habit leftover from communist times (see Chapter 28). So he decided to form the **Polish Beer-Lovers' Party** (Polska Partia Przyjaciół Piwa or PPPP in Polish) together with several colleagues who had worked on a popular 80s TV show about beer.

The party's main platform was to fight alcoholism by popularizing the pub as a forum for slow discussion over beer, rather than the quick downing of vodka shots as was the current fashion. However, the joke was on them when the party managed to win sixteen seats in the Polish Sejm in 1991. It turned out that so many Poles were sick of the disordered mess that was transition-era politics that the party received 3.27% of the national vote. Their slogan? "It won't be better, but it will surely be funnier." Cheers to that!

THE SPIRIT CONTINUES

Some people assumed that after the 1990s, everything would be fine and dandy in Poland, and no one would have any more reason to protest or rebel. Of course, examining any democracy can disprove that theory right away, and Poland is no different in that respect. Today, very diverse factions protest all kinds of ills or perceived ills, from issues such as environmental degradation and air quality (very serious problems to this day) to more artistic rebellions against everyday nuisances, like the Krakow student who used a ruler and a paintbrush to mark vehicles offending the 1.5 meter sidewalk rule and put his antics up on YouTube (legally, cars can park on the sidewalk in Poland, but they must leave at least 1.5 meters of space for pedestrians, a law that is woefully under-enforced). Social media campaigns, flash mobs, exhibitions, and good old fashioned protests and marches happen quite often in Poland's larger cities, where young and old alike campaign for animal rights, gay rights, retiree benefits, gender equality, saving national parkland, and all sorts of issues now open to criticism in Poland's modern democracy.

One of the more controversial protests that was also probably most confusing for outsiders to understand was over the placement of a cross in 2010. The events happened in the wake of the 2010 Smolensk airplane crash that took the lives of President Lech Kaczyński, the first lady, and ninety-four other high-ranking officials and crew. As news of the tragedy spread, all sorts of tributes began appearing in front of the presidential palace in Warsaw, from the usual flowers, candles and wreaths to elaborate artwork, posters, and other signs of a nation in shock and mourning. One of these tributes was a several-meter high wooden cross spontaneously erected by the Polish Scouts.

While all of Poland seemed to come together in the days following the crash, soon afterward the political divides reappeared, and what had been a simple token of solidarity became a symbol of deep-seated divisions in Polish society. The new President Bronisław Komorowski—who is a member of the opposition party to Kaczyński's PiS—suggested the cross be moved to a church. However, an opposing faction gave the **Smolensk cross** an almost sacred designation and vowed to stand vigil day and night should the authorities try to remove it. Some Poles saw defenders of the cross as conspiracy theorists and blind Kaczyński followers, while those defending the cross saw themselves as fighting for the right to express their religious and political beliefs. While to outsiders it may have looked like a silly argument over the placement of an oversized religious symbol, to Poles it was a struggle over the nation's very identity, and the traditional battle between older, more religious, and conservative factions and younger, more secular, and progressive ones. In the end, the cross was removed in the middle of the night without fanfare and now stands in St. Anne's Church down the street, but Poland's political and social divisions remain as strong as ever, just beneath the surface, and will no doubt rise again given the opportunity.

A.S.

FURTHER READING

Countdown: The Polish Upheavals of 1956, 1968, 1970, 1976, 1980 by Jakub Karpiński. Karz-Cohl Publishers, 1982.

Rebellious Satellite: Poland 1956 by Paweł Machcewicz. Stanford University Press, 2009.

Solidarity And Contention: Networks Of Polish Opposition by Maryjane Osa. University of Minnesota Press, 2003.

PART IV

POLES AROUND THE WORLD

CHAPTER 42

NATIONHOOD (& LACK THEREOF)

"The soul of Poland is indestructible... she will rise again like a rock, which may for a spell be submerged by a tidal wave, but which remains a rock."
–Sir Winston Churchill, speech to the House of Commons, 1939

There have been times in Poland's history when there was no Poland—at least not on any current map of Europe. Other times, it may have had physical borders and a capital, but it was not ruled by Poles in any meaningful sense. Nonetheless, Polish language and culture survived, evolved, and sometimes even thrived in these difficult conditions. And Poles learned how to retain a sense of *Polishness* against all odds. It is perhaps telling that Poland is the only nation in the world that came back from complete foreign dominance to form a free, democratic country.

HOW POLAND WAS LOST

Poland's slide into non-existence began in the days of the Polish-Lithuanian Commonwealth (see Chapter 4), well before its neighbors sliced it up between themselves (Chapter 7). In a sense, Poland's seemingly progressive democratic tendencies (in reality a grab for power by the ruling noble minority) led to its demise. When the rest of Europe was tending toward absolute monarchy, Poland introduced elected monarchs and a legislative body made up of the nobility, the Sejm, which kept the monarchy in check. However, due to its need for unanimity to get anything accomplished, the Sejm was wide open for political deadlock, corruption, and foreign interference through bribery. Education, culture, and the country's financial standing all suffered as a result. It also didn't help that the nobility largely ignored the problems of the peasantry that far outnumbered them, and whose loyalty declined along with their circumstances. While the nobility enjoyed the most progressive democratic and civil rights in Europe, the other ninety percent of the population fell increasingly under the economic control of the ruling elite.

What's more, Polish troops were exhausted from fighting a century of wars with Swedes, Muscovites, Tartars, Cossacks, and Ottomans (see Chapter 9). So while Poland contended with an over-stretched army and political inaction at the start of the eighteenth century, Prussia, Russia, and Austria—all of which had grown decidedly more powerful over the previous century, thanks in part to Poland's inattention—were already making plans to annex Polish lands. By the time the First Partition was declared in 1772, Polish troops were unable to fight off the simultaneous invasion from its three stronger neighbors, and the Prussians took most of northern and western Poland, Austria took Galicia (including Lviv but not Krakow at first), and Russia took what is today's Belarus and parts of Ukraine. All in all, half of Poland's population and a third of its territory was now gone, though the Commonwealth still existed, at least in name.

The next partition came two decades later, and was instigated by the passing of the May 3 Constitution in 1791. Though it was the first of its kind in Europe (and the second in the world only after the American one), the Constitution was more a last act of desperation than a declaration of independence. It corrected many of the errors of the old Sejm, introduced democratic reforms, and separated the three branches of government. Had it been allowed to be fully implemented, it may have created an effective government and the resurgence of the Commonwealth. Unfortunately, that was exactly what Poland's neighbors were afraid of, and in the Second Partition of 1793, Poland was reduced to just one-third of its original population.

The Third Partition came as a result of an uprising led by Tadeusz Kościuszko (see Chapter 47) in 1794, which was crushed by the Russian Empire. Seeing that an independent Poland would keep attacking the partitioning forces, they decided to get rid of the problem altogether, making the final partition in 1795.

BEING POLISH WHEN THERE WAS NO POLAND

Over the next 123 years, ethnic Poles had three choices: rebel militarily, rebel clandestinely, or emigrate. While many chose the latter (see Chapter 43), those who remained in occupied Polish lands found a multitude of ways to rebel against the ruling powers, many of them much more subtle than the January or November Uprisings.

In the Russian and Prussian Partitions, and to a much lesser extent in Austria, the official mission was to eliminate Polishness through any means necessary, including laws banning the teaching of Polish language or history, Russification and Germanization, deportations or outright killing. Due to these policies, the spread of Polish culture and nationalism to new generations moved underground and to the home.

Within the home, it was mainly a mother's job to make sure her children knew "real" Polish history, spoke Polish correctly, and were instilled with patriotism (see Chapter 20). As Russian or German became the only languages taught at schools, and after the January Uprising, when students were not even allowed to speak Polish among themselves, the home was the only place where the Polish language could survive and evolve. Children read Polish stories and literature, and more and more Polish grammar books were published clandestinely.

Underground, Polish artists and writers propagated nationalism through the clandestine press and publishers (see chapters 34–38). While hundreds of journals and newspapers appeared during the partition era, those published officially were subject to strong censorship, particularly those under Russian and Prussian rule. This led to a flourishing underground and émigré press tradition, with Paris and London leading the way, and most of the publications were of a political nature. They allowed for a continuing dialog between Polish speakers in partitioned lands and those spread throughout the world.

Another tradition that was popularized during the Partitions was that of the salon. Artists, poets, writers, and other intellectuals would meet in the living rooms or salons of private homes to share their works, which would often never be allowed in the open by the censors. In cities such as Krakow or Warsaw, these salons became legendary and often launched whole new movements in the arts or literature, while keeping Polish nationalism alive as well.

In a way, the growth of nationalism in the nineteenth century was helped by the growth of literacy among the peasant classes in the Partitions, as former serfs whose only ties had been to their land or region began to think of themselves as Poles. Conversely, the peoples who had been considered Polish subjects under the old Commonwealth—but spoke German or Lithuanian or were not Catholics—often lost any sense of Polishness, so those who considered themselves Poles were mainly Polish-speaking Catholics by the end of the nineteenth century. Through marriage or emigration, many Polish Catholics assimilated into new cultures, some taking their Polish identities (and surnames) with them, others leaving both behind.

This flux of peoples and underground society meant that as a whole, Polish culture and language survived for the 123 years it took for Poland to have a state again. However, it also means that the definition of being Polish went through many transformations as the people who considered themselves Poles changed with each generation.

REDUX

The lessons learned during the Partitions would be applied once again in 1939, and to an extent from 1945 to 1989. As Hitler's forces took over western Poland and Stalin's forces took the east, the teaching of Polish language and culture was once again banned and moved underground. This time, entire underground universities arose, with classes often taking place in private homes. While the Nazis banned all higher education, the vocational schools that were permitted also secretly conducted university-level courses. With the war still raging, the teaching of medicine was especially important, and medical schools were established wherever it was possible, including within the Warsaw Ghetto.

Poland had the largest underground society of any occupied country in World War II. In addition to the clandestine universities, there was an entire underground press network, including intelligence gathering that provided invaluable information to the Allied cause. While the Nazi and Soviet agendas included the wholesale elimination of the Polish intelligentsia and all signs of Polish culture, leaving behind only an uneducated labor class to perform the hardest physical work, Poles understood that the survival of Polish spirit and culture was far more important than the survival of individuals, often risking everything so that Polish literature, press, theater, and art could continue. Any student attending underground courses, any individual found with underground publications, any teacher found teaching the Polish language could, and often was, killed on the spot. Yet for five years of Nazi occupation, Polish culture not only survived, but also thrived.

When Poland once again reformed in 1945, its population as well as its borders had changed dramatically. Historically a cosmopolitan state comprised of multiple languages and faiths, Poland became more homogenous than ever in its new, postwar state, with its minorities either killed, expelled, or incorporated into the Soviet Empire. After the establishment of the People's Republic of Poland, communist censorship once again forced Polish culture underground, and the networks that had been established during the war would continue for the next fifty years (see Chapter 10). Nonetheless, through underground and émigré efforts, Polish culture would persevere once again, until a free Polish state arose for the third time in 1990.

A.S.

FURTHER READING

Fighting Warsaw: The Story of the Polish Underground State, 1939-1945 by Stefan Korbonski. Hippocrene Books, 2004.

Forgotten Holocaust: The Poles Under German Occupation, 1939-1944 by Richard C. Lukas. Hippocrene Books, 2001.

The Partitions of Poland 1772, 1793, 1795 by Jerzy Lukowski. Longman Publishing Group, 1998.

The Peasant Prince: Thaddeus Kosciuszko and the Age of Revolution by Alex Storozynski. St. Martin's Griffin, 2010.

Story of a Secret State: My Report to the World by Jan Karski. Penguin Books, 2011.

CHAPTER 43

EXILE & EMIGRATION

*"I see the whole world open before me; the only place that remains
sealed off is Poland, and suddenly I feel the atmosphere so close about me
that at times it is difficult to breathe."*
–Ignacy Domeyko

Today, there are nearly forty million people in Poland—and about half that number abroad that can claim Polish roots. Poles have a long history of emigrating, and there are Polish communities on every habitable continent. When a nation becomes an idea rather than a place on a map (see Chapter 42), it seems very reasonable to leave that homeland, as one can always carry an idea with them. This is exactly what Poles have done for hundreds of years, as history pushed them outside of Polish borders, whether they existed or not.

Polish emigration came in waves, usually following a cataclysmic event. Each wave had their own way of dealing with separation from their homeland, but every emigrant eventually faced two choices: to mentally remain behind on their native soil, imprinting a static image of the home of their memories on their new existence, or to cut oneself off from the past, immersing themselves in the new surrounding culture and resigning themselves to the thought that they won't return home.

Most of the time, émigrés and émigré communities found a balance between the two extremes, preserving some memories of a common past while resuming a normal life in their new surroundings.

Though the main reason for emigration was either economic or political, both types of migrants tended to come together, forming or joining *Polonia* communities that shared a language, history, and religion if not always an economic or political affiliation. We'll explore specific communities in the following chapters, but suffice it to say, over time Poles have managed to inhabit every continent on the planet.

THE GREAT EMIGRATION(S)

As with just about every aspect of Polish life, major emigrations were a product of Polish history. The first large-scale emigrations began after Poland was partitioned between its neighbors, and the subsequent ones followed the failed uprisings of 1830 and 1863. Together, the period of 1830–1870 is known as the Great Emigration, when the majority of émigrés left for political reasons—often when faced with the choice between emigration or death. France, Belgium, and Britain were the most popular destinations, and as most of the émigrés came from the professional or creative classes, they took their passions with them and founded vibrant literary and artistic communities in their new homelands.

The next great emigration began in the 1870s and lasted until 1918. Unlike the previous one, these émigrés usually left for economic reasons, and in much larger numbers. While today's young rural Poles seeking work in English towns might think of themselves as trailblazers, they're actually following a long tradition of economic migration from rural Poland to the West. By the time of the Partitions, the Polish countryside was severely overpopulated and lacking a source of income other than subsistence farming. While some first migrated to industrial Polish towns, many decided to seek their fortunes much farther away in the New World. Between 1870 and World War I, about three and a half million Poles left the territories that had once been Poland. Many of these Poles came from poor, rural backgrounds and immigrated to the American Midwest (see Chapter 47).

They differed from the earlier migrants in that they were largely uneducated and had few skills outside of agriculture. They settled throughout the Americas as well as Europe, where they usually took on the hardest manual jobs for little pay. Nonetheless, they made lives for themselves and ultimately for their children, who then became

true citizens of their adopted homelands, and could pursue the educational and professional opportunities
their parents had no hope for back in
partitioned Poland.

Joachim Lelewel (1786–1861)
(rook76 / Shutterstock.com)

TWENTIETH CENTURY EMIGRATION

Immediately before, during, and after
World War II, another Great Emigration from Poland took place.
When suspicions of Hitler's plans for the country began to circulate,
some Poles and many Jewish Poles sought new homes abroad, at least
until the danger passed. Others, like writer Witold Gombrowicz, were
already abroad when war broke out, making their return dangerous
or impossible. Many of the émigrés who left before or during the war
fully expected to return as soon as peace was restored. These plans
changed when the imposition of Soviet rule looked inevitable.

Another significant population of migrants were soldiers from the
Polish Armed Forces, most notably the Home Army (AK) and Anders'
Army. Stranded abroad when peace finally came, they had a choice of
returning home, where they would be branded enemies of the state
and often imprisoned by the new communist government, or staying
abroad—not surprisingly, most chose the latter option. In 1947, the
UK gave citizenship to over 200,000 Polish troops, allowing them to
remain in Britain and start the still-thriving British *Polonia* community.

NEW NEIGHBOURS—EU EXPANSION

When Poland joined the European Union in 2004, three EU nations—
the UK, Ireland, and Sweden—opened their doors to Polish workers right away, expecting a modest influx of job-seekers. What they
got instead, particularly in Great Britain, was a flood of economic
migrants, mostly young and from middle and lower classes, seeking the financial rewards that were still pipe dreams for all but the
few in the new Poland (see Chapter 12). By some estimates, about a
million Poles came to the UK for work following the EU expansion,
while the official number is closer to 400,000—though undocumented
workers were common enough to make official records quite unre-
liable. However, by 2007 Poland's financial situation had improved

Ellis Island, New York City, the onetime entry point for millions of immigrants to the United States (SeanPavonePhoto / Shutterstock.com)

while the global economic crisis was starting to hit the UK, and in the following years the tide of migration has slowed significantly, with many Poles returning to Poland with valuable skills and money to invest back home.

FAMOUS ÉMIGRÉS

Because of this Polish tendency to emigrate, some of the most famous Poles throughout history actually made their names abroad. We will cover Polish émigré artists, composers, and writers in Chapter 48, but there are plenty of others worth mentioning. Among them is scientist **Marie Skłodowska-Curie** (see Chapter 39), who emigrated not for political or financial reasons, but because as a woman she was not permitted to pursue higher education in Russian-controlled Warsaw. She followed her sister to Paris, where she could enroll at the University of Paris to study chemistry, mathematics, and physics.

Prince **Adam Czartoryski** was a nobleman who was initially involved in Russian politics as a foreign minister, though he then led the Polish National Government during the November 1830 Uprising against Russia. Sentenced to death for his rebellious activities, the sentence was then commuted to exile, and the prince immigrated to Paris and soon invested his energies back into politics, leading a political emigration party. He even made plans to found another Polish emigration settlement called Polonezköy, also known as Adampol, in Turkey.

Another famous Pole, historian and political activist **Joachim Lelewel**, also left Poland as a result of his involvement in the November 1830 Uprising and initially immigrated to Paris. On the request of Russia, he was banned from French territories and ended up settling in Brussels, where he would work with Karl Marx and Friedrich Engels to found the Democratic Society for Unity and Brotherhood of All Peoples. His histories of Poland continued to be popular and influential long after his death.

Less famous (at least outside of Australia) is **Sir Paweł Edmund Strzelecki**, an explorer and geologist best known to Poles for naming Australia's highest mountain Mount Kosciuszko, after he became the first person to scale it in 1840. Strzelecki chose the name because the mountain reminded him of the Kosciuszko Mound in Krakow.

Statesman **Zbigniew Brzeziński**, who was in Canada with his father, a diplomat, when World War II broke out, ended up staying and entering university when his family could not return to Poland following the war. He is best known for serving as National Security Advisor to U.S. President Jimmy Carter, as well as for his highly influential political science books, including *The Grand Chessboard*.

A.S.

FURTHER READING

On Cultural Freedom: An Exploration of Public Life in Poland and America by Jeffrey C. Goldfarb. University of Chicago Press, 1982.

Lost in Translation: A Life in a New Language by Eva Hoffman. Plunkett Lake Press, 2011.

Polish Roots by Rosemary A. Chorzempa. Genealogical Publishing Company, 2000.

CHAPTER 44

Polonia—The Polish Diaspora

"If you were to plant two Poles in the middle of the Sahara Desert, they would certainly start a newspaper."
–British Minister of Information Brendan Bracken

When Poles move abroad, as they are apt to do, the Polish communities they form in other lands are collectively known as *Polonia*. The term has been popularized in part because the Polish diaspora is one of the largest of any ethnic group in the world. The biggest communities number in the hundreds of thousands or even millions, as in Chicago, and can be found on every continent. Most form organizations that support Polish culture and help new émigrés adjust to life abroad. However, these communities are not without their problems, and they have not always been accepted by their host countries, as we shall see.

Problems Polonia faces

Perhaps the most important decision for Poles in Polish communities is whether to assimilate, and to what extent? This question largely depends on where émigrés end up settling. Some Polonia communities—notably Chicago, Detroit, New York, and London—were large enough that newly arriving Poles could keep their language and traditions intact by mainly associating with other Poles. In the largest communities, Poles with businesses often employed other Poles, so they could spend years in a foreign country without needing to learn anything above the most basic words in the host language. In many cases, the children of these émigrés would be the first ones to become fluent in the foreign tongue.

Then, there were the differences between the émigrés themselves. Each subsequent wave of immigrants had their own characteristics and reasons for emigrating. This meant that though members of a Polonia community from different emigrations may share the same language and cultural background, there was very little else that tied them together. Sometimes, these different waves would even form separate organizations or newspapers, often split into conservative and liberal factions.

THE POLISH JOKE—NOT SO FUNNY

But even Poles who did assimilate were not always accepted by native populations. A stark example of this situation is the phenomenon of the "Polack joke" that began in the 1950s in the U.S. and is still a part of American culture today, though not quite as noticeably as during its heyday in the 70s and 80s. The term "Polack" itself is a derogatory slur for a Pole, and is derived from the Polish word *Polak*, which simply means Polish male. Though the actual origins of Polack jokes are hard to pinpoint, they were very frequently perpetuated by the American media, especially during the Cold War, and stereotyped Poles as unintelligent and dirty, and Polish women as promiscuous, while Polish men seemed oddly preoccupied with bowling. A typical example:

> *Did you hear about the Polack who went to the doctor and asked him for advice on how to improve his sex life? The doctor told him to jog ten miles a day, for seven days, and then call him.*
>
> *A week later, the Polack telephoned.*
>
> *"Well," asked the doctor, "has jogging improved your sex life?"*
>
> *"I don't know," said the Polack. "I'm seventy miles from home!"*

And another:

> *Q: Why do Polish names end in "ski"?*
> *A: Because they can't spell toboggan.*

One theory as to their existence is that large numbers of Poles did not arrive in the U.S. until the late nineteenth century, when other immigrant populations who had been the targets of similar humor were already assimilated. Thus, Poles became easy prey for other immigrant communities who had faced this kind of discrimination earlier—particularly because this wave of economic immigrants consisted mostly of uneducated Poles from the countryside who often took on only the physically demanding and menial jobs available to them. Another theory is that German and Jewish immigrants to America before and during World War II brought this anti-Polish sentiment with them.

When surrounded by such stereotypes in popular culture, many Poles hid their origins, particularly those who were born abroad to Polish families. Many more changed or Anglicized their surnames, or even denied that they had anything to do with Poland. Even today, popular American comedy shows such as *Saturday Night Live* have featured Polack jokes—though one difference is that Polish-American organizations are quick to make formal complaints, and networks have been much quicker to apologize.

POLISH ORGANIZATIONS ABROAD

Wherever Poles settle en masse, they form a variety of Polonia organizations, including schools, cultural centers, newspapers, job placement assistance services, and of course the ubiquitous Polish church, which often functioned as the setting for these organizations.

Perhaps the most well known today is the **Kosciuszko Foundation**, which is based in New York City and has been active since 1925. The foundation offers scholarships and other assistance to promote educational and cultural exchanges between the U.S. and Poland. Many Americans of Polish descent have studied or conducted research in Poland thanks to this foundation, while at the same time Poles have gained the opportunity to study at American universities such as Harvard or Columbia.

In the UK, most Polish Londoners are familiar with the acronym POSK—the **Polish Social and Cultural Association.** Active since the 1960s, today POSK has its headquarters in the heart of London's Polonia community, Hammersmith, and within it is a theater, gallery, library—including an entire room devoted to Joseph Conrad—school facilities, a café, as well as the offices of the major Polish associations in the UK.

In Germany, which has the largest permanent European Polonia community (not counting migrant workers in the UK), the main organization is the **Congress of Polonia in Germany** (Kongres Polonii Niemieckiej).

In addition to these larger networks, most cities around the world with a significant Polish population have their own local Polonia website that lists news and Polonia-related events.

A PERSONAL TALE

What is life like as a member of a Polonia community today? In addition to others' accounts that have been published in numerous places, I can share my own story of growing up Polish in Houston in the 1990s. Though rarely referred to on the list of large Polish population centers such as Chicago and New York, this Texan metropolis has one of the largest and most active Polish communities in the U.S.

As a child, I was taken (or often dragged, away from my morning cartoons) to Polish school on Saturday mornings, run by the local Polish church, the Polish Parish of Our Lady of Częstochowa (still in existence and quite expanded since those days). I would learn Polish grammar as well as Polish history and culture, and we would often sing Polish songs or even put on plays during the holidays. Afterward, my mother and I would go shopping for Polish ham (imported from Chicago, naturally) and other goods in the Polish store, or on special occasions, have an early dinner at the Polish restaurant next door. Many Sundays we would drive a good hour to attend mass at the Polish church (where I received my first communion along with just about every Polish child of my generation in Houston), and afterwards my parents would meet with their friends, all speaking Polish, while I ran around with the other children, speaking in English unless addressed by adults. The way the community functioned, if you were Polish and living in Houston, you knew just about every other Polish person in the city, as well as their children, parents, and often intimate family details.

Though my parents came to America in the 1980s to escape communism, once Poland regained its independence, they remained in the

U.S., tied to their new home both emotionally and economically. They mainly surrounded themselves with other Polish speakers, though through their jobs and daily lives they became part of a larger, mixed community. And yet, fighting the tide of new economic migrants following Poland's EU membership, I would return to Poland in 2005, and every year I meet more and more Poles raised in America and the UK who have decided to come back and explore their roots in a free Poland. Perhaps that, more than anything, is a testament to the success of the Polonia communities in passing on Polish culture to new generations.

A.S.

FURTHER READING

American "Polonia" and Poland by Frank Mocha (Editor). East European Monographs, 1998.

Hollywood's War with Poland, 1939-1945 by M.B.B. Biskupski. University Press of Kentucky, 2009.

Polack (film) by James Kenney. 2010.

Traitors & True Poles by Karen Majewski. Ohio University Press, 2003.

CHAPTER 45

New Neighbours: Poles in the UK

> *"I have fought a good fight, I have finished my course,*
> *I have kept the faith."*
> (Inscription on the Polish War Memorial in London,
> from 2 Timothy 4:7)

Individual Poles had been traveling to the British Isles for centuries—including famous ones such as Joseph Conrad (see Chapter 48)—but the British Polonia did not become the populous community it is known as today until the early 1940s, when the war first drove Polish troops and civilians to France, and then to Britain. When the war ended, they found themselves facing two difficult choices: return to certain Soviet rule and likely persecution (especially those who had fought for the Home Army or had intellectual backgrounds), or remain in a country that was free, but was not home and had a hostile population. The Polish Resettlement Act of 1947 made the choice somewhat easier by granting British citizenship to some 200,000 Poles who decided to remain.

Post–World War II
Though the chaos and destruction of World War II left the British economy badly damaged, the country itself and its capital didn't bear the massive physical scars of France, Germany, or especially Poland. At the end of World War II, a peak of 250,000 Polish nationals remained

in the United Kingdom, with about 33,000 remaining in London itself in the 1950s, where a significant population settled around the Hammersmith area. The Poles found themselves in a somewhat hostile environment at the end of the war, with a general lack of sympathy in the British press and from the British public—more than half of Britons disapproved the government's decision to allow Polish troops to stay in the country, and only thirty percent approved. One exception might be British Catholics, who were particularly friendly to Poles— at least until Poles stopped going to British Catholic churches after setting up their own network of Polish ones.

In addition to former soldiers, the Polish Government-in-Exile made the UK its home as well. No longer recognized as the formal leadership of Poland after the Soviet takeover, the members of the government nonetheless remained active in supporting efforts for Polish independence and promoting the Polish cause in Britain and elsewhere abroad. It was not dissolved until 1990.

In general, the London Poles were anticommunist, holding an irreconcilable opposition to Soviet rule and a somewhat pessimistic hope for Polish independence. However, most resigned themselves to the fact that the UK would be their home for a long time, if not forever. Not only did they have to adjust to a new language, but a new lifestyle, including the boredom of the "British Sunday," or everyday life after years in the chaos of Europe. Part of this everyday life meant for some the reestablishment of the Polish press; some fifty periodicals were started by January 1946, though the majority were organs of various Polish political parties or other organizations such as the military or the Church; if nothing else, the wide diversity of periodicals shows the wide diversity of the Polish émigré community in England. In general, the aim of the émigré publications was to publish what couldn't be published in Poland because of the censor (especially before 1956), thus maintaining some sort of bridge between Poland and the rest of the world.

Just as the Parisian emigration had its literary and political mouthpiece, *Kultura* (see Chapter 46), the London Polonia had its own, called **Wiadomości** (*News*). While *Kultura* was often read and quite popular in Poland after 1956, *Wiadomości* remained more a publication aimed at and read by the émigré community, though it did often reach Poland as well. *Wiadomości*, and with it its editor, Mieczysław Grydzewski, claimed to remain apolitical and objective, keeping a distance from Polish politics even after 1956; instead, the weekly addressed the problems of emigration as regarding politics, culture, literature, and history. Unique in both its wide range of topics and its long existence, *Wiadomości* reflected the political leanings of the émigré community in London, which tended to be conservative in its views, remembering (almost to a fault) prewar Poland and wanting to have nothing to do with the politics of the People's Republic of Poland.

After 1956, some changes began to take place in the Polish community in Britain. First, the thaw meant a renewed flow of information and ideas between Poland and the rest of the world, but it also meant a new flow of immigrants to the already established émigré communities—immigrants with a clear picture of what life behind the Iron Curtain was really like. The death of prominent Polish leaders of the emigration in the late 60s and early 70s was symbolic of a change in the Polish community in Britain as a whole, as it was becoming better integrated into British society. This meant that a more open exchange between the Polish and British communities was possible, and enough time had passed for language barriers to become less of an issue. By the time communism fell in Poland, a new generation of British-born Poles was ready to take over the community and the promotion of Polish culture within the UK.

THE FLOODGATES OPEN

To see what an effect Poland's 2004 ascension to the EU has had on Polish migration to the UK, it's enough to look at two numbers: 60,711 vs. 579,000. The first is the number of Polish-born UK residents recorded in the 2001 census; the second is the same statistic for 2011. Of course, this figure only counts the Poles who were registered and working on the books, and who remained after the recession—the actual number, impossible to determine with certainty, is estimated to be much closer to one million. To many Britons, it seemed like Polish workers invaded its cities almost overnight, and the popular press reflected that, often publishing negative or even xenophobic accounts of the Central and Eastern European migration. Press outlets such as the *Daily Mail* have become notorious for preying on fears of rising crime rates or abused social services to push an anti-immigration agenda—often resulting in formal complaints from the Federation of Poles in Great Britain.

There have also been tensions between this new, economic migration and the postwar political migration that created the Polonia institutions in the UK. Similarly to the differences between the economic and political migrations in nineteenth-century America (see Chapter 47), the two migrations have very little in common besides a shared language and cultural background. More than three quarters of post-2004 migrants are under thirty-four, while those of the postwar migration who are still alive are well into their golden years. The economic migrants tend to be more progressive, secular, and eager for travel and adventure; most hardly remember life under communism or were not even born until the 90s. Many do not identify with the existing Polonia community anyway, choosing to socialize instead with their British peers. This should come as no surprise, given that the Poland they left behind is a free country, capable of promoting and preserving its own cultural heritage without their help. And should they start missing any aspect of home, it's just a cheap, three-hour flight away.

The recession of 2007–2008 significantly reduced the flow of Polish migration to the UK, and many Poles who had migrated in 2004 actually ended up returning to Poland, albeit with fuller bank accounts and improved English skills. This return led to debates in both the British and Polish press about just how permanent this migration is—and how dependent the UK had become on immigrant labor. Most scholars, however, predict that this latest migration will turn out to be temporary; as the Polish economy continues to outperform others in the region, many young Poles will want to return to apply the skills and knowledge they have gained into starting their own businesses or institutions and contributing to the future of their birth country. Others may want to move on to other European countries whose markets are now open to Poland—which, as the EU renders national borders more and more fluid, will likely be the future for many Poles.

A.S.

FURTHER READING

Hello, I'm Your Polish Neighbour: All about Poles in West London by Wiktor Moszczynski. AuthorHouse, 2010.

Victims of Stalin and Hitler: The Exodus of Poles and Balts to Britain by A. T. Lane. Palgrave Macmillan, 2004.

White Immigrants: A Portrait of the Polish Community in London by Belinda Brown. Institute of Community Studies, 2003.

CHAPTER 46

TAKING OVER THE CONTINENT: POLES IN EUROPE

"I really don't know whether any place contains more pianists than Paris, or whether you can find more asses and virtuosos anywhere."
–Fryderyk Chopin

As European borders have shifted over the centuries, so have the destinies of those Poles and Polish communities who settled throughout the continent, whether for political or economic reasons. Though Germany and France have the largest European Polonia communities (as well as the UK—see Chapter 45), Poles and Polish descendants can be found in just about every European country, particularly in Slavic countries to the east that were once a part of the Commonwealth. With Poland's ascension to the EU, Poles have taken advantage of existing Polonia networks to join earlier emigrations abroad.

GERMANY—THE LARGEST EUROPEAN POLONIA
The fact that Europe's largest population of Polonia is found in Germany has less to do with any particular appeal the country has for Poles, and much more to do with the turmoil of history. For that reason as well it's impossible to determine just how many Poles there are within German borders; if you count those who only hold Polish passports, the number is about 400,000. However, if you include those with dual citizenship, it's closer to 1.5 or two million. Finally, if you

include anyone of direct Polish descent, it might be even twice that. Nonetheless, no matter how you count them, Poles are a significant minority in Germany, and Polish surnames are very common there— just look at the line-up of the German national football team.

The existence of a significant Polish minority in Germany began with the Partitions, when part of Poland was incorporated into what was then Prussia (see Chapter 42). In addition to the Poles who suddenly found themselves Prussian citizens, the Industrial Revolution brought even more, as the rapidly developing Prussian lands demanded more manpower than the local population could produce. However, these early migrations were mostly forced to assimilate under Prussian rule, and German was the only language allowed to be taught at schools—not that this made much of a difference, as Poles stubbornly refused to give up their language and customs and developed even stronger nationalistic sentiments.

Immediately before and during World War II, many Poles who had remained in Germany would have to fully hide their identities, as the Nazi agenda was to treat Poles as an inferior race. However, many remained in what then became West Germany in order to avoid communism. Today, there are several large Polonia communities within Germany, most notably in the Ruhr Valley (called *Ruhrpolen*), comprised of the descendants of Poles who immigrated to the area during the Industrial Revolution, as well as Berlin and Hamburg, with smaller populations scattered throughout the country.

HôTEL LAMBERT AND THE FRENCH SCENE

Under the Partitions, Paris was the heart of the Polish émigré scene, and **Hôtel Lambert** was the heart of Paris for Poles. It was the destination of choice for the cultural and political elite, particularly following the failed uprisings of the 1830s and 60s, including Fryderyk Chopin, Adam Mickiewicz, and Marie Skłodowska-Curie (see Chapters 39 & 48). Purchased by Prince Adam Jerzy Czartoryski in 1843, this beautiful seventeenth century townhouse became part safe house, part think tank and salon for Polish political émigrés of the era. Chopin would play the piano in its halls while politicians and activists would debate and plot the liberation of their homeland. Later, a Polish school, library, and historical society were founded in the hotel.

When WWII broke out, Paris once again became the headquarters of Poland's intellectual leaders, as the Government-in-Exile was initially set up in the French capital and remained there until France capitulated. Many Polish refugees also fled to France when the war began, and would stay once the fate of Poland was decided. In October 1939, General Władysław Sikorski formed the Polish Army in France, which became part of the general French armed forces, though they were often undersupplied. The Polish divisions continued the fight even when the French leadership called for armistice and demobilization in June 1940, and were soon afterward evacuated to Great Britain to continue fighting for the Allied cause. Polish civilians, on the other hand, joined the French Resistance in 1941, carrying out acts of sabotage, spying, and distributing Polish language underground press throughout the war.

Under communism, one of the most influential Polish émigré publications, *Kultura*, was published in Paris for half a century. The monthly literary magazine held the pride of place among postwar émigré cultural organizations, and published such frequent contributors as Czesław Miłosz, Witold Gombrowicz, Wisława Szymborska, and Gustaw Herling-Grudziński (see Chapter 34). Edited from its start in 1947 by Jerzy Giedroyc, *Kultura* existed as the mouthpiece of Giedroyc's publishing house, the Literary Institute. The monthly, which often took on a political tone, significantly influenced Polish thought and discourse, as it was frequently smuggled into the country. By publishing writers and political commentators residing in Poland, the journal gave them a voice the censors had silenced in the "official" Polish press.

Today, about a million Poles still live in France, though mainly concentrated in the north around the town of Lille. While Paris is no longer the center of independent Polish thought and culture, its legacy as such survives in its libraries and museums that feature some of the greatest products of Polish minds.

ELSEWHERE IN EUROPE

Many Polish descendants can be found in areas that had historically belonged to Poland, such as Lviv, Ukraine and Vilnius, Lithuania (where they make up some twenty percent of the city's population).

However, though they may still have Polish surnames and keep some Polish customs, they don't necessarily make up the traditional Polonia, as rather than moving for political or economic reasons, these are mainly Poles who found themselves on the wrong side of the Soviet border at the end of World War II. They do not have the memory of leaving Poland behind to make their way in a new land; rather, the land that had always been theirs switched allegiances, so often they did as well.

As far as those who emigrated are concerned, other European countries with significant Polonia communities include Sweden, Austria, Italy, Hungary, and Greece; in fact, more European countries have at least a few thousand Poles than not. One curious fact that most Polish people don't even know is that Poles comprise Iceland's largest minority group. Granted, in actual numbers there are only about 8,000–9,000 Poles in the island nation—but because Iceland's population is so small, they make up nearly three percent of it. It's fair to say that whether due to history or economics, Poles have made the entire continent of Europe their home.

A.S.

Further Reading

Chopin in Paris: The Life and Times of the Romantic Composer by Tad Szulc. Da Capo Press, 1999.

Savage Continent: Europe in the Aftermath of World War II by Keith Lowe. St. Martin's Press, 2012.

Uprooted: How Breslau Became Wroclaw during the Century of Expulsions by Gregor Thum. Princeton University Press, 2011.

CHAPTER 47

JACKOWO!
POLES IN THE AMERICAS

"The newcomer from the disillusioned, tired, skeptical Europe feels a heartwarming glow in the sincere optimism of a nation that is on the whole contented and satisfied with its present. That form of patriotism, free from any ideological complications and histrionics, simple and straightforward, constitutes a source of moral strength that can never be overestimated."
–Melchior Wankowicz, Polish journalist who arrived in the U.S. after WWII

It's said that Chicago is the second largest Polish city in the world (after Warsaw, of course). And it's difficult to spend a day in that city without seeing a Polish store or hearing Polish being spoken (or shouted) on the street. But even before the birth of America in 1776, Poles had been immigrating to the New World in droves, and although their presence is most felt in the United States, large and diverse Polish communities can be found all over both continents to this day.

UNITED STATES
Of all the places where Poles have immigrated throughout history, the United States is unique in that the entire country is one of immigrants. Within America, the bubbles of *Polishness* Poles tended to congregate in were perfectly normal. What's Greenpoint in New York City's Brooklyn compared to Little Italy or Chinatown? Poles were just another group of fortune seekers in the land of opportunity—and yet, they managed to stand out in often unexpected ways.

The very first Polish settlers arrived in America in 1608, as part of Captain John Smith's Jamestown colony. Given the Poles' tendency to rebel (see Chapter 41) and the historical significance of trade unions in Polish history, perhaps it's not surprising that the first recorded strike in the New World was started by the Poles at the Jamestown colony over voting rights.

Over the next two centuries, small groups of Polish settlers continued to arrive, and in the late 1700s there were even plans for a Polish colony, though they soon collapsed with the First Partition of 1772. Nonetheless, around the time of the American Revolution, Polish soldiers and noblemen were drawn to America to take part in its struggle, and among them were **Kazimierz Pulaski**, called "the father of the American cavalry," who died in the Battle of Savannah, and **Tadeusz Kościuszko**. An officer trained in Poland and France, and a skilled engineer as well, Kościuszko joined the American war effort, where his strengthening of the fortifications at Saratoga led to a British defeat there in 1777 (a monument to Kościuszko still stands in Washington, D.C.). Afterward he returned to Poland, where he led the final uprising before the Third Partition.

In the nineteenth century, subsequent waves of immigrants would reflect historical events in Poland: many came following the final Partition in 1795 and after each failed uprising in the 1830s and 1860s. These Poles were political migrants, whose choices were between death, deportation to Siberia, or emigration. They were mainly educated, distinguished individuals, often skilled militarily. They spoke Latin and French and had no problem picking up other languages, which was a necessity as they were often the first Poles to arrive in a new American town, and it was up to them to found Polish institutions and communities. These initial Polish Americans spread as far as California, and some even participated in the Texas fight for independence.

The first truly Polish settlement was actually in Texas. Founded in 1854 near today's San Antonio, it was called Panna Maria in honor of the Virgin Mary. That year, the first Polish church in America was established, and in 1866 the first Polish school was also founded there. However, these settlers faced many hardships in an area that was mostly wilderness, and many families ended up moving to other parts of Texas and the west.

One of the other earliest destinations for Polonia was Wisconsin, and the first Polish church there was founded in 1865 in Milwaukee.

The General
Casimir (Kazimierz)
Pulaski Memorial in
Savannah, Georgia.
(Shutterstock.com)

Other states included Illinois, Indiana, Michigan, and Pennsylvania. By the time of the Civil War, Poles had already begun to assimilate into American life, and several thousand fought on both sides. However, the influx of Poles was just beginning.

Before 1870, there were about 40,000 Poles in America, with a quarter of them living in Chicago. By 1875, there were 200,000, and in 1889 there were some 800,000 and over a hundred schools and churches. This great migration came in the wake of the failure of the 1863 Uprising as well as the defeat of Polish ally France by Prussia, as the future of Poland looked increasingly bleak.

However, the migration of 1870 to 1920 differed in more than just size from previous waves. Most significantly, it was economically rather than politically motivated, and most of the migrants were poor, landless peasants and urban workers, uneducated and with few skills outside of agriculture. They didn't speak English, so they were at a disadvantage compared to the Irish and Scottish immigrants arriving at the same time. They took on the jobs no one else wanted, working in textile and lumber mills, railroads, mines, steel mills, and factories as manual laborers. A good third also worked in agriculture, though these immigrants often made fortunes farming harsh northern lands thought to be infertile by Americans.

The most popular cities for these Poles were those along the same latitudes and climates as home and included Chicago, Milwaukee,

Detroit, Buffalo, Cleveland, and Pittsburgh. The peak of the migration was 1912–1918; at the end of the First World War and Poland's reappearance on the map, migration nearly stopped. At that time, there were between five and six million Poles and Polish descendants in the United States. In 1940, there were almost 2.5 million Polish speakers. Though the economic migrants came uneducated and with few possessions, they worked hard and pushed education on their children, and future generations of Polish Americans usually joined the professional classes.

The next waves of Polish migration came once again as a result of catastrophes: World War II and the imposition of Soviet communism on Poland. These included a mixture of political and economic migrants, as well as a significant number of Jewish Poles who fled as a result of the Holocaust. Settling in already established and thriving Polish communities, with their own traditions and culture, these newly arriving émigrés often found themselves at odds with the "old" migration, who tended to be more conservative and held on to a picture of Poland that no longer existed, as well as speaking, in essence, a "dead" language, as the Polish spoken in Poland had been continually evolving. This was especially the case with political migrants following the upheavals in Poland in 1956, '68, and after martial law was imposed in the 1980s. Nonetheless, each wave of immigrants added to the definition of what it meant to be Polish American.

Poles arriving in America (and throughout the world) soon set up Polish churches, schools, and newspapers. In larger communities, they opened stores selling Polish foods like *kiełbasa* sausages or *pierogi* dumplings (see Chapter 26). Often, they carried regional traditions with them, including various holiday celebrations. Most importantly, they established a sense of community through shared history, language, and traditions, and they ensured that these were passed to their American-born children through institutions such as the church, Polish schools, festivals of Polish culture, and various Polish American associations like the Kosciuszko Foundation.

CANADA

As America's northern neighbor was being settled, Poles were trickling in as well, though the first significant migration of Poles into Canada didn't occur until 1858. These were Poles from northern,

Prussian-occupied Poland escaping oppression, and they mainly settled in Ontario. During the same period as the major American emigration, the 1870s until 1914, mostly improvised peasants settled in droves in Canada, establishing farms on its prairies. Later migrations, especially under communism, brought a more urban and educated population to Canada's cities, making Toronto its largest Polish community. These political émigrés were more concerned with the situation at home, and founded Polish-Canadian organizations that promoted Polish culture and supported the anticommunist movements of that era.

As in the United States, these immigrants founded Polish Catholic churches, schools, and Polish stores in places like Toronto, as well as printing Polish-language newspapers. Today, there are nearly a million Canadians of Polish descent living in the country, and famous names include physicist Leon Katz, many politicians, Geddy Lee of the band Rush, actors Lisa Ray and William Shatner and of course hockey legend Wayne Gretzky.

SOUTH AMERICA

Poles also sought opportunities and freedom in the southern hemisphere of the New World. Within Latin America, Polish engineers and scientists contributed greatly to the development of the railroads, launched naturalist expeditions to the rainforests, headed universities, and helped to develop the aeronautical industry in Argentina and Brazil, while Polish writers and artists contributed to local culture as well as launching émigré publications. Though small populations of Poles and Polish descendants can be found all throughout South America, the main countries where Poles settled were Brazil and Argentina.

Poles began arriving in Brazil in the 1860s, and initially came mainly from the Prussian partition of former Poland. Many of these immigrants were drawn by the country's well-paying mining jobs, particularly those used to working in Silesian coalmines. The first Polish school was set up in 1876 in the town of Orleans, and several Polish organizations were created soon thereafter. However, the major immigration to Brazil began in 1890, and like in North America, most of the migrants were poor peasants looking for work. This wave was dubbed the "Brazilian fever," and officially, some 40,000 Polish emigrants landed in Brazil in 1890–1891 alone. Of course, the first Polish newspaper in Brazil was launched the following year, and immigration continued until World War I. During World War II, the Brazilian Polonia, now some 200,000 strong, formed the Help for Poland Committee, which would send over 500 soldiers to contribute to the Allied effort. Following the war, the last major wave of immigrants arrived—those escaping the communist regime. These were mainly intellectuals and professionals, and would continue to support Polish efforts for independence from Brazil.

The Polish community of Argentina is well known to many Poles thanks to the writings of **Witold Gombrowicz** (see Chapter 48), particularly his *Diaries*. Gombrowicz found himself stuck on a ship bound for South America when Hitler invaded Poland, and ended up staying in Argentina until 1963, chronicling his life there as well as his thoughts on the situation in Poland.

In general, Polish immigration to Argentina followed similar patterns to that of Brazil, though exact numbers are not known until the twentieth century. The first Polish organization in the country was founded in 1890, and the Misiones Province was considered the hub of the Argentine Polish community, and still has the highest population of Poles within Argentina. Today, an estimated half to one million Argentinians are of Polish descent, making them one of the country's largest minorities.

A.S.

FURTHER READING

America's Polish Heritage by Joseph A. Wytrwal. Endurance Press, 1961.

Diary by Witold Gombrowicz. Yale University Press, 2012.

Poles in the United States of America 1776–1865 by Bogdan Grzeloński. Interpress, 1976.

Polish Americans by Andrzej Brożek. Interpress, 1985.

Trans-Atlantyk by Witold Gombrowicz. Yale University Press, 1995.

CHAPTER 48

NON-NATIVE REALMS: THE ARTS IN EMIGRATION

"It is well known that Poles, whenever they chance to come together, even in twos and threes, immediately found a journal and begin to publish in Polish."

–Marion Moore Coleman

It seems that the second a significant Polonia community forms, whether in Europe, the United States or elsewhere, three things are established: a Polish church, a Polish school, and a Polish press, around which a literary and artistic community soon starts to gather. Add to that a tendency for artists, writers, and other intellectuals to get in trouble with the authorities at times of occupation, and the result is one of the most creative and influential émigré traditions of any nation.

LITERATURE

It is no stretch to say that the most significant Polish literary traditions were born, or at least cultivated, abroad. We already mentioned **Adam Mickiewicz** at length (see Chapter 34), who composed some of his greatest masterpieces, such as *Pan Tadeusz*, while in Rome. Other writers of that era, such as **Henryk Sienkiewicz**, also provided a valuable look at another culture through the eyes of outsiders. His "Letters from America," a series of articles written for Polish newspapers while he lived in California, present an insightful and unbiased view of the United States in the late 1800s. The Great Emigration (see Chapter 43) of the nineteenth century also included such Polish literary greats as Romantic poets Zygmunt Krasiński, Juliusz Słowacki, and Cyprian Norwid.

Born Józef Teodor Konrad Nałęcz Korzeniowski, but better known as **Joseph Conrad** to the rest of the world, Conrad is one of the best-known Polish writers, perhaps because he wrote in English. He was born to a Polish noble family of revolutionaries in what is today's Ukraine, though he would live in Warsaw, then in exile in Russia after the January Uprising, followed by Lviv and Krakow, all by the age of eleven. By sixteen, he had set off for France to begin a long life at sea, where he would sail throughout the Mediterranean and to the West Indies and Africa, forming the basis for much of his fiction. He later joined the English Merchant Marine, thanks to which he learned English and sailed all the way to Australia, and eventually became a British citizen. Though written in English, his fiction is undoubtedly marked by his experiences in Poland and his upbringing, particularly the Romantic literature he was exposed to as a young boy. His most famous novel, *Heart of Darkness*, has many Romantic features, and his English had a distinct Polish and French flair.

During the era of communism, émigré literature significantly influenced literature in Poland thanks to its freedom from the censors. Its main centers were London and Paris (though with considerable readership and publications among the diasporas in the United States and Latin America), and émigré literary magazines such as Paris's *Kultura* and London's *Wiadomości* were frequently smuggled into the country, influencing an entire generation of young Polish writers. In fact, Polish writers abroad were usually more widely read in Poland than in their adopted countries, mainly because the previous immigration were of working-class or provincial origins, or had otherwise assimilated and lacked interest in reading literature in their ancestral tongue.

One of the single most pivotal Polish writers of the twentieth century was **Czesław Miłosz**, a Nobel laureate, poet, prose writer, and essayist. Born to a Polish family of the intelligentsia in what is today Lithuania, he grew up speaking Polish, Lithuanian, Russian, English, and French, though he would write in Polish. He spent World War II in Warsaw, where he attended an underground university, and took a position in the postwar Polish government that allowed him to defect. Soon thereafter, he published *The Captive Mind*, a non-fiction book that was hypercritical of communism and made Miłosz an international success. Continuing to write, Miłosz spent most of the 1950s in Paris before emigrating to the United States in 1960, and was completely banned in Poland from 1951 to 1956, allowed for two years, then banned again until 1980; in spite of this, he remained more popular in Poland than abroad, and he managed to keep close ties with writers in Poland.

Similarly, **Witold Gombrowicz** (1904–1969) was widely read in communist Poland despite being banned. When WWII broke out, he was on board a Polish cruise ship to South America. Unable to return (and ruled unfit to serve in the military), Gombrowicz would spend the next twenty-four years in Argentina. He tried to publish his works in Argentina, translated to Spanish, but they were not recognized until the 60s. Instead, from the 50s he published in the Parisian journal *Kultura*, and after 1956 his books were smuggled into Poland and read by Polish émigrés around the world.

Other significant émigré Polish writers of that era include **Gustaw Herling-Grudzinski**, who fought in the underground resistance during WWII, was arrested and sent to Siberia for two years, then escaped to Rome where he helped found *Kultura*. His most famous work is the memoir *A World Apart*, which describes his time in the Russian gulags. Similarly, **Józef Mackiewicz** was a staunch anticommunist who fled to Italy and then London, where he published in *Kultura* and other émigré publications, as his works were banned by the Polish authorities.

ART

Like literature, Polish art has a long history of thriving in emigration. During the Romantic era, many notable Polish artists became émigrés, mainly settling in Europe. They include painter **Piotr Michałowski**, who escaped to Paris after the November Uprising to avoid capture; he was unique in that he ended up returning to his hometown of Krakow a few years later, though he was greatly influenced by the French painters he had studied while abroad.

One of the most iconic and famous Polish émigré artists of the twentieth century is **Tamara de Lempicka**. Born Maria Górska in Warsaw, Tamara was a teenager living in St. Petersburg when the Russian Revolution broke out, and fled to Paris with her new husband, whom she had rescued from prison. As part of the Bohemian Paris scene, she would gain fame as much for her affairs as for her Art Deco and Cubist style paintings—she soon divorced her husband and became a hit in Parisian salons of the roaring 1920s, where she met Pablo Picasso, Jean Cocteau, and André Gide. In the 30s she became one of the most sought after portrait painters, immortalizing the royalty and aristocrats of the era. When war broke out in Europe she immigrated to the U.S. with her new husband and began painting the biggest Hollywood stars. Though her popularity faded in the 50s and 60s, before her death her artwork experienced a revival and is now a mainstay of American contemporary art museums.

MUSIC

Though Polish composers were less restricted by the censors, they often held political leanings or aristocratic backgrounds that made publishing in Poland impossible for them. Some even participated in the failed uprisings of the nineteenth century, thus sealing their fates as émigrés.

The greatest name in Polish music to this day, **Fryderyk Chopin**, became an émigré when he moved to France following the November Uprising in 1831 (see Chapter 38). Due to the political situation and his health, Chopin would never return to Poland, staying in Paris and becoming a French citizen in 1835. He would live in Paris most of his life, staying briefly in England and Scotland toward the end, though he often yearned for his homeland and was a part of the Parisian Polish diaspora. Upon his death, only his heart would return to his native Poland, smuggled back by his sister according to his request.

A contemporary of Chopin, **Henryk Wieniawski** was born in Lublin, but his immense talent was soon recognized and he was sent to the Paris Conservatoire at the age of eight. In Paris he met both Chopin and Adam Mickiewicz when he was still a boy. A violin virtuoso, Wieniawski spent many years touring around the world, including the United States in the 1870s. Wieniawski also lived in St. Petersburg, Brussels, and Moscow, where he died of a heart attack. Today, he is best known for his brilliant violin works.

FILM

It seems that Polish film is above all prone to its stars making their names abroad. Perhaps one reason is that its most innovative and prolific era happened to be right in the middle of communist rule, which, while spurring creativity in evading the censors, also made it impossible for many actors or directors to practice their art within Poland (see Chapter 36).

One of the first émigré Polish film stars was silent film icon **Pola Negri**, born Apolonia Chałupec, who began as a dancer and actress in Warsaw and immigrated to Hollywood in the interwar period to further her career. She would go on to become the richest woman in the film industry and a Hollywood legend during the silent era, where she swooned the likes of Charlie Chaplin and Rudolph Valentino. Meanwhile, behind the Hollywood scenes, Polish-Jewish film producer **Samuel Goldwyn** was born Schmuel Gelbfisz in Warsaw and left Poland for economic reasons, also ending up in America, where he would make his fortune producing films. Anyone who's ever heard the roar of the Metro-Goldwyn-Mayer lion knows his name well.

Among political émigrés is film director **Roman Polanski**, who left communist Poland initially for France, then to England to make films, and finally ended up in the United States, where he gained fame and then notoriety after being involved in a sex scandal. He has mostly lived in France since then, returning to Poland only for events related to his films. Similarly, director **Agnieszka Holland** left Warsaw and first immigrated to France just before martial law, and later made her career in Hollywood. **Andrzej Żuławski** is another well-known Polish director. He escaped to France when his second film was banned by the Polish authorities, and has made his career in the art film scene. Émigré Polish cinematographers have also seen success in Hollywood, most notably **Janusz Kamiński**, who filmed such classics as *Schindler's List*, *Saving Private Ryan*, *Jerry Maguire*, and *Lincoln*.

A.S.

Polish actress Pola Negri (1897–1987), the first European film star invited to Hollywood, became an iconic figure in America's silent film era.

FURTHER READING

Art in Exile: Polish Painters in Post-War Britain by Douglas Hall. Sansom & Company, 2008.

Breathing under Water and Other East European Essays by Stanisław Barańczak. Harvard University Press, 1990.

Memoirs of a Star by Pola Negri. Doubleday, 1970.

Native Realm: A Search for Self-Definition by Czesław Miłosz. Farrar, Straus and Giroux, 2002.

Roman by Roman Polanski. HarperEntertainment, 2003.

Traitors & True Poles by Karen Majewski. Ohio University Press, 2003.

Trans-Atlantyk by Witold Gombrowicz. Yale University Press, 1995.

CHAPTER 49

Bring on the Funding: Poland in the EU

"We are asking the nations of Europe between whom rivers of blood
have flowed to forget the feuds of a thousand years."
–Winston Churchill

On the evening of May 1, 2004, a barrage of fireworks rained down from the sky in Warsaw as the city, so often set ablaze by enemies, now had reason to light its skies in celebration. That day, Poland officially became a Member State of the European Union, now twenty-five nations strong. Unofficially, Poles could finally feel *safe*—safe that its neighbors who had caused it so much trouble in the past (see Chapter 7) were now either fellow members of a greater union, or could defend it in case its large neighbor to the east got any wrong ideas. Safe in the feeling that its democratic tendencies would finally be protected, not persecuted. Safe knowing Polish citizens were now fully European citizens, and after so many years of visa restrictions and denied travel, they could finally move around as they pleased. Though the EU is hardly a perfect entity, and there are plenty of eurosceptics within Polish borders as well, no one can say that Poland has been unaffected by its entry into the vast social and economic experiment that is the European Union.

Polish reactions
The range of emotions felt across Poland that day in May fell all over the spectrum, from elated to paranoid. Most, however, were relieved.

For better or worse, all those years of struggle, first to break free of communism, then to just survive the transition, were finally coming to an end, and the country could sit a spell because mother Brussels would help babysit the newborn economy for awhile. Some Poles also saw it as a confirmation that the country had "made it"—it was now officially, irreversibly part of Europe after being cut off for so long. To many, EU membership was simply the fulfillment of a destiny that was interrupted for fifty years.

And then there's the shiny influx of European money that would help build Polish roads, rails, and skyscrapers that had been neglected for so long—not to mention the cultural and small business initiatives that would now be supported. These days, it's quite difficult to find a banner over a public construction project or an exhibition without the words "co-financed by European Union funding" on it. While this trend cannot last forever and eventually Poland will have to begin supporting its own infrastructure projects and helping out even newer EU members, the first few years have been a wild ride of growth almost entirely funded by Brussels.

However, there have been plenty of adjustment pains in the process of ever closer union. EU membership came with many requirements, and not just the economic restrictions. Polish laws would have to be revised to match the democratic, environmental, human rights, and institutional provisions demanded by the European Constitution. That meant that Poland's long neglect of environmental issues (and its legacy of communist era pollution) would have to be addressed, while on the human rights side Poland would have to provide institutions that ensured the equality of all of its citizens and residents, punished discrimination, and protected minorities (something the country is still working on, admittedly).

Today, the majority of Poles are pro-EU, though some of the country's political parties have benefited from promoting a eurosceptic platform. Those with unfavorable views of the union voice concerns about the loss of national sovereignty and the declining role of religious institutions, particularly when it comes to social issues such as abortion and reproductive rights. They fear that EU membership will liberalize Poland, which tends toward conservatism and whose citizens are still largely supportive of the Catholic Church and traditional institutions. And these fears are not unfounded, as EU ascension has made Poland re-examine its approaches toward the rights of minorities and gender equality. However, this is a fate that Poland cannot escape if it wants to take its rightful place on the European stage.

NEW WAVES OF IMMIGRATION

Of course, one of the biggest and most visible consequences of Poland's entry into the EU was its mass exodus of workers searching for gold on the streets of London (see Chapters 12 & 45). But as Poles left Poland in droves, new residents began arriving as well, albeit in smaller numbers. This has resulted in a diverse expatriate community, mostly concentrated in Warsaw, Krakow, and the tri-city area. First of all, the influx of multinational companies brought its own workforce of managers and executives, mostly from the UK, U.S., and Western Europe. The predominately English-speaking professional ex-pat population mostly settled in gated suburban communities, near which American and British schools for their children (and the children of wealthy, ambitious Poles) quickly arose.

To contrast the image of the suburban expatriate, there's of course the traditional, bohemian stereotype: students or otherwise young (or young at heart) travelers from Western nations looking for romance and adventure in the wild east. First, in the 1990s Prague became for ex-pats what Paris was in Hemingway's day. Once that city lost its exotic flavor (and cheap beer prices), many headed east once again, this time to Krakow and other Polish cities. Today, their English-speaking expat communities are full of artists, musicians, ubiquitous English teachers, writers, students, and increasingly small business owners and start-ups (though rumors are that now Krakow is spent and Lviv, Ukraine is the next ex-pat hot spot). Exact numbers are hard to find as these communities are fluid by definition, but it's safe to assume that they number in the tens of thousands.

Nonetheless, Poland's overall immigrant population is relatively small—somewhere around 100,000 residence card holders. Granted, this does not include exchange students, unemployed EU citizens, or non-EU drifters who feel the sudden urge to travel to the Polish-Ukrainian border every ninety days. The overall figure is probably twice that, though that's still only about five percent of the country's

Euro Bank in Torun, Poland. (Tupungato / Shutterstock.com)

total population. And the largest group of migrants comes from Ukraine and other former Soviet countries, who usually emigrate for economic reasons and take many of the manual jobs left behind by the Poles who left to do them in the UK.

As far as non-European migrants go, Poland's largest ethnic minority is Vietnamese, a link that began when both countries were under communist rule. While many came illegally, in 2012 the Polish government granted such migrants amnesty when it realized the massive need for new sources of labor. Today, many economic migrants from Vietnam and other Asian countries as well as from Africa have decided to settle in Poland for good and are starting families—often giving their children Polish names, knowing they will go to Polish schools and become part of the revival of Poland's multicultural tradition. And it's no surprise: given that Poland is a nation with a migration habit (see Chapter 43), buried deep within each Pole is an understanding of the hardships of picking up and moving somewhere new, and thus an openness toward those who would do the same.

POLAND's EUROPEAN FUTURE

In the second half of 2011, Poland held the rotating presidency of the EU (or EU Council, to be specific)—a job title that meant setting the agenda and priorities of the Union for six months. Luckily, the presidency was seen as a success both by Brussels and the European press, and one of the key agendas it focused on was women's issues. As the largest of the ten countries that joined the EU in 2004 (as well as the two that joined in 2007), Poland is seen as a regional leader. Not only that, there have been increasing speculations in European media that the new center of EU power is shifting east, and will depend more and more on what decisions are made in Warsaw and Berlin than in Paris or London. Whether Poland is ready for its new leadership role remains to be seen, but it's safe to say that the country has stepped up in its desire to once again become a player on the world stage.

A.S.

FURTHER READING

Ever Closer Union: An Introduction to European Integration by Desmond Dinan. Lynne Rienner Publishers, 2010.

The New Atlanticist by Kerry Longhurst and Marcin Zaborowski. Chatham House, 2007.

PART V

POLES IN A NUTSHELL

CHAPTER 50

THE ESSENCE OF POLISHNESS

"And no invader has ever conquered the heart of Poland, that spirit which is the inheritance of sons and daughters, the private passion of families and the ancient, unbreakable tie to all those who came before."
–James A. Michener

In the end, we come to the question that is at the heart of this book: what does it mean to be Polish? Throughout history, Polish identity has been strongest when it has been under threat. Threats of Germanization and Russification inspired Poles of all social classes to work together, and were the reason Polish peasants developed a national consciousness. So this leads to an inevitable question: now that Poland is a free, democratic Member State of the European Union, is there an internal force that will preserve Polishness, or will the citizens of Poland see themselves as citizens of Europe, with no individual national identity to hold them together?

Already, Poles of the generation with little or no memory of communism have more in common with their peers across Europe than with their parents or grandparents who speak the same language. Many of the Poles who emigrated in 2004 have picked up British or Irish customs and accents as well as friends and often, husbands or wives. Will their children be Polish or British or simply European?

Unfortunately, there is no single answer to these questions, because the essence of Polishness is fluid; what it meant to be Polish in 1500 was different than what it meant to be Polish in 1861, which was different than what it meant to be Polish in 1947 or 2005, all of which are different from what it means to be Polish in 2013 and beyond. And yet, the common threads all Poles carry that tie them together are a complex history, a multicultural and democratic tradition, and an ever-evolving language.

THE POLISH COMPLEX

Perhaps one of the hardest things to understand about Poles, whether in Poland or abroad, is national pride, particularly in the context of something called the "Polish Complex." Roughly stated, the Polish Complex involves a national superiority complex and a sense of martyrdom wrapped up inside an inferiority complex in one big confusing, paradoxical mess.

Many Poles take great pride in Polish history, often glossing over the country's problems of the eighteenth century and blaming the loss of Polish independence solely on outside forces. When abroad, Poles are vehement in defending their nation from misconceptions, and the aging Polonia organizations seem to spend much of their time pointing out instances of anti-Polish bias in the media and demanding apologies.

And yet, despite this deep-seated belief of the enlightenment and superiority of the Polish nation, many Poles at the same time feel inferiority or anxiety when compared to other countries, particularly its neighbors to the west and—among the less educated—also the United States. A common paradoxical view is that something or someone that comes out of Poland cannot possibly be of value unless recognized as such by a more prestigious outsider. This contradictory attitude is ubiquitous within the arts in Poland today, where those artists or musicians held highest in esteem are the ones who make it big abroad; only then do many finally gain a following in their home country.

Where does this paradoxical thinking come from? On the one hand, Poland has had few individuals that have made a worldwide impact when compared to countries like Germany or England. On the other hand, the ones who have—Copernicus, Skłodowska-Curie, Chopin, Pope John Paul II—made a revolutionary impact few others have achieved. On the other, other hand, all of the previously mentioned individuals were Polish by birth and heritage, but made their careers abroad. This might explain some of the reasons Poles still hold more respect for their countrymen and women who have succeeded abroad than those making similar contributions within their own country.

POLAND THE MARTYR

Adam Mickiewicz, Poland's national bard, saw Poland as "Christ among nations," a martyr meant to suffer for the sins of the world, so that through Poland's pain the rest of the world could be set free. This was, to put it mildly, a difficult expectation to live up to, but it has become a part of the national consciousness, often used to explain away Poland's historical hardships. As "the chosen nation," Poles realize they may have to sometimes bear hardships for the sake of others.

Of course, just because one is a martyr doesn't mean one has to take it quietly. The Polish tendency to protest and resist goes back centuries and is not limited to Polish borders, former or otherwise. Some might even say it's in the Polish blood—how else does one explain the fact that the first ever recorded strike in the New World was begun by Poles in a seventeenth century British colony?

Throughout history, Poles tended to have great faith, and not just the religious kind. They lived their lives with an underlying sense that freedom and justice will prevail, even if it takes centuries. This is what allowed Poles to keep fighting during the Partitions, and is the reason that in the years 1939-1942, far before the tide of war turned in favor of the Allies, Poles kept fighting, knowing that eventually the side that was moral and right would triumph.

SARMATIAN TRADITION

In addition to the matyr status, the Sarmatian tradition is another explanation for the Polish Complex. Beginning in the fifteenth century, Polish nobles gained their legitimacy by declaring themselves descendants of an ancient Hellenic tribe of warriors known as the Sarmatians (in reality, the Iranian Ossetians of the Caucasus are their direct descendants). The Poles called themselves *Sarmaci*, a title that distinguished them from the peasant and merchant classes as well as from other European nobility. This also explains why all nobles saw themselves fit to rule, and so democracy (albeit one limited to the nobility) took hold quite early in Poland, modeled on the Greeks whose blood and traditions the nobility believed they were the heirs of.

Perhaps above all, Poles are proud of their democratic tradition, and see freedom and democracy as traits coursing through the veins of every Pole. At her proudest moments, Poland was freer than any other nation in Europe, and led the way as far as tolerance and egalitarianism were concerned. When kings were consolidating their powers throughout the world, in Poland they were being elected and bound by a constitution. While Jews and Catholics were being expelled from other nations, Poles welcomed all. And, like a good martyr, it was these noble qualities that led to her downfall in the face of ignoble enemies. Poland represented the most virtuous ideas, trying to survive in a world where force dominated.

Statue of poet and writer Adam Mickiewicz, Warsaw. (Fotokon / Shutterstock.com)

Of course, this is the romantic view of Poland, in which every sacrifice is worthy if made in the fight for freedom. Reality has been far more complicated, and many times it was the errors of Polish leadership that were as much responsible for her predicaments as any foreign intervention. Nonetheless, many Polish intellectuals have viewed the nation's history as a series of unsuccessful attempts to move closer to freedom and national independence.

THE POLISH PARADOX

This leads us to an essential paradox of Polishness. On the one hand, Poles love laughing at the absurdities of daily life in Poland, from trying to book a visit to the doctor's office to the latest political scandal. And yet, if an outsider points out these things, they get quite defensive and may even stress that most of these problems can be blamed on the last fifty years of occupation—and they wouldn't be wrong.

And while this is a paradox at face value, it's not without its own logic. Throughout history, Poles have had to fight for their very right to exist, to have their own language and culture and to defend it from outsiders. Any attack on Polish values or institutions, however small, can feel like foreign intervention, something that never really worked out well for the country. In the end, the ability to take criticism and use it to make improvements is a process that comes with the confidence of a nation that feels secure about its place in the world—and that's hard to come by for Poles, given history. Over time, Poland may come to accept its place on the European and world stages, as it has already as a regional leader, but these things cannot be rushed.

For 950 years of its over 1,000-year history, Poland was multicultural and multinational, and now the country is slowly reopening its borders and institutions to outsiders once again. But the lessons of history must be remembered, for there is no other way to understand the essence of Polishness, paradoxes and all.

A.S.

FURTHER READING

The Modern Polish Mind by Maria Kuncewicz, ed. Little, Brown and Company, 1962.

The Polish Complex by Tadeusz Konwicki. Dalkey Archive Press, 1998.

INDEX

Adamek, Tomasz, 248
Alexander I, 12
All Saints' Day (*Wszystkich
Świętych*), 120
Alternatywy 4, 156
Anders, General Władysław, 60
art/artists, 227–231, 288–289
Auschwitz II–Birkenau death
camp, 51

baca, 199
Bagna Biebrzańskie, 14
Balcerowicz, Leszek, 72, 79
Bareja, Stanisław, 224
barszcz (borscht), 169
Battle of Grunwald (1410), 42, 114
Belarus, 4, 12, 57
Białowieża National Park
(Białowieski Park
Narodowy), 8–12
Białowieża Primeval Forest
(Puszcza Białowieska), 12–13
Biebrza National Park
(Biebrzański Park
Narodowy), 14
Biskupin, 6
Biskupizna region, 194
Black Madonna, 10, 115–116
boazeria, 155
Bobola, Saint Andrzej, 107
Bogurodzica, 113
Bolesław the Brave (Bolesław I
Chrobry), 30–31
Bolesław, Duke, 49
Bonaparte, Napoleon, 44
borders of Poland, 4
Austria, 46–47
Belarus, 4, 12, 46, 57

Czech Republic, 46
Germany, 41–44, 46
Lithuania, 46
modern times, 46
Russia, 44–46
Slovakia, 46
Ukraine, 46
Borowski, Tadeusz, 213
Boy-Żeleński, Tadeusz, 219
Bretislaus I, 37
Brezhnev Doctrine, 70
Bryła, Stefan, 241
bryndza, 161
Brzeziński, Zbigniew, 265
Buczkowski, Leonard, 223

Carpathian Mountains, 10
Casimir III the Great (Kazimierz
III Wielki), 32–33, 49
Catholic Church, 98–100, 102
Catholicism, 23, 42, 44, 98–100
Charles, Duke, 56
Chmielowski, Saint Adam,
107–108
Chopin, Fryderyk, 8, 196, 233–234,
289
Christianity, 23, 26, 29–30, 32, 34,
98–101, see also Christmas
celebrations
Christmas celebrations
Christmas carols, 190–191
Christmas Eve table, 190
Christian rite of sharing
bread, 189–191
Christmas tree, 190
Wigilia supper, 190
Churchill, Winston, 62
Chwin, Stefan, 216

Cieszyn region, 195
Civic Platform (Platforma
    Obywatelska or PO) political
    party, 75, 77
coal mines, 8
communism, 73–74, 78–79
composers, 232–237, 289–290
Congress of Polonia in Germany, 269
Congress of Vienna, 44
Conrad, Joseph, 271, 287
Copernicus, Nicolaus, 238–239
Cossacks, 24
countryside, 3
cuisine
    bay leaves (*liście
    laurowe*), 161
    beetroot, 169–170
    bigos, 163–164
    borowiki (*Boletus*), 165
    cabbage, 164
    caraway seeds (*kminek*), 161
    czernina, 163
    dairy products, 161–162
    dill (*koperek*), 161
    dill pickles, 164
    dumplings, 167–168
    fish, 170
        herring (*śledź*), 170
    kasza, 165–166
    kiełbasa, 163
    kiszona kapusta, 164
    kluski (*noodles*), 167–168
    kotlet de volaille, 163
    kotlet schabowy, 162
    main meal of the day, 169
    marinating pickles (*ogórki
    konserwowe*), 164
    meat, 162–164
    mushrooms, 165
    oscypek, 161–162
        parsley (*pietruszka*), 161

pasztet, 163
    pierniki (honey-spice
    cakes), 161
    pierogi filling, 166–168
    potatoes, 168
    potrawka, 163
    roasted chicken (*kurczak z
    rożna*), 163
    rulers of Poland and, 161
    salads (*surówki*), 164
    savory and sweet fillings, 166
    soups (*kapuśniak, kwaśnica*),
    162, 164, 169
    spices, 161
    vegetarian, 164–166
    włoszczyzna ("Italian stuff"),
    161
Czartoryski, Prince Adam Jerzy,
    264, 277
Czech Republic, 4, 47, 247

d'Arquien, Marie, 35
Dąbrowska, Maria, 213
Davies, Norman, 64
demography, 4
diaspora (*Polonia*), *see also*
    emigration/immigration
    issues, 266–267
    organizations abroad, 268–269
    personal tale, 269–270
    Polack jokes, 267–268
Dobrava (Dąbrówka), Princess,
    29–30
Dolny Śląsk, 6
Dom Polonii, 8
Dragons, 19–20
drinking habits, see also cuisine
    average alcohol consumed,
    175–176
    bimber or *gorzała*, 177–178
    coffee, 179

drinking water, 179
Krupnik, 176
Luksusowa, 177
nalewka, 178
serving glass, 179
vodka, 175–176
wine, 178–179
Wyborowa, 177
Żubrówka, 177
Druzno lake, 5
dynasties
    Jagiellon dynasty, 33–34, 37
    Piast dynasty, 28–33, 37

Eagle's Nest Trail (Szlak Orlich
    Gniazd), 10
economy
    communism and, 78–79
    after EU membership, 81,
    292–294
    GDP, 82
    between 1999–2004, 80–81
    privatization and transition
    (1990s), 79–80
    process of Polish freedom, 80
    between 2005–2008, 81–82
    2008 onwards, 82–83
    unemployment issue, 80–82
Einsatzgruppen, 50
Elblag Canal, 5
emigration/immigration,
    294–295
    in Canada, 283–284
    after EU membership, 81,
    263–264, 276–279
    famous emigrants, 264–265
    the Great Emigration, 262–263
    of Jews, 52–53
    in South America, 284–285
    twentieth century, 263

in UK, 271–274
in USA, 280–283
endangered wild animals, 8
environmental protection
    systems, 15
"Euro-orphan," 150
European lowlands, 12

Fameg in Radomsko, 157
family
    divorce, 149
    "Euro-orphan,"150
    parent-child relationships, 150
    stable family model, 150
    ties, 149–150
Fibak, Wojciech, 247
films and film directors, 222–
    226, 290
    B- and C-class movies, 225
    communist era, 222–225
    1980s, 225
Fiszdon, Władysław, 242–243
folk traditions
    art, 192
    costumes, 192–196, 199–200
    dances, 193–195
    ornaments/jewelry, 193–
    195, 200
    traditional areas, 193–196
    Zakopane Style (*styl
    zakopiański*), 200–201
Fredro, Aleksander, 211, 219
Funk, Kazimierz, 241
Fydrych, Waldemar "Major," 251

gay pride marches, 143
Gdańsk, 4–5, 42–43
*Germany, 4, 13–14, 25, 41–44, 47,
    58–59, 80, 135, 138, 143, 150,
    157, 186, 210, 247, 271, 276–
    277, 299*

Giedroyc, Jerzy, 278
Gniezdo (Gniezno), 6, 17, 36–37, 111
Goldwyn, Samuel, 290
Gombrowicz, Witold, 213, 278,
    285, 288
Gopło Lake, 17–18
Gorbachev, Mikhail, 70
Górecki, Henryk Mikołaj, 235
Górny Sląsk, 8
Góry Stolowe, 10
Gothic castle of the Teutonic
    Order, 5
Great Masurian Lakes, 4
Great Plague of 1348, 32
Greater Poland (Wielkopolska), 6,
    37, 167
Gretzky, Wayne, 284

Habsburg, Elizabeth, 33
Hapsburg Austrians, 24
Henry V, Emperor, 31
Herbert, Zbigniew, 214
Herling-Grudziński, Gustaw,
    278, 288
Herman, Władysław, 31
highlanders (górale), 196, 198–200
Hildegard, 18
holidays
    Christmas, 188–191
    religious, 187
    St. Andrew's Eve
        (Andrzejki), 131–132
    St. Barbara's Day
        (Barbórka), 132
    St. John's Night (Noc
        świętojańska), 131
    St. Nicholas Day
        (Mikołajki), 132
Holland, Agnieszka, 290
Holocaust, 48, 50–52, 283
Holy Cross Mountains (Góry
    Świętokrzyskie), 9

Holy Roman Empire, 28, 30, 36,
    42, 46, 57, 98
Home Army (Armia Krajowa
    or AK), 40, 60–61, 223,
    263, 271
home
    bathroom, 158
    blokowiska, 156
    foreigner perspective, 158
    kawalerka ("bachelor
        pad"), 156
    living room (pokój
        dzienny), 157
    furniture, 157
    M-2, M-3, M-4 apartments, 156
    modern apartment, 156,
        158–159
    neighborhoods, 156
    meblościanka, 157
    windows, 157–158
homosexuals in Poland, 142–143
hospitality, see also Polish traits
    neighborly relations,
        171–172
    sense of community,
        171–172
    Sto lat, 172
    treating guests, 172–174
Hôtel Lambert, 234, 277
Huelle, Paweł, 216
Husaria, 34

Infeld, Leopold, 241–242
International Festival of Jewish
    Culture, 53
Iron Curtain, 43, 45, 64, 135
Iwaszkiewicz, Jarosław, 213

Jadwiga, Saint, 106
Jagiełło, Ladislaus II (Władysław
    Jagiełło), 34
Jagiellon dynasty, 23, 33–34, 37

Jagiellonian University, 33, 38, 64
Janiszewski, Jerzy, 231
Janów Podlaski, 8
January Uprising (1863), 57
Jarema, Maria, 220
Jarocin Festival, 237
Jasna Góra monastery, 9, 115
jazz music, 236
Jedwabne pogrom (1941), 51
Jewish Combat Organization
    (ŻOB), 52
Jewish population in Poland,
    25–26
    bills of rights and, 49
    emigration and communism,
    52–53
    Holocaust, 48, 50–52, 283
    before 1939, 48–50
    under Polish-Lithuanian
    Commonwealth, 49
    reemergence of, 53–54
    during World War I, 49
John XIX, Pope, 31

Kaczyński, Jarosław, 75
Kaczyński, Lech, 75
Kamiński, Janusz, 290–291
Kampinos National Park (Puszcza
    Kampinoska), 8
Kantor, Tadeusz, 220, 230
Kapuściński, Ryszard, 214
Karkonosze, 10
Kashubia, 4, 193
Katherine of Habsburg, 34
Katyn Massacre (1940), 45
Katz, Leon, 284
Kieślowski, Krzysztof, 222, 235
Kilar, Wojciech, 235
Kingdom of Prussia, 42
Kłobukowska, Ewa, 245–246
Kolbe, Saint Maksymilian, 108–109
Koliba, 200

Kołobrzeg or Międzyzdroje, 4
Kombinowanie, 66, 78
Komeda, Krzysztof, 236
Konwicki, Tadeusz, 215
Kosciuszko Foundation, 268
Kościuszko, Tadeusz, 281
Kossak, Juliusz, 56
Kostka, Saint Stanisław, 106–107
Koterski, Marek, 226
Kowalczyk, Justyna, 24
Kowalska, Saint Faustyna, 108
Krak, King, 19
Krakow Academy, 33
Krakow, 9, 23, 37–38, 47, 53,
    159, 191
Krakow-Częstochowa Upland, 9
Krasiński, Zygmunt, 211
Kraszewski, Józef Ignacy, 211
Kryszewski, Marian, 243
Kubica, Robert, 248
Kujawy region, 194
Kulej, Jerzy, 246
Kultura, 278
Kurpie region, 194–195

language, 84–85, 210, see also
    literature
    adjectives, 89
    cases, 89–92
    formal/informal, 95–96
    future tense, 94
    negating sentences, 92
    nouns, 87–88
    past tense, 93
    present tense, 92–93
    pronunciation and spelling,
    96–97
    verbs, 92
    words borrowed from
    English, 86–87
    word order, 94–95
Lato, Grzegorz, 247

League of Polish Families (Liga Polskich Rodzin or LPR), 77
legends
    Lech, Czech, and Rus, 16–17
    Popiel, king, 17–19
    Wawel dragon, 19–20
    sleeping knights, 20–22
Lelewel, Joachim, 265
Lem, Stanisław, 214
Lempicka, Tamara de, 230, 289
Leśmian, Bolesław, 213
Lesser Poland (Małopolska), 8–9, 32, 37, 130
Leszczyńska, Saint Stanisława, 109–110
literature, 286–288, *see also* language
    Catholicism and, 215
    clandestine publishing, 213
    under communism, 214
    modernist movement (*Młoda Polska*), 212–213
    1970s, 215
    post communism, 215–216
    Romanticism, 211–212
    travel narratives, 214
    during World War II, 213–214
Lithuania, 4, 10, 23, 25, 39, 47, 57–58, 100, 112
Louis of Anjou (Ludwik Andegaweński), 33
Łowicz region, 195

Machulski, Juliusz, 224
Mackiewicz, Józef, 288
Makowicz, Adam, 236
Malbork town, 5
Małysz, Adam, 248
man/men
    under communism, 141–142
    crisis of masculinity, 141–142

economic crisis and, 141–142
    embodiment of chivalry, 140
    historical perspective, 139–140
    homosexuality, 142–143
    unemployment, 141–142
marmot (*świstak*), 15
martyrs, 300
Masłowska, Dorota, 216
Matejko, Jan, 28, 56, 227–229
"matka polka" ("the Polish Mother"), 133–135, 138
May 3 Constitution, 24, 112, 257
Mazovia (Mazowsze), 6, 8
Mazowiecki, Duke Konrad, 42
Mazurek Dąbrowskiego, 114–115
Melomani, 236
Michałowski, Piotr, 288
Michnik, Adam, 215
Mickiewicz, Adam, 10, 211, 277, Adam, 286, Adam, 300
Mieszko I, 23, 28–30, 37, 42, 98
Miller, Grazyna, 216
Miłosz, Czesław, 214, 278, 287
Molotov–Ribbentrop Pact, 25, 45
Moniuszko, Stanisław, 234
Morskie Oko Lake, 10
Mrożek, Sławomir, 214
music, 232–237, 289–290
Muzeum Koronki, 199
Mysia Wieża (Mouse Tower), 19

names
    holy, 129–130
    common in 1950s, 130
    common in 1970s, 130
    foreign-sounding (and often non-Christian) names, 131
    name days, 131–132
national anthem, 113–115
National Independence Day, 112
national symbols, 111–112
Natowski, Zygmunt, 200

Nazis, 40, 44, 59–60
Negri, Pola, 290
Neisse (Nysa Łużycka) River, 43
Nogat River, 5
Norwid, 211
November Uprising (1830), 24, 57, 114

Oder (Odra) river, 43
Odra River, 8
Old Town, 9
Open'er Festival, 237
Otto I, 42
Otto III, Emperor, 31, 36

Paderewski, Ignacy Jan, 234–235
Pasikowski, Władysław, 225
Paul II, Pope John, 26, 101–103, 110, 299
Penderecki, Krzysztof, 235
People's Republic of Poland (PRL), 52, 65–68
Piast dynasty, 28–33, 37, 111
Pieniny Mountains, 197
Pierre, Marie Simon, 110
Pilch, Jerzy, 216
Piłsudski, Józef, 50, 58
Piwowski, Marek, 223
Plater, Emilia, 134
Płock, 8
poaching, 15
Podhale region, 10, 161, 169, 197, 199–200
Podlasie region, 6, 12, 14, 100, 166, 190, 194
Podolski, Lukas, 247
Polanski, Roman, 235, 290
Polish Armed Forces, 62
Polish Beer-Lovers' Party (Polska Partia Przyjaciół Piwa or PPPP), 252
Polish flag, 112–113
Polish–German relations, 43

Polish history, 256–260
    Catholicism, 98–100
    Christianity, 23, 26, 29–30, 32, 34, 98
    Communism, 26–27, 64–71, 72–73
    eighteenth century, 24
    establishment of kingdom, 23–24, 44–45
    under Nazi rule, 50–51
    between 1948 and 1956, 26
    1990s, 27, 72–73
    partitions, 24
    quasi-democratic system, 24
    Solidarity (Polish trade union), 26–27, 68–70
    during World War I and II, 25–26, 42–43
Polish hymn, 114–115
Polish–Lithuanian Commonwealth, 10, 23–24, 39, 42, 44, 46, 49, 56, 112, 211–212, 256
Polish Resettlement Act of 1947, 271
Polish–Russia relations, 45–46
Polish School of Posters, 231
Polish Sejm (Parliament), 112
Polish Social and Cultural Association, 268
Polish society, 114, 150
Polish–Soviet War (1919–21), 45, 58
Polish traits
    charity/philanthropy, 120
    cultural identity, 119, 148
    hospitality, 171–174
    national pride, 119–120, 258–259
    paradox of Polishness, 301–302
    "Polish Complex," 299
    Roman Catholic tradition, 119
    Sarmatian tradition, 300–301

sense of humor, 120–121, 267–268
sensitivity, 122
political parties, 74–77
Pomerania (Pomorze), 4
Poniatowski, Stanisław August, 39
Popiel, King, 17–19
Potsdam Agreement, 26
Poznań, 37
Prague Spring rebellion, 53
Preisner, Zbigniew, 236
Protestant churches in Poland, 100
protesters, rebels, and rabble-rousers, 249–253
Prus, Bolesław, 212
Prussians, 24
Przemysł II, 111
Pulaski, Kazimierz, 281
Pułtusk, 8
Raczki Elbląskie, 5
Radwańska, Agnieszka, 248
Radziwiłł, Barbara (Radziwiłłówna), 33
Ray, Lisa, 284
Red Army, 61, 64–65
Rejewski, Marian, 242
Roosevelt, Franklin D., 62
Round Table Talks (1989), 70
Różewicz, Tadeusz, 214
Różycki, Jerzy, 242
Russians, 24, 44–46, 56, 65, 138, 211
Rzeczpospolita, 5

Sarnecki, Tomasz, 231
Saturday Night Live, 268
school
    a day in class, 182–185
    dziennik (class register), 183–184
    gimnazjum (middle school), 182
    przedszkole (kindergarten), 182
    przepytywanie, 183–185

szkoła podstawowa (primary school), 182
wychowawca (homeroom teacher), 182–183
Schulz, Bruno, 213
scientists, 238–243
seacoast, 4
Seifert, Zbigniew, 236
Sforza, Queen Bona, 33, 170
Shatner, William, 284
shock therapy, 27, 72, 79
shopping
    bielizna, 153
    Centra Handlowe, 154
    chemiczny, 153
    cukiernia, 152
    for freshly baked goods, 152
    for fresh vegetables, 153
    Galerie Handlowe, 154
    gospodarczy, 153
    hypermarket, 154
    IKEA store, 157, 159
    kiosk, 153
    kwiaciarnia, 154
    mięsny, 152
    papierniczy, 153
    piekarnia, 152
    reklamówki, 154
    retail clothing chain, 154
    sklep meblowy, 153
    sklep obuwniczy, 153
    sklep odzieżowy, 153
    sklep warzywny, 153
    sklep z nabiałem, 152
    sklep z zabawkami, 153
    supermarkets, 154
Sienkiewicz, Henryk, 212, 286
Sigismund I the Old (Zygmunt I Stary), 33
Sigismund II Augustus, King, 23, 33–34
Sigismund III Vasa, King, 39, 56
Sikorski, General Władysław, 278

Skłodowska-Curie, Marie, 239–240, 264, 277
Slavic tribes, 16–17
Słowacki, Juliusz, 211, 219
Smolensk cross, 253
Śnieżka Mountain, 10
Sobieski, John III (Sobieski, Jan III), King, 33–34, 46, 56–57
Society for the Protection of European Bison, 13
Solidarity (Polish trade union), 26–27, 68–70, 79
Solidarność sign, 116
Soviet system, collapse of, 26
sports
athletics, 245–246, 248
boxing, 246
football, 245–247
in schools, 244
ski jumping, 248
tennis, 247–248
Stalin, Joseph, 62
Stanisław, Saint, 105–106
Stanko, Tomasz, 236
Stasiuk, Andrzej, 216
state symbolism, 112
Stryjeńska, Zofia, 230
Strzelecki, Sir Paweł Edmund, 265
Stuhr, Maciej, 221
Sudeten Mountains, 10
superstitions
connected with weddings, 127–128
connected with Wigilia, 128
events that bring bad luck, 123–126
ways to assure good luck, 126–127
Swedes, 24
Sylvester I, Pope, 30
synagogues, 54
Szczepanik, Jan, 241

Szewińska, Irena, 245
Szymanowska, Maria, 232–233
Szymanowski, Karol, 235
Szymborska, Wisława, 214, 278

tarpans, 13–14
Tatars, 34, 56, 99, 115
Tatra Mountains, 10, 15, 20, 22, 197
theater
Cricot Theater, 220
Green Balloon (Zielony Balonik) cabaret, 219–220
Potem (After), 220
romantic, 219
twenty-first century cabaret, 220–221
Thonet, Michael, 157
Tokarczuk, Olga, 216
Toruń, 161
Treaty of Versailles (1919), 25
tur, 15
Tusk, Donald, 75
twaróg, 161

Ukraine, 4, 25, 47, 57–58, 247, 257, 278, 287, 294–295
Union of Lublin, 24
Urbaniak, Michał, 236

vacations, 202–208
choice, 204–208
preferred destinations, 204
reasons for going on, 203
trends and statistics, 203–204
Valley of Five Lakes (Dolina Pięciu Stawów), 10
Vasa, King John II Casimir (Jan II Kazimierz Waza), 116
Vetulani, Tadeusz, 13
Vistula River, 5, 8, 20
Vladislaus II of Opole (Władysław Opolczyk), 115
voivodeships (województwa), 4

Wajda, Andrzej, 223, 235
Wałęsa, Lech, 27, 70–71, 249–250
wars
    Battle of Britain, 60
    Battle of Monte Cassino
    (1944), 60–61
    French Campaign of May–
    June (1940), 60
    January Uprising (1863), 57
    November Uprising (1830),
    24, 57, 114
    Polish–Ottoman war, 56–57
    Polish–Soviet War (1919–21),
    45, 58
    rebellions under partitions,
    57–58
    with Sweden, 56
    War on Terror, 62
    World War I, 25, 39, 42,
    45, 47, 49, 58, 112, 161,
    262, 285
    World War II, 25–26, 38–39,
    43, 45, 47, 50–52,
    55, 59–62, 64–65, 99,
    108–110, 112, 119, 135, 213,
    220, 222, 238, 242, 259–260,
    263, 268, 271, 277, 279, 283,
    285, 288
Warsaw, 8, 23–24, 36, 38–40, 42,
    44, 49, 56–57, 61, 69–70, 74,
    100–102, 107–109, 166, 212,
    220, 233, 235, 237
Warsaw Ghetto Uprising (1943),
    39–40, 50, 52, 54, 61, 65, 223
Warsaw Mermaid, 8
Wat, Aleksander, 213
Wawel Castle, 9, 37
wedding
    cake, 147
    church, 145
    dance of newlyweds, 146
    day of, 145

    drinking at (Vodka), 147
    invitation to, 144–145
    menu, 146
    music on day of, 146
    oczepiny at midnight, 147
    official ceremony of
    newlyweds, 147
    płonąca szynka, 147
    reception, 146
    zaproszenie, 144–145
    zawiadomienie, 144–145
Wiadomości, 272–273
Wieliczka Salt Mine, 9, 33
Wielka Orkiestra Świątecznej
    Pomocy (The Great Orchestra
    of Christmas Charity), 120
Wieniawski, Henryk, 289
Wigierski Park, 8
Witkiewicz, Stanisław Ignacy
    (Witkacy), 200, 220, 230
Władysław the Exile (Władysław
    Wygnaniec), 32
Wojciech, Saint, 30–31, 104–105
Wojtek the Soldier Bear, 61
Wojtyła, Karol, see Paul II,
    Pope John
Wolszczan, Aleksander, 243
woman/women
    education level, 136
    employment status, 136
    feminism, 137
    foreigners and, 137–138
    marriage age for, 136
    myth of *"matka polka"*
    ("the Polish Mother"), 133–
    135, 138
    "New Woman," 135
    wage discrepancies, 136
World War I, 25, 39, 42, 45, 47, 49,
    58, 112, 161, 262, 285
World War II, 25–26, 38–39, 43, 45,
    47, 50–52, 55, 59–62, 64–65,

99, 108–110, 112, 119, 135, 213,
220, 222, 238, 242, 259–260,
263, 268, 271, 277, 279, 283,
285, 288
Wróblewski, Andrzej, 231
Wrymouth, Bolesław III
    (Krzywousty, Bolesław III),
    31–32
Wybicki, Józef, 114
Wyspiański, Stanisław, 229

Yalta Conference, 45, 62

Zakopane, 10, 20
Zamość, 9
Zanussi, Krzysztof, 235
Żelazowa Wola, 8
Ziemia Krakowska, 195–196
Ziemia Lubuska, 195
Zubilewicz, Tomasz, 6–7
żubr (European bison), 12–14
Żuławy delta area, 5
Żuławski, Andrzej, 290
Zygalski, Henryk, 242

Eastern Europe!

Everything You Need to Know About the History (and More) of a Region that Shaped Our World and Still Does

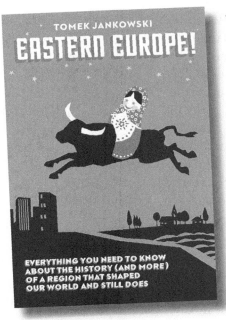

978-0-98250623-2-3

"A veritable intellectual feat. . . . A must-read."
—**Laszlo Borhi, Indiana University, Hungarian Academy of Sciences**

"A well researched and engaging introduction to Central and Eastern Europe and the Balkans. . . . [A] joy to read."
—**John Ashbrook, Sweet Briar College**

"Compact, inclusive, and accessible, this book is an enjoyable and thorough account of the Eastern European past."
—**Nate Weston, Seattle Central Community College**

New Europe Books

New Europe Books
Williamstown, Massachusetts

Find our titles wherever books are sold, or visit
www.NewEuropeBooks.com
for order information.

About the Authors

Anna Spysz is the former editor-in-chief of the *Krakow Post*, Poland's English-language newspaper. Born in Warsaw, she moved to Texas of all places with her parents at the age of six. She graduated in 2004 from the University of Texas at Austin with a BA in English and subsequently moved to Krakow, where she earned an MA in Central and East-
ern European Studies from the Jagiellonian University. She currently lives in Krakow, where in addition to working as a freelance writer and translator, she dabbles in photography, graphic design, and music. Her website is www.annaspysz.com.

Marta Turek moved from Poland to the United States with her parents in 1981, when she was four years old. Settling first in Chicago and later in Seattle, her whole family returned to Poland in 1993. She finished high school in Poznań and graduated from Adam Mickiewicz University with an MA in English Linguistics in 2001. She has taught English as
a second language at private schools and universities on both sides of the Atlantic. Marta currently lives in Rokietnica, Poland, and specializes in proofreading translations and English-language texts.